GRAY'S ENGLISH POEMS

GRAY'S ENGLISH POEMS

ORIGINAL AND TRANSLATED FROM THE NORSE AND WELSH

EDITED BY

D. C. TOVEY, M.A.

FORMERLY CLARK LECTURER AT TRINITY COLLEGE, CAMBRIDGE

CAMBRIDGE:
AT THE UNIVERSITY PRESS
1922

CAMBRIDGE
UNIVERSITY PRESS

University Printing House, Cambridge CB2 8BS, United Kingdom

Published in the United States of America by Cambridge University Press, New York

Cambridge University Press is part of the University of Cambridge.

It furthers the University's mission by disseminating knowledge in the pursuit of education, learning and research at the highest international levels of excellence.

www.cambridge.org
Information on this title: www.cambridge.org/9781107665682

First edition 1898
Reprinted 1904, 1911, 1914, 1922
First published 1922
First paperback edition 2014

A catalogue record for this publication is available from the British Library

ISBN 978-1-107-66568-2 Paperback

PREFACE.

THE editor has arranged, as far as possible, the English Poems of Gray in chronological order and has illustrated them from Gray's correspondence. So much biographical detail will be found in the notes, that the account of the poet's life in the Introduction is necessarily short. If therein one or two circumstances are less briefly treated, this is because they have needed hitherto to be more exactly stated.

The editor wishes to thank Dr Aldis Wright, Vice-Master of Trinity College, Cambridge, Dr Henry Jackson, Mr J. M. Image and Mr W. C. D. Whetham, Fellows of that College, the Rev. W. C. Green, translator of the *Egilssaga,* Professor Villiers Stanford, Professor Dowden, and Mr W. George of Bristol, for kind assistance and information. He has also found great help in the little work on Gray in the Athenæum Press Series by Professors Phelps of Yale, and Kittredge of Harvard College.

CONTENTS.

INTRODUCTION.

THOMAS GRAY was born on the 26th of December, 1716. His father was Philip Gray, said to have been a scrivener or broker. This man amid other sources of income owned a house and shop in Cornhill which in the year 1706, or thereabouts, was let to two sisters Mary and Dorothy Antrobus. At this date, approximately, Philip was on the eve of marriage with Dorothy, and their marriage-contract left her still a partner with her sister in the business (millinery), they paying Philip Gray rent for his shop, and the three, apparently, living together in the house connected with it. Dorothy Gray was financially independent of her husband, with whom she lived unhappily, and from whom in 1735 she endeavoured to get a separation. She had at this time given birth to twelve children, of whom Thomas, the fifth, was the only survivor; the rest had died in infancy; and the future poet might have shared their fate but that his mother opened one of his veins with her own hand.

To his mother Gray owed his education both at Eton and Cambridge. There is nothing to contradict the impression made by Mrs Gray's 'Case for Counsel' (1735)[1] that his father was a brute, and perhaps crazy[2]. The straitened circumstances

[1] First published by Mitford. Gray's *Works*, vol. I. pp. xcvi sq.

[2] 'He daily threatens he will pursue her with all the vengeance possible, and will *ruin himself to undo her, and his only son*; in order to which he hath given warning to her sister to quit his shop, where they have carried on their trade so successfully, which will almost be their ruin' &c. Mrs Gray's 'Case for Counsel.'

of the poet's earlier years, compared with the ease and comfort with which he lived at Cambridge after his father's death, point to the inference that it was not poverty but callous selfishness that made Philip Gray put the task of providing for his son upon this 'careful, tender mother.'

Dorothy Gray's nephew[1], William Antrobus, was an assistant master at Eton, and thither in 1727 Gray was sent, perhaps[2] as his pupil. There is some reason to believe that Mrs Gray was a humble friend of Lady Walpole[3] (the daughter of Alderman Shorter); this perhaps was the starting point of the friendship at Eton between Horace Walpole and Gray. Two other names are linked with this friendship, Richard West and Thomas Ashton. West was the son of the Lord Chancellor of Ireland, and, on his mother's side, the grandson of Bishop Burnet. At Eton he was reckoned the most brilliant of the little *coterie*, there known by the name of the Quadruple Alliance. His early death in 1742 was to Gray a never-forgotten sorrow[4]. Ashton, the least interesting member of this group, entered into holy orders, and achieved some promotion in the Church; but became at last estranged from Walpole, his affection, as Walpole suggests, cooling when his friend ceased to be a prime minister's son, and hopes of preferment in that quarter lapsed in consequence.

Both Gray and Walpole were delicate children; and it speaks well for the Eton of that day that they were allowed to follow their own studious bent unmolested, and that our poet loved those fields in which he moved with little or no share or skill in the sports of boyhood.

Gray left Eton for Cambridge in 1734. He became a pensioner at Peterhouse. Another uncle, Robert Antrobus, had been a fellow of that college[5]. Gray had little sympathy with

[1] See Appendix.

[2] See note 4 *infra*.

[3] See *Gray and His Friends*, pp. 4, 5, 60, 61.

[4] *Gray and His Friends*, pp. 15—17.

[5] Dr Bradshaw says that this *Robert* was Gray's tutor at Eton. Mason also affirms that Gray's tutor there was a fellow of S. Peter's

Cambridge studies, as then pursued; he gave up attending lectures; and in 1739 he went with Horace Walpole for a continental tour, of which Walpole bore the principal expense. That incompatibility of temper which travel so often discovers broke out in an acute form at last, and ended in the separation of the friends at Reggio in 1741[1]. Gray went off with two friends of his and Walpole's, John Chute and Francis Whithed, to Venice, and thence returned home, accompanied only by a servant, arriving in London on the 1st of Sept. 1741. His father died on the 6th of November following.

Gray spent some time between London and Stoke Pogis (whither his mother and his aunt Mary Antrobus had gone to live with their widowed sister, Mrs Rogers), and finally, after hesitating between his old college and Trinity Hall[2], returned to Peterhouse (this time, I believe, as a fellow-commoner), in the autumn of 1742, graduating as LL.B. in 1744. His choice, even before he started on his foreign travels, was ostensibly the bar, but he never made any attempt to pursue that vocation, preferring that life of secluded study to which the possession of a competency enabled him to devote himself.

In November 1745 a reconciliation was effected between Gray and Walpole[3]. The young men had never lost esteem for each other. Walpole especially wrote of Gray kindly even during their estrangement, and mentioned him always with

College (*William* was of King's). Since Robert died in 1729, it is clear that Gray, even if he entered Eton under him, must have passed into other hands before he left school. Perhaps from Robert to William? But see Appendix.

[1] A close examination of Gray's correspondence would show that Ashton was a mischief-maker in this matter, probably by retailing to Walpole some unkind comments received from Gray.

[2] I have not space to exhibit the evidence on which these statements are based. Gray's correspondence has never been published with any care for chronological sequence; if it ever should be, it will be found that my statements are correct.

[3] A lady is said to have done much to bring this about. This lady I conjecture, doubtfully, to have been a maiden sister of John Chute.

pride and affection, modified only by gentle complaints of his censorious temper.

From this point the history of Gray is more and more identical with that growth of his mind and of his studies which I have tried to trace in my notes. In 1756 he removed from Peterhouse to Pembroke College on the other side of the street, in consequence of a cruel practical joke attémpted upon him by some fellow-commoners, of which the college authorities refused to take sufficient notice. It should be remembered that he was at this time the famous author of the *Elegy*.

In 1762 he attempted indirectly through Walpole and Sir Henry Erskine, a creature of Lord Bute's, to obtain the Professorship of Modern History at Cambridge. It was given to a Mr Brockett, of Trinity, who had been tutor to Sir James Lowther, son-in-law of the prime minister. In 1768 it was offered to Gray unsolicited, probably at the suggestion of Stonhewer, secretary to the Duke of Grafton. Gray accepted it, but delivered no lectures.

Cambridge was in the main the poet's residence during the whole of his life from 1742 to his death in 1771. The year 1759 was spent by him for the most part in London, in researches in the British Museum; he stayed at times with his mother and aunts at Stoke Pogis; and was occasionally the guest of Walpole, Wharton and other friends. He visited different parts of England and Scotland, and was one of the first Englishmen to appreciate the beauty of lake and mountain scenery. He died in Pembroke College on the 30th of July, 1771, and was buried in Stoke Pogis Churchyard, in the same tomb with his mother.

In the notes attention has designedly been called to the hostile criticisms of Johnson upon Gray's poetry. I have felt that this prejudice is not to be dismissed in a word; like all Johnson's antipathies it is well worth investigating. I have referred it elsewhere to the dislike which the man who has written for his bread is inclined to feel towards the man who writes for his own amusement, and there was certainly in the matter of literary taste and bias a line of demarcation which might be overstepped, but which is very clearly traceable, between the adventurers who came up to town to live by their wits, and the *dilettantists* who from a secure social or academic position could make or welcome experiments. The hardworking man of letters believed in the conditions under which he had slowly made his way to fame. It is only his prose style that can be said to be quite distinctive of Johnson, by virtue perhaps of an inevitable law which in one direction or the other makes the style the man. When he wrote 'London' and 'The Vanity of Human Wishes,' the language of the age was, a few conventionalisms apart, rapidly becoming the language of its poetry, the very thing which Gray declared it never could be for a permanence, except in French. A less exact observer than Gray, Johnson had not perhaps noticed how largely not only Dryden but Pope had borrowed from the older diction of Shakespeare and Milton[1]. At any rate he set his face against any attempt to repeat that example; he hated these borrowings from antiquity, these things strange yet not new, whether they were offered him by Gray or by Percy, whether they appeared with 'strutting dignity,' as he would call it, in a revived ornateness, or in the simplicity of ballad poetry; and he struck out both to the right and to the left. Accustomed as we are to think of the simple pathos of the *Elegy* as clothed in language sufficiently trite, it should startle us to find that the man whose name is often used as a synonyme for pompous diction found it blemished by that defect, as well as by offensive archaisms and affected inversions. We get to the root of Johnson's objections in one clear instance which sets his meaning beyond mistake. He made two versions of a chorus of the Medea. One of these is an attempt without bias; it represents his own notion of how the thing ought to be done; he gave it to Burney for his History of Music:—

The rites deriv'd from ancient days
With thoughtless reverence we praise,

[1] See Gray to West, April, Thursday, 1742 (quoted in part on *Agrippina*).

The rites that taught us to combine
The joys of music and of wine,
And bad the feast and song and bowl
O'erfill the saturated soul;
But ne'er the Flute or Lyre apply'd
To cheer despair or soften pride,
Nor call'd them to the gloomy cells
Where Want repines and Vengeance swells,
Where Hate sits musing to betray
And Murder meditates his prey.
To dens of guilt and shades of care
Ye sons of Melody repair,
Nor deign the festive dome to cloy
With superfluities of joy.
Ah, little needs the Minstrel's power
To speed the light convivial hour;
The board with varied plenty crown'd
May spare the luxuries of sound.

Here there is scarcely a word that would seem affected in the conversation either of Johnson's day or our own; and the same may be said of most of Johnson's verse no less than of Goldsmith's. But now take the same passage rendered by him in the style, as he conceived it, of the Elegy:

Err shall they not, who resolute explore
Times gloomy backward with judicious eyes;
And scanning right the practices of yore,
Shall deem our *hoar progenitors* unwise.

They to the dome where smoke with curling play
Announced the dinner to the regions round,
Summon'd the *singer blythe* and *harper gay*
And aided time with *dulcet-streaming* sound.

The better use of notes, or sweet or shrill,
By quiv'ring string, or modulated wind,
Trumpet or lyre—to their *harsh* bosoms *chill*
Admission ne'er had sought, or could not find.

Oh! send them to the *sullen* mansions *dun*
His baleful eyes where Sorrow rolls around;
Where *gloom-enamour'd* Mischief loves to dwell
And Murder, all *blood-bolter'd*, schemes the wound.

Where *cates luxuriant* pile the spacious dish,
And purple nectar glads the festive hour,
The guest without a want, without a wish,
Can yield no room to Music's soothing pow'r.

Mrs Piozzi calls this a burlesque and a parody, and that it was written, as she says, 'with some merry malice' is undoubtedly true; an absurd touch here and there, as in the second line, betrays this; otherwise we might almost take it quite seriously, indeed an unguarded critic might be betrayed into quoting it as distinctively Johnsonian. But the adjectives following their substantives, the archaisms, the epithets double and hyphenated and always indispensable, belong to Gray, not to Johnson, and have much to do with that charge of obscurity which sounds so strange to modern ears. The inversions too of subject or object with the verb are Gray's, and no one else perhaps in his day would have written, as he undoubtedly did,

Awaits alike th' inevitable hour,

to the bewilderment of printers ever since. But chiefly by reviving and consequently enlarging our poetic vocabulary does Gray appear as an innovator. He was of all the innovators of his day in this respect perhaps the most conscious and deliberate, a fact which justifies the pains which Mitford and others have taken in tracing his diction to its probable sources.

In another and later direction the results of Gray's effort, so tardy and in volume so scanty, were still more noteworthy. The fact that the 'Progress of Poesy' and the 'Bard' were published together has obscured for us the generic difference between them. Before he wrote the 'Bard' Gray's mind had received a new bias; he had begun those studies in Scandinavian literature which modified his treatment of that poem. His characteristic hesitation over it might have left it a belated fragment but for the music of Parry, the blind Welsh harper, which gave him a stimulus just in time. Its effect, especially in combination with the two 'Norse Odes,' was far-reaching indeed. In the huge Ossianic mirror Gray saw, without recognizing, his own distorted image. Yet he had helped to prepare a public for Macpherson. The wand which the student-poet waved so cautiously, in bolder hands conjured up wider visions, many of which were only phantasmagoric. But when the world had shaken off these portentous shadows, it found its poetic horizon mysteriously enlarged; it was in this case a happiness that there is no controlling power to keep due measure between a novel experiment in literature and its possible effect. Between Gray and Scott intervene not only the Ossianic Mist, but the *Reliques* and that tide of Romanticism of which Percy and Macpherson, involuntary associates, opened the floodgates; a tide which returned to us in greater volume from abroad. Still the two poets somehow contrive to join hands; in that spiritual succession which criticism loves to trace back, we pass by such names as Mason and Warton and find in the 'Bard' and the 'Norse Odes' the first memorable exemplars of new studies put to poetic use by a mind delicate, fastidious, and a little hampered by conventions belonging to a very different tradition; and with these and 'Christabel' we link the 'Lay of the Last Minstrel.' It was given to Gray and to Coleridge, minds most critical, most receptive, but in the way of production most inert, to stimulate and fashion the labours of a spirit more robust, and capable, in that new world of romance in which Gray was a pioneer, of working with surprising rapidity and a versatile energy almost inexhaustible.

I. ODE ON THE SPRING.

Lo! where the rosy-bosom'd Hours,
  Fair VENUS' train appear,
Disclose the long-expecting flowers,
  And wake the purple year!
The Attic warbler pours her throat,
Responsive to the cuckow's note,
  The untaught harmony of spring:
While whisp'ring pleasure as they fly,
Cool Zephyrs thro' the clear blue sky
  Their gather'd fragrance fling. 10

Where'er the oak's thick branches stretch
  A broader browner shade;
Where'er the rude and moss-grown beech
  O'er-canopies the glade,
Beside some water's rushy brink
With me the Muse shall sit, and think
  (At ease reclin'd in rustic state)
How vain the ardour of the Crowd,
How low, how little are the Proud,
  How indigent the Great! 20

Still is the toiling hand of Care:
  The panting herds repose:
Yet hark, how thro' the peopled air
  The busy murmur glows!
The insect youth are on the wing,
Eager to taste the honied spring,
  And float amid the liquid noon:
Some lightly o'er the current skim,
Some shew their gayly-gilded trim
  Quick-glancing to the sun. 30

To Contemplation's sober eye
  Such is the race of Man:
And they that creep, and they that fly,
  Shall end where they began.
Alike the Busy and the Gay
But flutter thro' life's little day,
  In fortune's varying colours drest:
Brush'd by the hand of rough Mischance,
Or chill'd by age, their airy dance
  They leave, in dust to rest. 40

Methinks I hear in accents low
  The sportive kind reply:
Poor moralist! and what art thou?
  A solitary fly!
Thy Joys no glittering female meets,
No hive hast thou of hoarded sweets,
  No painted plumage to display:
On hasty wings thy youth is flown;
Thy sun is set, thy spring is gone—
  We frolick, while 'tis May. 50

II. SONNET

ON THE DEATH OF RICHARD WEST.

IN vain to me the smileing Mornings shine,
  And redning Phœbus lifts his golden Fire:
The Birds in vain their amorous Descant joyn;
  Or chearful Fields resume their green Attire:
These Ears, alas! for other Notes repine,
  A different Object do these Eyes require:
My lonely Anguish melts no Heart but mine;
  And in my Breast the imperfect Joys expire.
Yet Morning smiles the busy Race to chear,
  And new-born Pleasure brings to happier Men: 10
The Fields to all their wonted Tribute bear;
  To warm their little Loves the Birds complain:
I fruitless mourn to him that cannot hear,
  And weep the more because I weep in vain.

III. ODE

ON A DISTANT PROSPECT OF ETON COLLEGE.

Ἄνθρωπος· ἱκανὴ πρόφασις εἰς τὸ δυστυχεῖν.—MENANDER.

YE distant spires, ye antique towers,
  That crown the watry glade,
Where grateful Science still adores
  Her HENRY's holy Shade;
And ye, that from the stately brow
Of WINDSOR's heights th' expanse below
  Of grove, of lawn, of mead survey,
Whose turf, whose shade, whose flowers among
Wanders the hoary Thames along
  His silver-winding way: 10

Ah, happy hills, ah, pleasing shade,
  Ah, fields belov'd in vain,
Where once my careless childhood stray'd,
  A stranger yet to pain!
I feel the gales, that from ye blow,
  A momentary bliss bestow,
  As waving fresh their gladsome wing,
My weary soul they seem to sooth,
And, redolent of joy and youth,
  To breathe a second spring. 20

Say, father THAMES, for thou hast seen
  Full many a sprightly race
Disporting on thy margent green
  The paths of pleasure trace,
Who foremost now delight to cleave
With pliant arm thy glassy wave?
  The captive linnet which enthral?
What idle progeny succeed
To chase the rolling circle's speed,
  Or urge the flying ball? 30

While some on earnest business bent
  Their murm'ring labours ply
'Gainst graver hours, that bring constraint
  To sweeten liberty:
Some bold adventurers disdain
The limits of their little reign,
  And unknown regions dare descry:
Still as they run they look behind,
They hear a voice in every wind,
  And snatch a fearful joy. 40

Gay hope is theirs by fancy fed,
  Less pleasing when possest;
The tear forgot as soon as shed,
  The sunshine of the breast:
Theirs buxom health of rosy hue,
Wild wit, invention ever-new,
  And lively chear of vigour born;
The thoughtless day, the easy night,
The spirits pure, the slumbers light,
  That fly th' approach of morn. 50

Alas, regardless of their doom
  The little victims play!
No sense have they of ills to come,
  Nor care beyond to-day:
Yet see how all around 'em wait
The Ministers of human fate,
  And black Misfortune's baleful train!
Ah, shew them where in ambush stand
To seize their prey the murth'rous band!
  Ah, tell them, they are men! 60

These shall the fury Passions tear,
  The vulturs of the mind,
Disdainful Anger, pallid Fear,
  And Shame that sculks behind;
Or pineing Love shall waste their youth,
Or Jealousy with rankling tooth,
  That inly gnaws the secret heart,
And Envy wan, and faded Care,
Grim-visag'd comfortless Despair,
  And Sorrow's piercing dart. 70

Ambition this shall tempt to rise,
  Then whirl the wretch from high,
To bitter Scorn a sacrifice,
  And grinning Infamy.
The stings of Falshood those shall try,
And hard Unkindness' alter'd eye,
  That mocks the tear it forc'd to flow;
And keen Remorse with blood defil'd,
And moody Madness laughing wild
  Amid severest woe. 80

Lo, in the vale of years beneath
  A griesly troup are seen,
The painful family Death,
  More hideous than their Queen:
This racks the joints, this fires the veins,
That every labouring sinew strains,
  Those in the deeper vitals rage:
Lo, Poverty, to fill the band,
That numbs the soul with icy hand,
  And slow-consuming Age. 90

To each his suff'rings: all are men,
  Condemn'd alike to groan,
The tender for another's pain;
  Th' unfeeling for his own.
Yet, ah! why should they know their fate?
Since sorrow never comes too late,
  And happiness too swiftly flies.
Thought would destroy their paradise.
No more; where ignorance is bliss,
  'Tis folly to be wise. 100

IV. HYMN TO ADVERSITY.

Ζῆνα . . . . . .
τὸν φρονεῖν βροτοὺς ὁδώ-
σαντα, τῷ πάθει μαθὰν
θέντα κυρίως ἔχειν.
ÆSCHYLUS, *in Agamemnone.*

DAUGHTER of JOVE, relentless Power,
Thou Tamer of the human breast,
Whose iron scourge and tort'ring hour
The Bad affright, afflict the Best!
Bound in thy adamantine chain,
The Proud are taught to taste of pain,
And purple Tyrants vainly groan
With pangs unfelt before, unpitied and alone.

When first thy Sire to send on earth
Virtue, his darling Child, design'd, 10
To thee he gave the heav'nly Birth,
And bad to form her infant mind.
Stern rugged Nurse! thy rigid lore
With patience many a year she bore:
What sorrow was, thou bad'st her know,
And from her own she learn'd to melt at others' woe.

Scared at thy frown terrific, fly
Self-pleasing Folly's idle brood,
Wild Laughter, Noise, and thoughtless Joy,
And leave us leisure to be good. 20

Light they disperse, and with them go
The summer Friend, the flatt'ring Foe;
By vain Prosperity received,
To her they vow their truth, and are again believed.

Wisdom in sable garb array'd
Immers'd in rapt'rous thought profound,
And Melancholy, silent maid
With leaden eye, that loves the ground,
Still on thy solemn steps attend:
Warm Charity, the general Friend, 30
With Justice to herself severe,
And Pity, dropping soft the sadly-pleasing tear.

Oh, gently on thy Suppliant's head,
Dread goddess, lay thy chast'ning hand!
Not in thy Gorgon terrors clad,
Not circled with the vengeful Band
(As by the Impious thou art seen)
With thund'ring voice, and threat'ning mien,
With screaming Horror's funeral cry,
Despair, and fell Disease, and ghastly Poverty: 40

Thy form benign, oh Goddess, wear,
Thy milder influence impart,
Thy philosophic Train be there
To soften, not to wound my heart.
The gen'rous spark extinct revive,
Teach me to love and to forgive,
Exact my own defects to scan,
What others are, to feel, and know myself a Man.

V. HYMN TO IGNORANCE.

A FRAGMENT.

HAIL, horrors, hail! ye ever gloomy bowers,
Ye gothic fanes, and antiquated towers,
Where rushy Camus' slowly-winding flood
Perpetual draws his humid train of mud:
Glad I revisit thy neglected reign,
Oh take me to thy peaceful shade again.
But chiefly thee, whose influence breathed from high
Augments the native darkness of the sky,
Ah, Ignorance! soft salutary power!
Prostrate with filial reverence I adore. 10
Thrice hath Hyperion roll'd his annual race,
Since weeping I forsook thy fond embrace.
Oh say, successful dost thou still oppose
Thy leaden ægis 'gainst our ancient foes?
Still stretch, tenacious of thy right divine,
The massy sceptre o'er thy slumb'ring line?
And dews Lethean through the land dispense
To steep in slumbers each benighted sense?
If any spark of wit's delusive ray
Break out, and flash a momentary day, 20

With damp, cold touch forbid it to aspire,
And huddle up in fogs the dang'rous fire?
  Oh say—she hears me not, but, careless grown,
Lethargic nods upon her ebon throne.
Goddess! awake, arise! alas, my fears!
Can powers immortal feel the force of years?
Not thus of old, with ensigns wide unfurl'd,
She rode triumphant o'er the vanquish'd world;
Fierce nations own'd her unresisted might,
And all was Ignorance, and all was Night. 30
  Oh! sacred age! Oh! times for ever lost!
(The schoolman's glory, and the churchman's boast.)
For ever gone—yet still to Fancy new,
Her rapid wings the transient scene pursue,
And bring the buried ages back to view.
  High on her car, behold the grandam ride
Like old Sesostris with barbaric pride;
* * * a team of harness'd monarchs bend

* * * *

The ponderous waggon lumbered slowly on.

VI.

ODE

On The Death Of A
Favourite Cat,
Drowned In A Tub Of Gold Fishes

'Twas on a lofty Vase's side,
Where China's gayest Art had dyed
  The azure Flowers, that blow:
Demurest of the Tabby Kind,
The pensive Selima reclined
  Gazed on the Lake below. (6)

Her conscious Tail her Joy declared.
The fair round Face, the snowy Beard,
  The Velvet of her Paws,
Her Coat that with the Tortoise vyes,
Her Ears of Jett, and Emerald Eyes
  She saw, and purr'd Applause. (12)

Still had she gazed; but midst the Tide
Two angel-Forms were seen to glide,
  The Genii of the Stream:
Their scaly Armour's Tyrian Hue
Thro' richest Purple to the View
  Betray'd a golden Gleam. (18)

The Hapless Nymph with Wonder saw
A Whisker first and then a Claw,
  With many an ardent Wish,
She stretch'd in vain to reach the Prize.
What female Heart can Gold despise?
  What Cat's averse to Fish? (24)

Presumptuous Maid! with Looks intent
Again she stretch'd, again she bent
  Nor knew the Gulph between.
Malignant Fate sate by and smil'd
The slippery Verge her Feet beguiled:
  She tumbled headlong in. (30)

Eight Times emerging from the Flood
She mew'd to every watry God,
  Some speedy Aid to send
No Dolphin came, no Nereïd stirr'd;
No cruel Tom, nor Susan heard.
  A Fav'rite has no Friend! (36)

From hence, ye Beauties, undeceiv'd
Know, one false step is ne'er retrieved,
  And be with Caution bold.
Not all that tempts your wand'ring Eyes
And heedless Hearts is lawful Prize,
  Nor all that glisters, Gold. (42)

VII. AGRIPPINA

A FRAGMENT OF A TRAGEDY.

DRAMATIS PERSONÆ.

AGRIPPINA, the Empress-mother.
NERO, the Emperor.
POPPÆA, believed to be in love with OTHO.
OTHO, a young man of quality, in love with POPPÆA.
SENECA, the Emperor's Preceptor.
ANICETUS, Captain of the Guards.
DEMETRIUS, the Cynic, friend to SENECA.
ACERONIA, Confidant to AGRIPPINA.

SCENE—*The Emperor's villa at Baiæ.*

ARGUMENT.

"THE drama opens with the indignation of Agrippina at receiving her son's orders from Anicetus to remove from Baiæ, and to have her guard taken from her. At this time Otho having conveyed Poppæa from the house of her husband Rufus Crispinus, brings her to Baiæ, where he means to conceal her among the crowd; or, if his fraud is discovered, to have recourse to the Emperor's authority; but, knowing the lawless temper of Nero, he determines not to have recourse to that expedient but on the utmost necessity. In the meantime he commits her to the care of Anicetus, whom he takes to be his friend, and in whose age he thinks he may safely confide. Nero is not yet come to Baiæ: but Seneca, whom he sends before him, informs Agrippina of the accusation concerning Rubellius Plancus, and desires her to clear herself, which she does briefly: but demands to see her son, who, on his arrival, acquits her of all suspicion, and restores her to her honours. In the mean while, Anicetus, to whose care Poppæa had been intrusted by Otho, contrives the following plot to ruin Agrippina: he betrays his trust to Otho, and brings Nero, as it were by chance, to the sight of the beautiful Poppæa; the Emperor is immediately struck with her charms, and she, by a feigned resistance, increases his passion: though, in reality, she is from the first dazzled with the prospect of empire, and forgets Otho: she therefore joins with Anicetus in his design of ruining Agrippina, soon perceiving that it will be for her interest. Otho hearing that the Emperor had seen Poppæa, is much enraged; but not knowing that this interview was obtained through the treachery of Anicetus, is readily persuaded by him to see Agrippina in secret, and acquaint her with his fears that her son Nero would marry Poppæa. Agrippina, to support her own power, and to wean the Emperor from the love of Poppæa, gives Otho encouragement, and promises to support him. Anicetus secretly introduces Nero to hear their discourse; who resolves immediately on his mother's death, and, by Anicetus's means, to destroy her by drowning. A solemn feast, in honour of their reconciliation, is to be made; after which she being to go by sea to Bauli, the ship is so contrived as to sink or crush her; she escapes by accident, and returns to Baiæ. In this interval Otho has an interview with Poppæa; and being duped a second time by Anicetus and her, determines to fly with her into Greece, by means of a vessel which is to be furnished by Anicetus; but he, pretending to remove Poppæa on board in the night, conveys her to Nero's apartment: she then encourages and determines Nero to banish Otho, and finish the horrid deed he had attempted on his mother. Anicetus undertakes to execute his resolves; and, under pretence of a plot upon the Emperor's life, is sent with a guard to murder Agrippina, who is still at Baiæ in imminent fear, and irresolute how to conduct herself. The account of her death, and the Emperor's horror and fruitless remorse, finishes the drama."—[*Mason*, who professes to have united the plot and underplot, as he found these drawn up on two detached papers by Gray.]

ACT I. Scene I.

Agrippina. Aceronia.

Agrip. 'Tis well, begone! your errand is perform'd,
[*Speaks as to* Anicetus *entering.*
The message needs no comment. Tell your master,
His mother shall obey him. Say you saw her
Yielding due reverence to his high command:
Alone, unguarded and without a lictor,
As fits the daughter of Germanicus.
Say, she retir'd to Antium; there to tend
Her household cares, a woman's best employment.
What if you add, how she turn'd pale and trembled:
You think, you spied a tear stand in her eye, 10
And would have dropp'd, but that her pride restrain'd it?
(Go! you can paint it well) 'twill profit you,
And please the stripling. Yet 'twould dash his joy
To hear the spirit of Britannicus
Yet walks on earth: at least there are who know
Without a spell to raise, and bid it fire
A thousand haughty hearts, unus'd to shake
When a boy frowns, nor to be lured with smiles
To taste of hollow kindness, or partake
His hospitable board: they are aware 20
Of th' unpledg'd bowl, they love not aconite.
Acer. He's gone: and much I hope these walls alone
And the mute air are privy to your passion.
Forgive your servant's fears, who sees the danger

Which fierce resentment cannot fail to raise
In haughty youth, and irritated power.
Agrip. And dost thou talk to me, to me of danger,
Of haughty youth and irritated power,
To her that gave it being, her that arm'd
This painted Jove, and taught his novice hand 30
To aim the forked bolt; while he stood trembling,
Scar'd at the sound, and dazzled with its brightness?
'Tis like, thou hast forgot, when yet a stranger
To adoration, to the grateful steam
Of flattery's incense, and obsequious vows
From voluntary realms, a puny boy,
Deck'd with no other lustre, than the blood
Of Agrippina's race, he liv'd unknown
To fame, or fortune; haply eyed at distance
Some edileship, ambitious of the power 40
To judge of weights and measures; scarcely dar'd
On expectation's strongest wing to soar
High as the consulate, that empty shade
Of long-forgotten liberty: when I
Oped his young eye to bear the blaze of greatness;
Shew'd him where empire tower'd, and bade him strike
The noble quarry. Gods! then was the time
To shrink from danger; fear might then have worn
The mask of prudence; but a heart like mine,
A heart that glows with the pure Julian fire, 50
If bright ambition from her craggy seat
Display the radiant prize, will mount undaunted,
Gain the rough heights, and grasp the dangerous honour.
Acer. Through various life I have pursued your steps,
Have seen your soul, and wonder'd at its daring:
Hence rise my fears. Nor am I yet to learn
How vast the debt of gratitude which Nero

To such a mother owes; the world, you gave him,
Suffices not to pay the obligation.
 I well remember too (for I was present) 60
When in a secret and dead hour of night,
Due sacrifice perform'd with barb'rous rites
Of mutter'd charms, and solemn invocation,
You bade the Magi call the dreadful powers,
That read futurity, to know the fate
Impending o'er your son: their answer was,
If the son reign, the mother perishes.
Perish (you cried) the mother! reign the son!
He reigns, the rest is heav'n's; who oft has bade,
Ev'n when its will seem'd wrote in lines of blood, 70
Th' unthought event disclose a whiter meaning.
Think too how oft in weak and sickly minds
The sweets of kindness lavishly indulg'd
Rankle to gall; and benefits too great
To be repaid, sit heavy on the soul,
As unrequited wrongs. The willing homage
Of prostrate Rome, the senate's joint applause,
The riches of the earth, the train of pleasures
That wait on youth, and arbitrary sway:
These were your gift, and with them you bestow'd 80
The very power he has to be ungrateful.
 Agrip. Thus ever grave and undisturb'd reflection
Pours its cool dictates in the madding ear
Of rage, and thinks to quench the fire it feels not.
Say'st thou I must be cautious, must be silent,
And tremble at the phantom I have raised?
Carry to him thy timid counsels. He
Perchance may heed 'em: tell him too, that one
Who had such liberal power to give, may still
With equal power resume that gift, and raise 90

A tempest that shall shake her own creation
To its original atoms—tell me! say
This mighty emperor, this dreaded hero,
Has he beheld the glittering front of war?
Knows his soft ear the trumpet's thrilling voice,
And outcry of the battle? Have his limbs
Sweat under iron harness? Is he not
The silken son of dalliance, nurs'd in ease
And pleasure's flow'ry lap?—Rubellius lives,
And Sylla has his friends, though school'd by fear 100
To bow the supple knee, and court the times
With shows of fair obeisance; and a call,
Like mine, might serve belike to wake pretensions
Drowsier than theirs, who boast the genuine blood
Of our imperial house. [Cannot my nod]
Rouse [up] eight hardy legions, wont to stem
With stubborn nerves the tide, and face the rigour
Of bleak Germania's snows [?] Four, not less brave,
That in Armenia quell the Parthian force
Under the warlike Corbulo, by me 110
Mark'd for their leader: these, by ties confirm'd,
Of old respect and gratitude, are mine.
Surely the Masians[1] too, and those of Egypt,
Have not forgot my sire: the eye of Rome,
And the Prætorian camp have long rever'd
With custom'd awe, the daughter, sister, wife,
And mother of their Cæsars.
Ha! by Juno,
It bears a noble semblance. On this base
My great revenge shall rise; or say we sound
The trump of liberty; there will not want, 120
Even in the servile senate, ears to own

[1] [Qu.? Asians].

Her spirit-stirring voice; Soranus there,
And Cassius; Vetus too, and Thrasea,
Minds of the antique cast, rough, stubborn souls,
That struggle with the yoke. How shall the spark
Unquenchable, that glows within their breasts,
Blaze into freedom, when the idle herd
(Slaves from the womb, created but to stare,
And bellow in the Circus) yet will start,
And shake 'em at the name of liberty, 130
Stung by a senseless word, a vain tradition,
As there were magic in it? Wrinkled beldams
Teach it their grandchildren, as somewhat rare
That anciently appear'd, but when, extends
Beyond their chronicle—oh! 'tis a cause
To arm the hand of childhood, and rebrace
The slacken'd sinews of time-wearied age.
Yes, we may meet, ungrateful boy, we may!
Again the buried Genius of old Rome
Shall from the dust uprear his reverend head, 140
Rous'd by the shout of millions: there before
His high tribunal thou and I appear.
Let majesty sit on thy awful brow,
And lighten from thy eye: around thee call
The gilded swarm that wantons in the sunshine
Of thy full favour; Seneca be there
In gorgeous phrase of labour'd eloquence
To dress thy plea, and Burrhus strengthen it
With his plain soldier's oath, and honest seeming.
Against thee, liberty and Agrippina: 150
The world, the prize; and fair befall the victors.
But soft! why do I waste the fruitless hours
In threats unexecuted? Haste thee, fly
These hated walls that seem to mock my shame,

And cast me forth in duty to their lord.
  My thought aches at him; not the basilisk
More deadly to the sight, than is to me
The cool injurious eye of frozen kindness.
I will not meet its poison. Let him feel
Before he sees me. Yes, I will be gone, 160
But not to Antium—all shall be confess'd,
Whate'er the frivolous tongue of giddy fame
Has spread among the crowd; things, that but whisper'd
Have arch'd the hearer's brow, and riveted
His eyes in fearful extasy: no matter
What; so't be strange, and dreadful.—Sorceries,
Assassinations, poisonings—the deeper
My guilt, the blacker his ingratitude.
  And you, ye manes of ambition's victims,
Enshrined Claudius, with the pitied ghosts 170
Of the Syllani, doom'd to early death,
(Ye unavailing horrors, fruitless crimes!)
If from the realms of night my voice ye hear,
In lieu of penitence, and vain remorse,
Accept my vengeance. Though by me ye bled,
He wàs the cause. My love, my fears for him,
Dried the soft springs of pity in my heart,
And froze them up with deadly cruelty.
Yet if your injur'd shades demand my fate,
If murder cries for murder, blood for blood, 180
Let me not fall alone; but crush his pride,
And sink the traitor in his mother's ruin. [*Exeunt.*

Scene II.

OTHO, POPPÆA.

Otho. Thus far we're safe. Thanks to the rosy queen
Of amorous thefts: and had her wanton son
Lent us his wings, we could not have beguil'd
With more elusive speed the dazzled sight
Of wakeful jealousy. Be gay securely;
Dispel, my fair, with smiles, the tim'rous cloud
That hangs on thy clear brow. So Helen look'd,
So her white neck reclin'd, so was she borne 190
By the young Trojan to his gilded bark
With fond reluctance, yielding modesty,
And oft reverted eye, as if she knew not
Whether she fear'd, or wish'd to be pursued.

* * * *

VIII. THE ALLIANCE OF EDUCATION AND GOVERNMENT.

A FRAGMENT.

ESSAY I.

. . . *Πόταγ', ὦ 'γαθέ· τὰν γὰρ ἀοιδὰν*
Οὔτι πα εἰς 'Αΐδαν γε τὸν ἐκλελάθοντα φυλαξεῖς.
THEOCRITUS, *Id.* I. 63.

As sickly Plants betray a niggard Earth,
Whose barren Bosom starves her generous Birth,
Nor genial Warmth, nor genial Juice retains
Their Roots to feed, and fill their verdant Veins;
And as in Climes, where Winter holds his Reign,
The Soil, tho' fertile, will not teem in vain,
Forbids her Gems to swell, her Shades to rise,
Nor trusts her Blossoms to the churlish Skies;
So draw Mankind in vain the vital Airs,
Unform'd, unfriended, by those kindly Cares, 10
That Health and Vigour to the Soul impart,
Spread the young Thought, and warm the opening Heart.
So fond Instruction on the growing Powers
Of Nature idly lavishes her Stores,
If equal Justice with unclouded Face

Smile not indulgent on the rising Race,
And scatter with a free, though frugal, Hand
Light golden Showers of Plenty o'er the Land.
But Tyranny has fix'd her Empire there,
To check their tender Hopes with chilling Fear, 20
And blast the blooming Promise of the Year.
  This spacious animated Scene survey
From where the rowling Orb, that gives the Day,
His sable Sons with nearer Course surrounds
To either Pole, and Life's remotest Bounds,
How rude soe'er th' exterior Form we find,
Howe'er Opinion tinge the varied Mind,
Alike to all the Kind impartial Heav'n
The Sparks of Truth and Happiness has given.
With Sense to feel, with Mem'ry to retain, 30
They follow Pleasure, and they fly from Pain;
Their Judgment mends the Plan their Fancy draws,
Th' Event presages, and explores the Cause.
The soft Returns of Gratitude they know,
By Fraud elude, by Force repell the Foe,
While mutual Wishes, mutual Woes endear
The social Smile, the sympathetic Tear.
  Say then, thro' Ages by what Fate confined
To different Climes seem diff'rent Souls assign'd?
Here measured Laws and philosophic Ease 40
Fix and improve the polish'd Arts of Peace:
There Industry and Gain their Vigils keep,
Command the Winds, and tame th' unwilling Deep.
Here Force and hardy Deeds of Blood prevail:
There languid Pleasure sighs in every Gale.
Oft o'er the trembling Nations from afar
Has Scythia breath'd the living Cloud of War;
And where the Deluge burst, with sweepy sway

Their Arms, their Kings, their Gods were roll'd away.
As oft have issued, Host impelling Host, 50
The blue-eyed Myriads from the Baltic Coast.
The prostrate South to the Destroyer yields
Her boasted Titles and her golden Fields;
With grim Delight the Brood of Winter view
A brighter Day and Heavens of azure Hue;
Scent the new Fragrance of the breathing Rose,
And quaff the pendant Vintage as it grows.
Proud of the yoke, and pliant to the rod,
Why yet does Asia dread a Monarch's nod,
While European Freedom still withstands 60
Th' encroaching Tide, that drowns her lessening lands,
And sees far off with an indignant groan,
Her native plains, and empires once her own?
Can opener skies, and suns of fiercer flame
O'erpower the fire that animates our frame;
As Lamps that shed at Ev'n a cheerfull ray
Fade and expire beneath the eye of day?
Need we the influence of the northern star
To string our nerves and steel our hearts to war?
And where the face of nature laughs around, 70
Must sick'ning virtue fly the tainted ground?
Unmanly Thought! what seasons can controul,
What fancied Zone can circumscribe the Soul,
Who conscious of the source from whence she springs,
By Reason's light on Resolution's wings,
Spite of her frail companion dauntless goes
O'er Libya's deserts and through Zembla's snows?
She bids each slumb'ring energy awake,
Another touch, another temper take,
Suspends th' inferior laws that rule our clay: 80
The stubborn elements confess her sway,

Their little wants, their low desires refine,
And raise the mortal to a height divine.
Not but the human fabrick from the birth
Imbibes a flavour of its parent earth,
As various tracts enforce a various toil,
The manners speak the idiom of their soil.
An Iron race the mountain cliffs maintain,
Foes to the gentler genius of the plain:
For where unwearied sinews must be found 90
With side-long plough to quell the flinty ground,
To turn the torrent's swift-descending flood,
To brave the savage rushing from the wood,
What wonder, if to patient valour train'd
They guard with spirit what by strength they gain'd?
And while their rocky ramparts round they see,
The rough abode of want and liberty,
(As lawless force from confidence will grow)
Insult the plenty of the vales below?
What wonder in the sultry climes, that spread 100
Where Nile redundant o'er his Summer bed
From his broad bosom life and verdure flings
And broods o'er Egypt with his wat'ry wings,
If with adventrous oar and ready sail
The dusky people drive before the gale;
Or on frail floats to distant cities ride,
That rise and glitter o'er the ambient tide

* * * *

When love could teach a monarch to be wise,
And gospel-light first dawn'd from Bullen's eyes.

COMMENTARY.

THE author's subject being (as we have seen) *The necessary alliance between a good form of government and a good mode of education, in order to produce the happiness of mankind*, the Poem opens with two similes; an uncommon kind of exordium: but which I suppose the poet intentionally chose, to intimate the analogical method he meant to pursue in his subsequent reasonings. 1st, He asserts that men without education are like sickly plants in a cold or barren soil (l. 1 to 5, and 8 to 12); and, 2dly, he compares them, when unblest with a just and well-regulated government, to plants that will not blossom or bear fruit in an unkindly and inclement air (l. 5 to 9, and l. 13 to 22). Having thus laid down the two propositions he means to prove, he begins by examining into the characteristics which (taking a general view of mankind) all men have in common one with another (l. 22 to 39); they covet pleasure and avoid pain (l. 31); they feel gratitude for benefits (l. 34); they desire to avenge wrongs, which they effect either by force or cunning (l. 35); they are linked to each other by their common feelings, and participate in sorrow and in joy (l. 36, 37). If then all the human species agree in so many moral particulars, whence arises the diversity of national characters? This question the poet puts at line 38, and dilates upon to l. 64. Why, says he, have some nations shown a propensity to commerce and industry; others to war and rapine; others to ease and pleasure? (l. 42 to 46). Why have the northern people overspread, in all ages, and prevailed over the southern? (l. 46 to 58). Why has Asia been, time out of mind, the seat of despotism, and Europe that of freedom? (l. 59 to 64). Are we from these instances to imagine men necessarily enslaved to the inconveniences of the climate where they were born? (l. 64 to 72). Or are we not rather to suppose there is a natural strength in the human mind, that is able to vanquish and break through them? (l. 72 to 84). It is confest, however, that men receive an early tincture from the situation they are placed in, and the climate which produces them (l. 84 to 88). Thus the inhabitants of the mountains, inured to labour and patience, are naturally trained to war (l. 88 to 96); while those of the plain are more open to any attack, and softened by ease and plenty (l. 96 to 99). Again, the Ægyptians, from the nature of their situation, might be the inventors of home navigation, from a necessity of keeping up an intercourse between their towns during the inundation of the Nile (l. 99 to * * *). Those persons would naturally have the first turn to commerce who inhabited a barren coast like the Tyrians, and were persecuted by some neighbouring tyrant; or were drove to take refuge on some shoals, like the Venetian and Hollánder; their discovery of some rich island, in the infancy of the world, described. The Tartar hardened to war by his rigorous climate and pastoral life, and by his disputes for water and herbage in a country without land-marks, as also by skirmishes between his rival clans, was consequently fitted to conquer his rich southern neighbours, whom ease and luxury had enervated: yet this is no proof that liberty and valour may not exist in southern climes, since the Syrians and Carthaginians gave noble instances of both; and the Arabians carried their conquests as far as the Tartars. Rome also (for many centuries) repulsed those very nations which, when she grew weak, at length demolished her extensive empire * * * *.—Gray.

The reader will perceive that the Commentary goes further than the text. The reason for which is, that the Editor found it so on the paper from which he formed that comment; and as the thoughts seemed to be those which Gray would have next graced with the harmony of his numbers, he held it best to give them in continuation. There are other maxims on different papers, all apparently relating to the same subject, which are too excellent to be lost; these therefore (as the place in which he meant to employ them cannot be ascertained) I shall subjoin to this note, under the title of detached Sentiments:—

"Man is a creature not capable of cultivating his mind but in society, and in that only where he is not a slave to the necessities of life.

"Want is the mother of the inferior arts, but Ease that of the finer; as eloquence, policy, morality, poetry, sculpture, painting, architecture, which are the improvements of the former.

"The climate inclines some nations to contemplation and pleasure; others to hardship, action, and war; but not so as to incapacitate the former for courage and discipline, or the latter for civility, politeness, and works of genius.

"It is the proper work of education and government united to redress the faults that arise from the soil and air.

"The principal drift of education should be to make men *think* in the northern climates, and *act* in the southern.

"The different steps and degrees of education may be compared to the artificer's operations upon marble; it is one thing to dig it out of the quarry, and another to square it, to give it gloss and lustre, call forth every beautiful spot and vein, shape it into a column, or animate it into a statue.

"To a native of free and happy governments his country is always dear;

'He loves his old hereditary trees:' Cowley.

while the subject of a tyrant has no country; he is therefore selfish and base-minded; he has no family, no posterity, no desire of fame; or, if he has, of one that turns not on its proper object.

"Any nation that wants public spirit, neglects education, ridicules the desire of fame, and even of virtue and reason, must be ill governed.

"Commerce changes entirely the fate and genius of nations, by communicating arts and opinions, circulating money, and introducing the materials of luxury; she first opens and polishes the mind, then corrupts and enervates both that and the body.

"Those invasions of effeminate southern nations by the warlike northern people, seem (in spite of all the terror, mischief, and ignorance which they brought with them) to be necessary evils; in order to revive the spirit of mankind, softened and broken by the arts of commerce, to restore them to their native liberty and equality, and to give them again the power of supporting danger and hardship; so a comet, with all the horrors that attend it as it passes through our system, brings a supply of warmth and light to the sun, and of moisture to the air.

"The doctrine of Epicurus is ever ruinous to society; it had its rise when Greece was declining, and perhaps hastened its dissolution, as also that of Rome; it is now propagated in France and in England, and seems likely to produce the same effect in both.

"One principal characteristic of vice in the present age is the contempt of fame.

"Many are the uses of good fame to a generous mind: it extends our existence and example into future ages; continues and propagates virtue, which otherwise would be as short-lived as our frame; and prevents the prevalence of vice in a generation more corrupt even than our own. It is impossible to conquer that natural desire we have of being remembered; even criminal ambition and avarice, the most selfish of all passions, would wish to leave a name behind them."

Thus, with all the attention that a connoisseur in painting employs in collecting every slight outline as well as finished drawing which led to the completion of some capital picture, I have endeavoured to preserve every fragment of this great poetical design. It surely deserved this care, as it was one of the noblest which Mr Gray ever attempted; and also, as far as he carried it into execution, the most exquisitely finished. That he carried it no further is, and must ever be, a most sensible loss to the republic of letters.—Mason.

IX. ELEGY WRITTEN IN A COUNTRY CHURCH-YARD.

THE Curfew tolls the knell of parting day,
The lowing herd wind slowly o'er the lea,
The plowman homeward plods his weary way,
And leaves the world to darkness and to me.

Now fades the glimmering landscape on the sight,
And all the air a solemn stillness holds,
Save where the beetle wheels his droning flight,
And drowsy tinklings lull the distant folds:

Save that from yonder ivy-mantled tow'r
The mopeing owl does to the moon complain 10
Of such as, wand'ring near her secret bow'r,
Molest her ancient solitary reign.

Beneath those rugged elms, that yew-tree's shade,
Where heaves the turf in many a mould'ring heap,
Each in his narrow cell for ever laid,
The rude Forefathers of the hamlet sleep.

The breezy call of incense-breathing Morn,
  The swallow twitt'ring from the straw-built shed,
The cock's shrill clarion, or the echoing horn,
  No more shall rouse them from their lowly bed. 20

For them no more the blazing hearth shall burn,
  Or busy housewife ply her evening care:
No children run to lisp their sire's return,
  Or climb his knee the envied kiss to share.

Oft did the harvest to their sickle yield,
  Their furrow oft the stubborn glebe has broke:
How jocund did they drive their team afield!
  How bow'd the woods beneath their sturdy stroke!

Let not Ambition mock their useful toil,
  Their homely joys, and destiny obscure; 30
Nor Grandeur hear with a disdainful smile
  The short and simple annals of the poor.

The boast of heraldry, the pomp of pow'r,
  And all that beauty, all that wealth e'er gave,
Awaits alike th' inevitable hour.
  The paths of glory lead but to the grave.

Nor you, ye Proud, impute to These the fault,
  If Mem'ry o'er their Tomb no Trophies raise,
Where through the long-drawn isle and fretted vault
  The pealing anthem swells the note of praise. 40

Can storied urn or animated bust
  Back to its mansion call the fleeting breath?
Can Honour's voice provoke the silent dust,
  Or Flatt'ry soothe the dull cold ear of death?

Perhaps in this neglected spot is laid
  Some heart once pregnant with celestial fire;
Hands, that the rod of empire might have sway'd,
  Or wak'd to extasy the living lyre.

But Knowledge to their eyes her ample page
  Rich with the spoils of time did ne'er unroll; 50
Chill Penury repress'd their noble rage,
  And froze the genial current of the soul.

Full many a gem of purest ray serene,
  The dark unfathom'd caves of ocean bear:
Full many a flower is born to blush unseen,
  And waste its sweetness on the desert air.

Some village-Hampden, that with dauntless breast
  The little Tyrant of his fields withstood,
Some mute inglorious Milton here may rest,
  Some Cromwell guiltless of his country's blood. 60

Th' applause of list'ning senates to command,
  The threats of pain and ruin to despise,
To scatter plenty o'er a smiling land,
  And read their hist'ry in a nation's eyes,

Their lot forbad: nor circumscrib'd alone
  Their growing virtues, but their crimes confin'd;
Forbad to wade through slaughter to a throne,
  And shut the gates of mercy on mankind,

The struggling pangs of conscious truth to hide,
  To quench the blushes of ingenuous shame, 70
Or heap the shrine of Luxury and Pride
  With incense kindled at the Muse's flame.

Far from the madding crowd's ignoble strife,
  Their sober wishes never learn'd to stray;
Along the cool sequester'd vale of life
  They kept the noiseless tenor of their way.

Yet ev'n these bones from insult to protect
  Some frail memorial still erected nigh,
With uncouth rhimes and shapeless sculpture deck'd,
  Implores the passing tribute of a sigh. 80

Their name, their years, spelt by th' unletter'd muse,
  The place of fame and elegy supply:
And many a holy text around she strews,
  That teach the rustic moralist to die.

For who to dumb Forgetfulness a prey,
  This pleasing anxious being e'er resign'd,
Left the warm precincts of the chearful day,
  Nor cast one longing ling'ring look behind?

On some fond breast the parting soul relies,
  Some pious drops the closing eye requires; 90
E'en from the tomb the voice of Nature cries,
  E'en in our Ashes live their wonted Fires.

For thee, who mindful of th' unhonour'd Dead,
  Dost in these lines their artless tale relate;
If chance, by lonely contemplation led,
  Some kindred spirit shall inquire thy fate,—

Haply some hoary-headed Swain may say,
  "Oft have we seen him at the peep of dawn
Brushing with hasty steps the dews away
  To meet the sun upon the upland lawn. 100

[Him have we seen the Green-wood Side along,
While o'er the Heath we hied, our Labours done,
Oft as the Woodlark piped her farewell Song,
With whistful eyes pursue the setting Sun.]

"There at the foot of yonder nodding beech,
That wreathes its old fantastic roots so high,
His listless length at noontide would he stretch,
And pore upon the brook that babbles by.

"Hard by yon wood, now smiling as in scorn,
Mutt'ring his wayward fancies he would rove, 110
Now drooping, woeful-wan, like one forlorn,
Or craz'd with care, or cross'd in hopeless love.

"One morn I miss'd him on the custom'd hill,
Along the heath, and near his fav'rite tree;
Another came; nor yet beside the rill,
Nor up the lawn, nor at the wood was he:

"The next, with dirges due in sad array
Slow thro' the church-way path we saw him born.—
Approach and read (for thou can'st read) the lay,
Grav'd on the stone beneath yon aged thorn." 120

[There scatter'd oft, the earliest of the Year,
By Hands unseen are Showers of Violets found;
The Redbreast loves to build and warble there,
And little Footsteps lightly print the Ground.]

THE EPITAPH.

Here rests his head upon the lap of Earth
A Youth, to Fortune and to Fame unknown.
Fair Science frown'd not on his humble birth,
And Melancholy mark'd him for her own.

Large was his bounty, and his soul sincere,
Heav'n did a recompence as largely send: 130
He gave to Mis'ry all he had, a tear,
He gain'd from Heav'n ('twas all he wish'd) a friend.

No farther seek his merits to disclose,
Or draw his frailties from their dread abode,
(There they alike in trembling hope repose,)
The bosom of his Father and his God.

X. A LONG STORY.

In Britain's Isle, no matter where,
  An ancient pile of building stands:
The Huntingdons and Hattons there
  Employ'd the power of Fairy hands

To raise the cieling's fretted height,
  Each pannel in achievements cloathing,
Rich windows that exclude the light,
  And passages, that lead to nothing.

Full oft within the spatious walls,
  When he had fifty winters o'er him, 10
My grave Lord-Keeper led the Brawls;
  The Seal, and Maces, danc'd before him.

His bushy beard, and shoe-strings green,
  His high-crown'd hat, and satin-doublet,
Mov'd the stout heart of England's Queen,
  Tho' Pope and Spaniard could not trouble it.

What, in the very first beginning!
  Shame of the versifying tribe!
Your Hist'ry whither are you spinning?
  Can you do nothing but describe? 20

A House there is, (and that's enough)
  From whence one fatal morning issues
A brace of Warriors, not in buff,
  But rustling in their silks and tissues.

The first came cap-a-pee from France
  Her conqu'ring destiny fulfilling,
Whom meaner Beauties eye askance,
  And vainly ape her art of killing.

The other Amazon kind Heaven
  Had arm'd with spirit, wit, and satire: 30
But COBHAM had the polish given
  And tip'd her arrows with good-nature.

To celebrate her eyes, her air——
  Coarse panegyricks would but teaze her.
Melissa is her Nom de Guerre.
  Alas, who would not wish to please her!

With bonnet blue and capucine,
  And aprons long they hid their armour,
And veil'd their weapons bright and keen
  In pity to the country-farmer. 40

Fame, in the shape of Mr. Purt,
  (By this time all the Parish know it)
Had told, that thereabouts there lurk'd
  A wicked Imp they call a Poet,

Who prowl'd the country far and near,
  Bewitch'd the children of the peasants,
Dried up the cows, and lam'd the deer,
  And suck'd the eggs, and kill'd the pheasants.

My Lady heard their joint petition,
  Swore by her coronet and ermine, 50
She'd issue out her high commission
  To rid the manour of such vermin.

The Heroines undertook the task,
  Thro' lanes unknown, o'er stiles they ventur'd,
Rap'd at the door, nor stay'd to ask,
  But bounce into the parlour enter'd.

The trembling family they daunt,
  They flirt, they sing, they laugh, they tattle,
Rummage his Mother, pinch his Aunt,
  And up stairs in a whirlwind rattle. 60

Each hole and cupboard they explore,
  Each creek and cranny of his chamber,
Run hurry-skurry round the floor,
  And o'er the bed and tester clamber,

Into the Drawers and China pry,
  Papers and books, a huge Imbroglio!
Under a tea-cup he might lie,
  Or creased, like dogs-ears, in a folio.

On the first marching of the troops
  The Muses, hopeless of his pardon, 70
Convey'd him underneath their hoops
  To a small closet in the garden.

So Rumor says. (Who will, believe.)
  But that they left the door a-jarr,
Where, safe and laughing in his sleeve,
  He heard the distant din of war.

Short was his joy. He little knew
  The power of Magick was no fable.
Out of the window, whisk, they flew,
  But left a spell upon the table. 80

The words too eager to unriddle,
  The Poet felt a strange disorder:
Transparent birdlime form'd the middle,
  And chains invisible the border.

So cunning was the Apparatus,
  The powerful pothooks did so move him,
That will he, nill he, to the Great-house
  He went, as if the Devil drove him.

Yet on his way (no sign of grace,
  For folks in fear are apt to pray) 90
To Phœbus he prefer'd his case,
  And beg'd his aid that dreadful day.

The Godhead would have back'd his quarrel,
  But with a blush on recollection
Own'd, that his quiver and his laurel
  'Gainst four such eyes were no protection.

The Court was sate, the Culprit there,
  Forth from their gloomy mansions creeping
The Lady *Janes* and *Joans* repair,
  And from the gallery stand peeping: 100

Such as in silence of the night
  Come (sweep) along some winding entry
(*Styack* has often seen the sight)
  Or at the chappel-door stand sentry;

In peaked hoods and mantles tarnish'd,
  Sour visages, enough to scare ye,
High Dames of honour once, that garnish'd
  The drawing-room of fierce Queen Mary.

The Peeress comes. The Audience stare,
  And doff their hats with due submission: 110
She curtsies, as she takes her chair,
  To all the People of condition.

The bard, with many an artful fib,
  Had in imagination fenc'd him,
Disprov'd the arguments of *Squib*,
  And all that *Groom* could urge against him.

But soon his rhetorick forsook him,
  When he the solemn hall had seen;
A sudden fit of ague shook him,
  He stood as mute as poor *Macleane*. 120

Yet something he was heard to mutter,
  "How in the park beneath an old-tree
(Without design to hurt the butter,
  Or any malice to the poultry,)

"He once or twice had pen'd a sonnet;
  Yet hop'd, that he might save his bacon:
Numbers would give their oaths upon it,
  He ne'er was for a conj'rer taken."

The ghostly Prudes with hagged face
  Already had condemn'd the sinner. 130
My Lady rose, and with a grace——
  She smiled, and bid him come to dinner.

"Jesu-Maria! Madam Bridget,
  Why, what can the Viscountess mean?"
(Cried the square Hoods in woful fidget)
  "The times are alter'd quite and clean!

"Decorum's turn'd to mere civility;
  Her air and all her manners shew it.
Commend me to her affability!
  Speak to a Commoner and Poet!" 140

[*Here* 500 *stanzas are lost*]

And so God save our noble King,
  And guard us from long-winded Lubbers,
That to eternity would sing,
  And keep my Lady from her Rubbers.

XI. STANZAS TO MR RICHARD BENTLEY.

In silent gaze the tuneful choir among,
  Half pleas'd, half blushing, let the Muse admire,
While Bentley leads her sister-art along,
  And bids the pencil answer to the lyre.

See, in their course, each transitory thought
  Fix'd by his touch a lasting essence take;
Each dream, in fancy's airy colouring wrought
  To local symmetry and life awake!

The tardy rhymes that us'd to linger on,
  To censure cold, and negligent of fame, 10
In swifter measures animated run,
  And catch a lustre from his genuine flame.

Ah! could they catch his strength, his easy grace,
  His quick creation, his unerring line;
The energy of Pope they might efface,
  And Dryden's harmony submit to mine.

But not to one in this benighted age
  Is that diviner inspiration giv'n,
That burns in Shakespeare's or in Milton's page,
  The pomp and prodigality of heav'n, 20

As when conspiring in the diamond's blaze,
  The meaner gems that singly charm the sight,
Together dart their intermingled rays,
  And dazzle with a luxury of light.

Enough for me, if to some feeling breast
  My lines a secret sympathy . . . .
And as their pleasing influence . . . .
  A sigh of soft reflection . . . .

Φωνᾶντα συνετοῖσιν· ἐς δὲ τὸ πᾶν ἑρμηνέων
χατίζει. PINDAR, *Olymp.* II [85, 86].

XII. THE PROGRESS OF POESY.

A PINDARIC ODE.

I. 1.

AWAKE, Æolian lyre, awake,
And give to rapture all thy trembling strings.
From Helicon's harmonious springs
A thousand rills their mazy progress take:
The laughing flowers, that round them blow,
Drink life and fragrance as they flow.
Now the rich stream of music winds along
Deep, majestic, smooth, and strong,
Thro' verdant vales, and Ceres' golden reign:
Now rowling down the steep amain, 10
Headlong, impetuous, see it pour;
The rocks, and nodding groves rebellow to the roar.

I. 2.

Oh! Sovereign of the willing soul,
Parent of sweet and solemn-breathing airs,
Enchanting shell! the sullen Cares
And frantic Passions hear thy soft controul.
On Thracia's hills the Lord of War
Has curb'd the fury of his car,

And drop'd his thirsty lance at thy command.
Perching on the scept'red hand 20
Of Jove, thy magic lulls the feather'd king
With ruffled plumes, and flagging wing:
Quench'd in dark clouds of slumber lie
The terror of his beak, and light'nings of his eye.

I. 3.

Thee the voice, the dance, obey,
Temper'd to thy warbled lay.
O'er Idalia's velvet-green
The rosy-crownèd Loves are seen
On Cytherea's day
With antic Sports, and blue-eyed Pleasures, 30
Frisking light in frolic measures;
Now pursuing, now retreating,
  Now in circling troops they meet:
To brisk notes in cadence beating,
  Glance their many-twinkling feet.
Slow melting strains their Queen's approach declare:
  Where'er she turns the Graces homage pay.
With arms sublime, that float upon the air,
  In gliding state she wins her easy way:
O'er her warm cheek, and rising bosom, move 40
The bloom of young Desire, and purple light of Love.

II. 1.

  Man's feeble race what Ills await,
Labour, and Penury, the racks of Pain,
Disease, and Sorrow's weeping train,
  And Death, sad refuge from the storms of Fate!

The fond complaint, my Song, disprove,
And justify the laws of Jove.
Say, has he giv'n in vain the heav'nly Muse?
Night, and all her sickly dews,
Her Spectres wan, and Birds of boding cry, 50
He gives to range the dreary sky:
Till down the eastern cliffs afar
Hyperion's march they spy, and glitt'ring shafts of war.

II. 2.

In climes beyond the solar road,
Where shaggy forms o'er ice-built mountains roam,
The Muse has broke the twilight-gloom
To chear the shiv'ring Native's dull abode.
And oft, beneath the od'rous shade
Of Chili's boundless forests laid,
She deigns to hear the savage Youth repeat 60
In loose numbers wildly sweet
Their feather-cinctur'd Chiefs, and dusky Loves.
Her track, where'er the Goddess roves,
Glory pursue, and generous Shame,
Th' unconquerable Mind, and Freedom's holy flame.

II. 3.

Woods, that wave o'er Delphi's steep,
Isles, that crown th' Egæan deep,
Fields, that cool Ilissus laves,
Or where Mæander's amber waves
In lingering Lab'rinths creep, 70
How do your tuneful Echo's languish,
Mute, but to the voice of Anguish?

Where each old poetic Mountain
  Inspiration breath'd around:
Ev'ry shade and hallow'd Fountain
  Murmur'd deep a solemn sound:
Till the sad Nine in Greece's evil hour,
  Left their Parnassus for the Latian plains.
Alike they scorn the pomp of tyrant-Power,
  And coward Vice, that revels in her chains. 80
When Latium had her lofty spirit lost,
They sought, oh Albion! next thy sea-encircled coast.

III. 1.

  Far from the sun and summer-gale,
In thy green lap was Nature's Darling laid,
What time, where lucid Avon stray'd,
  To Him the mighty Mother did unveil
Her aweful face: The dauntless Child
Stretch'd forth his little arms, and smiled.
This pencil take (she said) whose colours clear
Richly paint the vernal year: 90
Thine too these golden keys, immortal Boy!
This can unlock the gates of Joy;
Of Horrour that, and thrilling Fears,
Or ope the sacred source of sympathetic Tears.

III. 2.

  Nor second He, that rode sublime
Upon the seraph-wings of Extasy,
The secrets of th' Abyss to spy.
  He pass'd the flaming bounds of Place and Time:

The living Throne, the saphire-blaze,
Where Angels tremble, while they gaze, 100
He saw; but blasted with excess of light,
Closed his eyes in endless night.
Behold, where Dryden's less presumptuous car,
Wide o'er the fields of Glory bear
Two Coursers of ethereal race,
With necks in thunder cloath'd, and long-resounding pace.

III. 3.

Hark, his hands the lyre explore!
Bright-eyed Fancy hov'ring o'er
Scatters from her pictur'd urn
Thoughts, that breath, and words, that burn. 110
But ah! 'tis heard no more——
Oh! Lyre divine, what daring Spirit
Wakes thee now? tho' he inherit
Nor the pride, nor ample pinion,
  That the Theban Eagle bear
Sailing with supreme dominion
  Thro' the azure deep of air:
Yet oft before his infant eyes would run
  Such forms, as glitter in the Muse's ray,
With orient hues, unborrow'd of the Sun: 120
  Yet shall he mount, and keep his distant way
Beyond the limits of a vulgar fate,
Beneath the Good how far—but far above the Great.

XIII. THE BARD.

A PINDARIC ODE.

I. 1.

'RUIN seize thee, ruthless King!
'Confusion on thy banners wait,
'Tho' fann'd by Conquest's crimson wing
'They mock the air with idle state.
'Helm, nor Hauberk's twisted mail,
'Nor even thy virtues, Tyrant, shall avail
'To save thy secret soul from nightly fears,
'From Cambria's curse, from Cambria's tears!'
Such were the sounds, that o'er the crested pride
Of the first Edward scatter'd wild dismay, 10
As down the steep of Snowdon's shaggy side
He wound with toilsome march his long array.
Stout Glo'ster stood aghast in speechless trance:
To arms! cried Mortimer, and couch'd his quiv'ring lance.

I. 2.

On a rock, whose haughty brow
Frowns o'er old Conway's foaming flood,
Robed in the sable garb of woe,
With haggard eyes the Poet stood;

(Loose his beard, and hoary hair
Stream'd, like a meteor, to the troubled air) 20
And with a Master's hand, and Prophet's fire,
Struck the deep sorrows of his lyre.
'Hark, how each giant-oak, and desert cave,
'Sighs to the torrent's aweful voice beneath!
'O'er thee, oh King! their hundred arms they wave,
'Revenge on thee in hoarser murmurs breath;
'Vocal no more, since Cambria's fatal day,
'To high-born Hoel's harp, or soft Llewellyn's lay,

I. 3.

'Cold is Cadwallo's tongue,
'That hush'd the stormy main: 30
'Brave Urien sleeps upon his craggy bed:
'Mountains, ye mourn in vain
'Modred, whose magic song
'Made huge Plinlimmon bow his cloud-top'd head.
'On dreary Arvon's shore they lie,
'Smear'd with gore, and ghastly pale:
'Far, far aloof th' affrighted ravens sail;
'The famish'd Eagle screams, and passes by.
'Dear lost companions of my tuneful art,
'Dear, as the light that visits these sad eyes, 40
'Dear, as the ruddy drops that warm my heart,
'Ye died amidst your dying country's cries—
'No more I weep. They do not sleep.
'On yonder cliffs, a griesly band,
'I see them sit, they linger yet,
'Avengers of their native land:
'With me in dreadful harmony they join,
'And weave with bloody hands the tissue of thy line.'

II. 1.

"Weave the warp, and weave the woof,
"The winding-sheet of Edward's race. 50
"Give ample room, and verge enough
"The characters of hell to trace.
"Mark the year, and mark the night,
"When Severn shall re-eccho with affright
"The shrieks of death, thro' Berkley's roofs that ring,
"Shrieks of an agonizing King!
"She-Wolf of France, with unrelenting fangs,
"That tear'st the bowels of thy mangled Mate,
"From thee be born, who o'er thy country hangs
"The scourge of Heav'n. What Terrors round him wait!
"Amazement in his van, with Flight combined, 61
"And sorrow's faded form, and solitude behind.

II. 2.

"Mighty Victor, mighty Lord!
"Low on his funeral couch he lies!
"No pitying heart, no eye, afford
"A tear to grace his obsequies.
"Is the sable Warriour fled?
"Thy son is gone. He rests among the Dead.
"The Swarm, that in thy noon-tide beam were born?
"Gone to salute the rising Morn. 70
"Fair laughs the Morn, and soft the Zephyr blows,
"While proudly riding o'er the azure realm
"In gallant trim the gilded Vessel goes;
"Youth on the prow, and Pleasure at the helm;
"Regardless of the sweeping Whirlwind's sway,
"That, hush'd in grim repose, expects his evening-prey.

II. 3.

"Fill high the sparkling bowl,
"The rich repast prepare,
"Reft of a crown, he yet may share the feast:
"Close by the regal chair 80
"Fell Thirst and Famine scowl
"A baleful smile upon their baffled Guest.
"Heard ye the din of battle bray,
"Lance to lance, and horse to horse?
"Long Years of havock urge their destined course,
"And thro' the kindred squadrons mow their way.
"Ye Towers of Julius, London's lasting shame,
"With many a foul and midnight murther fed,
"Revere his Consort's faith, his Father's fame,
"And spare the meek Usurper's holy head. 90
"Above, below, the rose of snow,
"Twined with her blushing foe, we spread:
"The bristled Boar in infant-gore
"Wallows beneath the thorny shade.
"Now, Brothers, bending o'er th' accursed loom
"Stamp we our vengeance deep, and ratify his doom.

III. 1.

"Edward, lo! to sudden fate
"(Weave we the woof. The thread is spun)
"Half of thy heart we consecrate.
"(The web is wove. The work is done.)" 100
'Stay, oh stay! nor thus forlorn
'Leave me unblessed, unpitied, here to mourn:
'In yon bright track, that fires the western skies,
'They melt, they vanish from my eyes.

'But oh! what solemn scenes on Snowdon's height
'Descending slow their glitt'ring skirts unroll?
'Visions of glory, spare my aching sight,
'Ye unborn Ages, crowd not on my soul!
'No more our long-lost Arthur we bewail.
'All hail, ye genuine Kings, Britannia's Issue, hail! 110

III. 2.

'Girt with many a Baron bold
'Sublime their starry fronts they rear;
'And gorgeous Dames, and Statesmen old
'In bearded majesty, appear.
'In the midst a Form divine!
'Her eye proclaims her of the Briton-Line;
'Her lyon-port, her awe-commanding face,
'Attemper'd sweet to virgin-grace.
'What strings symphonious tremble in the air,
'What strains of vocal transport round her play! 120
'Hear from the grave, great Taliessin, hear;
'They breathe a soul to animate thy clay.
'Bright Rapture calls, and soaring, as she sings,
'Waves in the eye of Heav'n her many-colour'd wings.

III. 3.

'The verse adorn again
'Fierce War, and faithful Love,
'And Truth severe, by fairy Fiction drest.
'In buskin'd measures move
'Pale Grief, and pleasing Pain,
'With Horrour, Tyrant of the throbbing breast. 130

'A Voice, as of the Cherub-Choir,
'Gales from blooming Eden bear;
'And distant warblings lessen on my ear,
'That lost in long futurity expire.
'Fond impious Man, think'st thou, yon sanguine cloud,
'Rais'd by thy breath, has quench'd the Orb of day?
'To-morrow he repairs the golden flood,
'And warms the nations with redoubled ray.
'Enough for me: With joy I see
'The different doom our Fates assign. 140
'Be thine Despair, and scept'red Care,
'To triumph, and to die, are mine.'
He spoke, and headlong from the mountain's height
Deep in the roaring tide he plung'd to endless night.

XIV. ODE

ON THE PLEASURE ARISING FROM VICISSITUDE.

FRAGMENT.

Now the golden Morn aloft
  Waves her dew-bespangled wing,
With vermeil-cheek and whisper soft
  She woo's the tardy spring:
Till April starts, and calls around
The sleeping fragrance from the ground;
And lightly o'er the living scene
Scatters his freshest, tenderest green.

New-born flocks, in rustic dance,
  Frisking ply their feeble feet; 10
Forgetful of their wintry trance,
  The Birds his presence greet:
But chief, the Sky-lark warbles high
His trembling thrilling ecstasy;
And, lessening from the dazzled sight,
Melts into air and liquid light.

Rise, my soul! on wings of fire,
  Rise the rapturous choir among;
Hark! 'tis nature strikes the lyre,
  And leads the general song: 20

. . . .

. . . .

. . . .

. . . .

Yesterday the sullen year
  Saw the snowy whirlwind fly;
Mute was the musick of the air,
  The Herd stood drooping by:
Their raptures now that wildly flow,
No yesterday, nor morrow know;
'Tis man alone that Joy descries
With forward and reverted eyes.

Smiles on past Misfortune's brow
  Soft Reflection's hand can trace; 30
And o'er the cheek of Sorrow throw
  A melancholy grace;
While Hope prolongs our happier hour,
Or deepest shades, that dimly lower
And blacken round our weary way,
Gilds with a gleam of distant day.

Still, where rosy Pleasure leads,
  See a kindred Grief pursue;
Behind the steps that Misery treads,
  Approaching Comfort view: 40
The hues of Bliss more brightly glow,
Chastised by sabler tints of woe;
And blended form, with artful strife,
The strength and harmony of Life.

See the Wretch, that long has tost
  On the thorny bed of Pain,
At length repair his vigour lost,
  And breathe and walk again:

The meanest flowret of the vale,
The simplest note that swells the gale, 50
The common Sun, the air, the skies,
To him are opening Paradise.

Humble quiet builds her cell,
  Near the source whence Pleasure flows;
She eyes the clear chrystalline well,
  And tastes it as it goes.
Far below, the crowd

Broad and turbulent it grows

with resistless sweep
They perish in the boundless deep. 60

Mark where Indolence and Pride,

Softly rolling, side by side,
  Their dull, but daily round

XV. TOPHET.

THUS Tophet look'd; so grinned the brawling fiend,
While frighted prelates bow'd and called him friend;
I saw them bow, and while they wished him dead,
With servile simper nod the mitred head.
Our mother-church, with half-averted sight,
Blush'd as she bless'd her griesly proselyte:
Hosannas rung through hell's tremendous borders,
And Satan's self had thoughts of taking orders.

XVI. EPITAPH ON MRS JANE CLARKE.

Lo! where the silent marble weeps,
A friend, a wife, a mother sleeps:
A heart, within whose sacred cell
The peaceful virtues lov'd to dwell.
Affection warm, and faith sincere,
And soft humanity were there.
In agony, in death, resign'd,
She felt the wound she left behind;
Her infant image here below,
Sits smiling on a father's woe: 10
Whom what awaits, while yet he strays
Along the lonely vale of days?
A pang, to secret sorrow dear;
A sigh; an unavailing tear;
Till time shall every grief remove,
With life, with memory, and with love.

XVII. EPITAPH ON A CHILD.

HERE, freed from pain, secure from misery, lies
A child, the darling of his parents' eyes:
A gentler Lamb ne'er sported on the plain,
A fairer flower will never bloom again:
Few were the days allotted to his breath;
Now let him sleep in peace his night of death

XVIII. THE FATAL SISTERS.

AN ODE

(From the Norse-Tongue)

in the

Orcades of Thormodus Torfæus; Hafniæ, 1697, Folio; and also in Bartholinus.

Vitt er orpit fyrir valfalli, etc.

Now the storm begins to lower
(Haste, the loom of Hell prepare,)
Iron-sleet of arrowy shower
Hurtles in the darken'd air.

Glitt'ring lances are the loom,
Where the dusky warp we strain,
Weaving many a Soldier's doom,
Orkney's woe, and *Randver's* bane.

See the griesly texture grow!
('Tis of human entrails made) 10
And the weights, that play below,
Each a gasping Warriour's head.

Shafts for shuttles, dipt in gore,
  Shoot the trembling cords along.
Sword, that once a Monarch bore,
  Keep the tissue close and strong.

Mista black, terrific Maid,
  Sangrida, and *Hilda* see,
Join the wayward work to aid:
  'Tis the woof of victory. 20

Ere the ruddy sun be set,
  Pikes must shiver, javelins sing,
Blade with clattering buckler meet,
  Hauberk crash, and helmet ring.

(Weave the crimson web of war)
  Let us go, and let us fly,
Where our Friends the conflict share,
  Where they triumph, where they die.

As the paths of fate we tread,
  Wading through th' ensanguin'd field, 30
Gondula, and *Geira*, spread
  O'er the youthful King your shield.

We the reins to slaughter give,
  Ours to kill, and ours to spare:
Spite of danger he shall live.
  (Weave the crimson web of war.)

They, whom once the desart-beach
  Pent within its bleak domain,
Soon their ample sway shall stretch
  O'er the plenty of the plain. 40

Low the dauntless Earl is laid,
  Gor'd with many a gaping wound:
Fate demands a nobler head;
  Soon a King shall bite the ground.

Long his loss shall Eirin weep,
  Ne'er again his likeness see;
Long her strains in sorrow steep:
  Strains of Immortality!

Horror covers all the heath,
  Clouds of carnage blot the sun. 50
Sisters, weave the web of death;
  Sisters, cease, the work is done.

Hail the task, and hail the hands!
  Songs of joy and triumph sing!
Joy to the victorious bands;
  Triumph to the younger King.

Mortal, thou that hear'st the tale,
  Learn the tenour of our song.
Scotland, thro' each winding vale
  Far and wide the notes prolong. 60

Sisters, hence with spurs of speed:
  Each her thundering faulchion wield;
Each bestride her sable steed.
  Hurry, hurry to the field.

XIX. THE DESCENT OF ODIN.

AN ODE

(From the Norse Tongue,)

in

Bartolinus, de causis contemnendæ mortis; Hafniæ, 1689, quarto.

Upreis Odinn allda gautr, etc.

Uprose the King of Men with speed,
And saddled strait his coal-black steed;
Down the yawning steep he rode,
That leads to Hela's drear abode.
Him the Dog of Darkness spied,
His shaggy throat he open'd wide,
While from his jaws, with carnage fill'd,
Foam and human gore distill'd:
Hoarse he bays with hideous din,
Eyes that glow, and fangs, that grin; 10
And long pursues, with fruitless yell,
The Father of the powerful spell.
Onward still his way he takes
(The groaning earth beneath him shakes,)
Till full before his fearless eyes
The portals nine of hell arise.

Right against the eastern gate,
By the moss-grown pile he sate;
Where long of yore to sleep was laid
The dust of the prophetic Maid. 20
Facing to the northern clime,
Thrice he traced the runic rhyme;
Thrice pronounc'd, in accents dread,
The thrilling verse that wakes the Dead:
Till from out the hollow ground
Slowly breath'd a sullen sound.

Pr. What call unknown, what charms presume
To break the quiet of the tomb?
Who thus afflicts my troubled sprite,
And drags me from the realms of night? 30
Long on these mould'ring bones have beat
The winter's snow, the summer's heat,
The drenching dews, and driving rain!
Let me, let me sleep again.
Who is he, with voice unblest,
That calls me from the bed of rest?

O. A Traveller, to thee unknown,
Is he that calls, a Warriour's Son.
Thou the deeds of light shalt know;
Tell me what is done below, 40
For whom yon glitt'ring board is spread,
Drest for whom yon golden bed.

Pr. Mantling in the goblet see
The pure bev'rage of the bee,
O'er it hangs the shield of gold;
'Tis the drink of *Balder* bold:

Balder's head to death is giv'n.
Pain can reach the Sons of Heav'n!
Unwilling I my lips unclose:
Leave me, leave me to repose. 50

O. Once again my call obey,
Prophetess, arise, and say,
What dangers *Odin's* Child await,
Who the Author of his fate.

Pr. In *Hoder's* hand the Heroe's doom:
His Brother sends him to the tomb.
Now my weary lips I close;
Leave me, leave me to repose.

O. Prophetess, my spell obey,
Once again arise, and say, 60
Who th' Avenger of his guilt,
By whom shall *Hoder's* blood be spilt.

Pr. In the caverns of the west,
By *Odin's* fierce embrace comprest,
A wond'rous Boy shall *Rinda* bear,
Who ne'er shall comb his raven-hair,
Nor wash his visage in the stream,
Nor see the sun's departing beam,
Till he on *Hoder's* corse shall smile
Flaming on the fun'ral pile. 70
Now my weary lips I close:
Leave me, leave me to repose.

O. Yet awhile my call obey;
Prophetess, awake, and say,
What Virgins these, in speechless woe,
That bend to earth their solemn brow,

That their flaxen tresses tear,
And snowy veils, that float in air.
Tell me, whence their sorrows rose:
Then I leave thee to repose. 80

Pr. Ha! no Traveller art thou,
King of Men, I know thee now;
Mightiest of a mighty line——

O. No boding Maid of skill divine
Art thou, nor Prophetess of good;
But Mother of the giant-brood!

Pr. Hie thee hence, and boast at home,
That never shall Enquirer come
To break my iron-sleep again,
Till *Lok* has burst his tenfold chain; 90
Never, till substantial Night
Has reassum'd her ancient right;
Till wrapt in flames, in ruin hurl'd,
Sinks the fabric of the world.

XX. EPITAPH ON SIR WILLIAM WILLIAMS.

HERE, foremost in the dang'rous paths of fame,
  Young Williams fought for England's fair renown;
His mind each Muse, each Grace adorn'd his frame,
  Nor envy dar'd to view him with a frown.

At Aix, uncall'd his maiden sword he drew,
  There first in blood his infant glory seal'd;
From fortune, pleasure, science, love, he flew,
  And scorn'd repose when Britain took the field.

With eyes of flame, and cool intrepid breast,
  Victor he stood on Bellisle's rocky steeps— 10
Ah, gallant youth! this marble tells the rest,
  Where melancholy friendship bends, and weeps.

XXI. SKETCH OF HIS OWN CHARACTER.

WRITTEN IN 1761, AND FOUND IN ONE OF HIS POCKET-BOOKS.

Too poor for a bribe, and too proud to importune,
He had not the method of making a fortune:
Could love, and could hate, so was thought somewhat odd;
No very great wit, he believed in a God:
A place or a pension he did not desire,
But left church and state to Charles Townshend and Squire.

XXII. AMATORY LINES.

With beauty, with pleasure surrounded, to languish—
To weep without knowing the cause of my anguish:
To start from short slumbers, and wish for the morning—
To close my dull eyes when I see it returning;
Sighs sudden and frequent, looks ever dejected—
Words that steal from my tongue, by no meaning connected!
Ah! say, Fellow-swains, how these symptoms befell me?
They smile, but reply not—Sure Delia will tell me!

XXIII. SONG.

Thyrsis, when we parted, swore
Ere the spring he would return—
Ah! what means yon violet flower
And the buds that deck the thorn?
'Twas the Lark that upward sprung!
'Twas the Nightingale that sung!

Idle notes! untimely green!
Why this unavailing haste?
Western gales and skies serene
Speak not always winter past. 10
Cease, my doubts, my fears to move,
Spare the honour of my love.

XXIV. THE TRIUMPHS OF OWEN.

A FRAGMENT.

FROM

Mr Evan's Specimens of the Welch Poetry;
London. 1764. Quarto.

OWEN'S praise demands my song,
OWEN swift, and OWEN strong;
Fairest flower of Roderic's stem,
Gwyneth's shield, and Britain's gem.
He nor heaps his brooded stores,
Nor on all profusely pours;
Lord of every regal art,
Liberal hand, and open heart.

Big with hosts of mighty name,
Squadrons three against him came; 10
This the force of Eirin hiding,
Side by side as proudly riding,
On her shadow long and gay
Lochlin plows the watry way;
There the Norman sails afar
Catch the winds, and join the war:
Black and huge along they sweep,
Burthens of the angry deep.

Dauntless on his native sands
The Dragon-Son of Mona stands; 20
In glitt'ring arms and glory drest,
High he rears his ruby crest.
There the thund'ring strokes begin,
There the press, and there the din;
Talymalfra's rocky shore
Echoing to the battle's roar.
[Check'd by the torrent-tide of blood,
Backward Meinai rolls his flood;
While, heap'd his master's feet around,
Prostrate warriors gnaw the ground.] 30
Where his glowing eye-balls turn,
Thousand Banners round him burn:
Where he points his purple spear,
Hasty, hasty Rout is there,
Marking with indignant eye
Fear to stop, and shame to fly:
There Confusion, Terror's child,
Conflict fierce, and Ruin wild,
Agony, that pants for breath,
Despair and honourable Death. 40

* * * *

XXV. THE DEATH OF HOEL.

AN ODE. SELECTED FROM THE GODODIN.

HAD I but the torrent's might,
With headlong rage and wild affright
Upon Deïra's squadrons hurl'd
To rush, and sweep them from the world!

Too, too secure in youthful pride,
By them, my friend, my Hoel, died,
Great Cian's son: of Madoc old
He ask'd no heaps of hoarded gold;
Alone in nature's wealth array'd,
He ask'd and had the lovely maid. 10

To Cattraeth's vale in glitt'ring row
Twice two hundred warriors go:
Every warrior's manly neck
Chains of regal honour deck,
Wreath'd in many a golden link:
From the golden cup they drink
Nectar that the bees produce,
Or the grape's extatic juice.
Flush'd with mirth and hope they burn:
But none from Cattraeth's vale return, 20
Save Aëron brave, and Conan strong,
(Bursting through the bloody throng)
And I, the meanest of them all,
That live to weep and sing their fall.

XXVI. CARADOC.

HAVE ye seen the tusky boar,
Or the bull, with sullen roar,
On surrounding foes advance?
So Caràdoc bore his lance.

XXVII. CONAN.

CONAN'S name, my lay, rehearse,
Build to him the lofty verse,
Sacred tribute of the bard,
Verse, the hero's sole reward.
As the flame's devouring force;
As the whirlwind in its course;
As the thunder's fiery stroke,
Glancing on the shiver'd oak;
Did the sword of Conan mow
The crimson harvest of the foe. 10

XXVIII. WILLIAM SHAKESPEARE to MRS ANNE, Regular Servant to the REV. MR PRECENTOR of York.

A MOMENT'S patience, gentle Mistris Anne:
  (But stint your clack for sweet St Charitie)
'Tis Willy begs, once a right proper man,
  Though now a book, and interleav'd you see.

Much have I borne from canker'd critic's spite,
  From fumbling baronets and poets small,
Pert barristers, and parsons nothing bright,
  But what awaits me now is worst of all.

'Tis true, our master's temper natural
  Was fashion'd fair in meek and dove-like guise; 10
But may not honey's self be turn'd to gall
  By residence, by marriage, and sore eyes?

If then he wreak on me his wicked will,
  Steal to his closet at the hour of prayer;
And (when thou hear'st the organ piping shrill)
  Grease his best pen, and all he scribbles, tear.

Better to bottom tarts and cheesecakes nice,
  Better the roast meat from the fire to save,
Better be twisted into caps for spice,
  Than thus be patch'd and cobbled in one's grave. 20

So York shall taste what Clouet never knew,
  So from our works sublimer fumes shall rise;
While Nancy earns the praise to Shakespeare due,
  For glorious puddings and immortal pies.

XXIX. IMPROMPTU,

SUGGESTED BY A VIEW, IN 1766, OF THE SEAT AND RUINS OF A NOBLEMAN, AT KINGSGATE, KENT.

OLD, and abandon'd by each venal friend,
  Here Holland form'd the pious resolution
To smuggle a few years, and strive to mend
  A broken character and constitution.

On this congenial spot he fix'd his choice;
  Earl Goodwin trembled for his neighbouring sand;
Here sea-gulls scream, and cormorants rejoice,
  And mariners, though shipwreck'd, dread to land.

Here reign the blustering North and blighting East,
  No tree is heard to whisper, bird to sing; 10
Yet Nature could not furnish out the feast,
  Art he invokes new horrors still to bring.

Here mouldering fanes and battlements arise,
  Turrets and arches nodding to their fall,
Unpeopled monast'ries delude our eyes,
  And mimic desolation covers all.

"Ah!" said the sighing peer, "had Bute been true,
  Nor Shelburne's, Rigby's, Calcraft's friendship vain,
Far better scenes than these had blest our view,
  And realis'd the beauties which we feign: 20

"Purg'd by the sword, and purified by fire,
  Then had we seen proud London's hated walls;
Owls would have hooted in St Peter's choir,
  And foxes stunk and litter'd in St Paul's."

XXX. CONCLUDING LINES OF EPITAPH ON MRS MASON.

TELL them, though 'tis an awful thing to die,
  ('Twas e'en to thee) yet the dread path once trod,
Heaven lifts its everlasting portals high,
  And bids the pure in heart behold their God.

XXXI. COUPLET ABOUT BIRDS.

THERE pipes the woodlark, and the song-thrush there
Scatters his loose notes in the waste of air.

XXXII. ODE FOR MUSIC.

AIR.

"HENCE, avaunt, ('tis holy ground)
Comus, and his midnight crew,
And Ignorance with looks profound,
And dreaming Sloth of pallid hue,
Mad Sedition's cry profane,
Servitude that hugs her chain,
Nor in these consecrated bowers
Let painted Flatt'ry hide her serpent-train in flowers.

CHORUS.

Nor Envy base, nor creeping Gain,
Dare the Muse's walk to stain, 10
While bright-eyed Science watches round:
Hence, away, 'tis holy ground!"

RECITATIVE.

From yonder realms of empyrean day
Bursts on my ear th' indignant lay:
There sit the sainted sage, the bard divine,
The Few, whom Genius gave to shine

Thro' every unborn age, and undiscover'd clime.
Rapt in celestial transport they: (*accomp.*)
Yet hither oft a glance from high
They send of tender sympathy 20
To bless the place, where on their opening soul
First the genuine ardour stole.
'Twas *Milton* struck the deep-ton'd shell,
And, as the choral warblings round him swell,
Meek *Newton's* self bends from his state sublime,
And nods his hoary head, and listens to the rhyme.

AIR.

"Ye brown o'er-arching groves,
That contemplation loves,
Where willowy *Camus* lingers with delight!
Oft at the blush of dawn 30
I trod your level lawn,
Oft woo'd the gleam of *Cynthia* silver-bright
In cloisters dim, far from the haunts of Folly,
With Freedom by my side, and soft-eyed Melancholy."

RECITATIVE.

But hark! the portals sound, and pacing forth
With solemn steps and slow,
High Potentates, and Dames of royal birth,
And mitred Fathers in long order go:
Great *Edward*, with the lilies on his brow
From haughty *Gallia* torn, 40
And sad *Chatillon*, on her bridal morn

That wept her bleeding Love, and princely *Clare*,
And Anjou's Heroine, and the paler Rose,
The rival of her crown and of her woes,
And either *Henry* there,
The murther'd Saint and the majestic Lord,
That broke the bonds of *Rome*.
(Their tears, their little triumphs o'er, (*accomp.*)
Their human passions now no more,
Save Charity, that glows beyond the tomb) 50
All that on *Granta's* fruitful plain
Rich streams of regal bounty pour'd,
And bad these awful fanes and turrets rise,
To hail their *Fitzroy's* festal morning come;
And thus they speak in soft accord
The liquid language of the skies:

QUARTETTO.

"What is grandeur, what is power?
Heavier toil, superior pain.
What the bright reward we gain?
The grateful mem'ry of the Good. 60
Sweet is the breath of vernal shower,
The bee's collected treasures sweet,
Sweet music's melting fall, but sweeter yet
The still small voice of Gratitude."

RECITATIVE.

Foremost and leaning from her golden cloud
The venerable *Marg'ret* see!
"Welcome, my noble Son, (she cries aloud)
To this, thy kindred train, and me:

Pleas'd in thy lineaments we trace
A *Tudor's* fire, a *Beaufort's* grace." 70

AIR.

"Thy liberal heart, thy judging eye,
The flow'r unheeded shall descry,
And bid it round heav'n's altars shed
The fragrance of its blushing head:
Shall raise from earth the latent gem
To glitter on the diadem."

RECITATIVE.

"Lo! *Granta* waits to lead her blooming band,
Not obvious, not obtrusive, she
No vulgar praise, no venal incense flings;
Nor dares with courtly tongue refin'd 80
Profane thy inborn royalty of mind:
She reveres herself and thee.
With modest pride to grace thy youthful brow,
The laureate wreath, that *Cecil* wore, she brings,
And to thy just, thy gentle hand,
Submits the Fasces of her sway,
While Spirits blest above and Men below
Join with glad voice the loud symphonious lay."

GRAND CHORUS.

"Thro' the wild waves as they roar,
With watchful eye and dauntless mien 90
Thy steady course of honour keep,
Nor fear the rocks, nor seek the shore:
The star of *Brunswick* smiles serene,
And gilds the horrors of the deep."

NOTES.

I. ODE ON THE SPRING.

THIS poem is touchingly connected with the story of Gray's friendship with Richard West. In his Commonplace Books (sometimes called the Stonhewer MSS.) preserved at Pembroke College, Cambridge, Gray's transcript of it bearing the title "Noon-tide, an ode" has the note "at Stoke, the beginning of June 1742 sent to Fav: not knowing he was then Dead." It was a response to the verses which West, whom, playing on his name, Gray was wont to call 'Favonius' (the Western Wind), had sent him (May 5, 1742), invoking 'May.' These verses Gray acknowledged on the 8th of May; received another from West in cheering strain enclosing translations from Catullus on the 11th; responded brightly on the 27th; and must have written once more about a week later a letter enclosing the poem before us, which was returned to him unopened[1], West, as he afterwards discovered, having died on the first of June. The first of Gray's and the last of West's original efforts in English Verse were on the same theme, and both these kindred spirits as they wrote thought more of friendship than of fame.

Gray's MS. at Pembroke does not, as far as I remember, exhibit any essential variation from the text of Mason, except perhaps in the more frequent use of capitals: accordingly the text is here given from vol. 1 of Mason's 4 vol. edition 1778, as printed by A. Ward and sold by Dodsley and others.

Mitford has illustrated the poem with his customary care and diligence, and almost all the fire of quotation which has been brought to bear on it has been derived from his magazines. In 1768 Gray

[1] See *Gray and His Friends*, pp. 164—172.

added notes of his own, which must be taken to indicate the passages which he really had in mind; and to these are added the more precise references which Mitford supplied.

Mason inferred from the title 'Noon-tide' that Gray originally intended to write three poems descriptive of Morning, Noon, and Evening. He remarks that the *Elegy* opens with a picture of Evening, and the fragment on *Vicissitude* with a picture of Morning. We have seen however under what conditions the *Ode on the Spring* was in fact produced; and it is perhaps not possible to say at what date Gray transcribed the poem and headed it otherwise. But if, as I think, his transcript contains the reading of ll. 19, 20 as we here print it, the correspondence which Mason attributes to original design was an afterthought, if it entered into Gray's mind at all[1]. It is not the time of day which is Gray's subject in any of the three poems; but it would be very like him designedly to distinguish them by adapting in each case the hour to the theme.

It may be, as Mitford affirms, that the Ode is founded on 'Horace's Ode *ad Sestium* (I. iv.)'; but the resemblance goes no further than this, that Horace passes from a description of the return of Spring, not much resembling Gray's, to reflections on the brevity of human life.

1. **the rosy-bosom'd Hours.** The expression is traced by Wakefield to Milton, *Comus* 986:

"Along the crispèd shades and bowers
Revels the spruce and jocund Spring:
The Graces and the rosy-bosomed Hours
Thither all their bounties bring."

Thomson, as Mitford indicates, had already borrowed from Milton in

"The *rosy-bosomed Spring*
To weeping fancy pines." (*Spring*, 1010.)

Did Milton take the word from the Greek ῥοδόκολπος, which is to be found in a Lyric fragment preserved by Stobaeus (*Ecl.* I. 174) as an epithet of εὐνομία? It may be difficult to fix the sense of ῥοδόκολπος as used in this fragment; but whether Milton had come across it or not, he probably used 'rosy-bosomed' after the analogy of ῥοδοδάκτυλος 'rosy-fingered' as an epithet of Morn in Homer. So also Thomson and Gray; Dr Bradshaw's suggestion that the meaning may be 'with bosom full of roses' after the analogy of 'rosy-crowned,' *Progress of Poesy* 28, is

[1] For, with the earlier reading of these lines, the poem was certainly called "*Ode on the Spring.*" See n. ad loc.

not so likely, though it is a little sanctioned by Mitford's quotation from Apuleius, 'Horae *rosis* et caeteris floribus *purpurabant* omnia.'"

2. **Venus'**. Of course a dissyllable. Cf.

"The fickle pensioners of Morpheus' train."

Milton, *Il Penseroso* 10.

train. Mitford quotes *Hymn to Venus* II. 5, and *to Apollo*, l. 194, for the Hours as attendants on Venus. His citation from Hesiod, *Works and Days* I. 75, is not apposite; there the Hours are described as decking *Pandora*.

3. **long-expecting**. Dryden, *Astraea Redux* 122:

"Frosts that constrain the ground, and birth deny
To flowers that in its womb *expecting* lie."

Rogers.

4. **the purple year**. Vergil, *Ecl.* IX. 40 "ver purpureum"; also in Columella. Whether any English poet before Pope in his *Pastorals* (1709) said 'purple year' I cannot discover; he probably did most to make the phrase familiar. Milton, *Lycidas* 141, writes "purple all the ground with vernal flowers"; and the word in this connection is used generally of all bright colours. Cf. n. 1 ad fin.

5. **The Attic warbler**. Cf. out of many classical instances Propertius II. 16. 5, 6

"Non tam nocturna *volucris* funesta querela
Attica Cecropiis obstrepit in foliis."

But the passages more or less in Gray's mind and fixing his phraseology are Milton, *Paradise Regained* IV. 245

"See there the olive-grove of Academe,
Plato's retirement, where the *Attic bird*
Trills her thick-warbled notes the summer long"

and Pope, *Essay on Man* III. 33

"Is it for thee the linnet *pours his throat*?"

Mark Pattison here, after noting Gray's imitation, adds "Pope more correctly *his throat*, the female bird having no song. Milton errs in the same way, *Par. Lost* 4. 600

'All but the wakeful nightingale:
She all night long her amorous descant sung.'"

But surely the 'error' is inevitable, at any rate in connection with the nightingale: the poets are still under the spell of the old-world legend of the daughter of Pandion king in Attica,—Philomela (or her sister

Procne as some said) transformed into a nightingale, and lamenting for ever her sorrows. Even Keats who quite ignores the legend, and like Gray seems to find more joy than sadness in the bird's song, betrays this 'error' in gender when he writes, "thou, light-wingèd *Dryad* of the trees." Byron is on the safe side, because he follows the *Persian* fable:

> "For there the Rose, o'er crag or vale,
> Sultana of the Nightingale,
> The maid for whom his melody,
> His thousand songs are heard on high,
> Blooms blushing to her lover's tale."
>
> *The Giaour.*

In Matthew Arnold the old Greek story and the consequent offence against natural history return together full-fledged:

> "Dost thou again peruse
> With hot cheeks and sear'd eyes
> The too clear web, and thy dumb sister's shame?
> Dost thou once more assay
> Thy flight, and feel come over thee,
> Poor fugitive, the feathery change
> Once more, and once more seem to make resound
> With love and hate, triumph and agony,
> Lone Daulis, and the high Cephissian vale?"

Pattison l.c. adds "To 'pour' song or sound is an expression used by many poets after Simonides of Ceos, *Fr.* 153. 8 ἡδὺ πνεῦμα χέων." He suggests also that the harshness of the metaphor 'pour *his throat*' is subdued by the repetition of the idea in the next line

> "Loves of his own and raptures *swell the note.*"

But it still remains a bold and questionable trespass upon such expressions as "liquidum tenui gutture cantat avis" (Ovid, *Amores* I. 13. 8) from which it is derived. Gray would not have employed it if Pope had not given it vogue.

6, 7. **note...spring.** Thomson (strangely misquoted in this place by Luke) writes (*Spring* 579):

> "...while I deduce,
> From the first note the hollow cuckoo sings,
> The symphony of Spring."

'Harmony' is in apposition with the general sense of ll. 5, 6, a construction corresponding to a common use of the Greek accusative; it is scarcely exact to say, with Dr Bradshaw, that it is in apposition with *throat and note.* Gray may have had Ovid, *Tristia* III. 12. 7, 8 somewhere in his mind:

"Prataque pubescunt variorum flore colorum
Indocilique loquax gutture *vernat* avis."

14. **O'er-canopies.**

"A bank......
O'er-canopied with luscious woodbine."
Shakespeare, *Mids. Night's Dream* [II. i. 251].

Gray (who here follows the text of Pope).

17. **reclin'd,** says Dr Bradshaw, "agrees with *me*, l. 16." Surely not; if the Muse can be imagined to sit with the poet, she can also be imagined to recline in rustic *state*. Gray gives her the honours proper to the scene; and treats her as he might some woodland goddess or fairy queen.

18. **ardour.** Horace's *civium ardor*, *C.* III. iii. 2.

19, 20. "'**How low, how indigent the Proud,**
How little are the Great.'

Thus it stood in Dodsley's *Miscellany* [1748], where it was first published. The author corrected it on account of the point of *little* and *great*. It certainly had too much the appearance of a Concetto, though it expressed his meaning better than the present reading." Mason.

23. Cf. Pope, *Essay on Man* I. 210—"the green myriads in the *peopled grass*."

26. **the honied spring.** Let us hear Johnson on this passage, by way of warning against hasty criticism:

"There has *of late* arisen a practice of giving to adjectives, derived from substantives, the termination of participles; such as the *cultured* plain, the *daisied* bank; but I was sorry to see, in the lines of a scholar like Gray, the *honied* Spring."

To this Lord Grenville (*Nugae Metricae*, privately printed) quoted by Mitford in his *Life of Gray* has replied: "A scholar like Johnson ought to have remembered that *mellitus* is used by Catullus, Cicero and Horace, and that *honied* itself is found both in Shakespeare and Milton." [*Henry V.* I. i. 50, "to steal his sweet and honeyed sentences." *Samson Agonistes* 1066, "the bait of honied words." Nearer still to Gray "quaint enamell'd eyes That on the green turf suck the *honied* showers," *Lycidas* 140, and "the bee with *honied* thigh," *Il Penseroso* l. 143.] Lord Grenville further remarks that "the ready conversion of our substantives into verbs, participles, and participial adjectives is of the very essence of our tongue." He cites *inter alia* such words as *plough*, *witness*, *ornament* (we may add *father*); and notes how participles of verbs thus derived pass into adjectives as in *winged*, *feathered*, *thatched*; and how there is the closest analogy between these participial adjectives, and words like *honied*, *daisied*, *tapestried*, *slipper'd*, which differ from the others only in not being referable to any yet established verb. He instances *sugared*, as an epithet the use of which was probably anterior to that of the verb, of which it appears to be the participle. He points out that Johnson's canon would banish from the language such expressions as *four-footed*, *open-hearted*, *short-sighted*, *good-natured*; the '*well-envyned frankelein*' of Chaucer; and *even-handed*, *high-flighted*, *trumpet-tongued*, *full-voiced*, *flowery-knitted*, *fiery-wheel'd* of Shakespeare or Milton.

27. **And float...noon.** "Nare per aestatem liquidam," Virgil. *Georg.* lib. IV. [59]. Gray.

30. "......sporting with quick glance
Shew to the sun their wav'd-coats dropt with gold."
Milton's *Par. Lost*, b. VII. [410]. Gray.

Milton here speaks of *fishes*, in describing the six days of Creation.

31. **To Contemplation's** &c. "While insects from the threshold preach &c." M. Green in the *Grotto*. Dodsley's *Misc.* vol. V. p. 161. Gray.

Matthew Green died in 1737. He printed and gave away a few copies of the *Grotto* in 1732. It was "written under the name of Peter Drake, a fisherman of Brentford." The subject of the poem was otherwise called the Queen's Hermitage, or Merlin's Cave at Richmond, a fancy or folly of Queen Caroline's; of it Stephen Duck (hence 'Peter Drake') the thresher-poet was Librarian; the cave and its custos were both the objects of Pope's ridicule. See *Gray and His Friends*, p. 89 n. In a letter to Walpole of 1748 Gray says that the thought on which his *Ode on Spring* turns is "manifestly stolen" from the *Grotto*; "not," he adds, "that I knew it at the time, but having seen this many years before, to be sure it imprinted itself on my memory, and, forgetting the Author, I took it for my own." (Cf. note on Ode III. l. 21.).

It is noteworthy that one of Gray's favourite French poets, his contemporary Gresset, had the same characteristic as Green, a sort of careless facility and diffuseness often akin to prose; and that Gray, in borrowing from both, compresses their thoughts, whilst he adopts a more stately and artificial manner:

"While insects from the threshold preach,
And minds disposed to musing teach;
Proud of strong limbs and painted hues,

They perish by the slightest bruise;
Or maladies begun within
Destroy more slow life's frail machine:
From maggot-youth, thro' change of state,
They feel like as the turns of fate:
Some born to creep have liv'd to fly,
And chang'd earth's cells for dwellings high:
And some that did their six wings keep,
Before they died, been forced to creep.
They politics, like ours, profess:
The greater play upon the less.
Some strain on foot huge loads to bring,
Some toil incessant on the wing:
Nor from their vigorous schemes desist
Till death; and then they are never mist.
Some frolic, toil, marry, increase,
Are sick and well, have war and peace;
And broke with age in half a day,
Yield to successors, and away."

But this is only one of the many motives in Green's poem, which in discursiveness and variety is in the manner of the 17th century, Andrew Marvell's manner for instance, whereas Gray has *but* this leading notion, to which the whole poem is focuss'd.

Wakefield, says Mitford, has traced Gray's stanza to Thomson's *Summer* 342 sq. I give the passage as it stood in 1730:

"Upward and downward, thwarting and convolved,
The quivering nations sport; with tempest wing,
Till Winter sweeps them from the face of day.
Even so luxurious men, unheeding, pass
An idle summer life in fortune's shine—
A season's glitter! [In soft-circling Robes
Which the hard hand of industry has wrought
The human insects glow; by Hunger fed,
And chear'd by toiling Thirst,] they rowl about
From Toy to Trifle, Vanity to Vice
Till, blown away by death, oblivion comes
Behind, and strikes them from the book of life."

The thought in brackets was omitted in 1744 and 1746, and the whole passage as we now read it strikingly resembles Gray's stanza. Gray praised Thomson grudgingly; and, if he was indebted to him, would never have acknowledged as much to Walpole, who sneered at Thomson habitually. Both Green and Gray before they wrote their own lines had in all probability read the passage in *Summer* in the form in which it is cited above.

42. **The sportive kind reply.** We must defer to the overwhelming weight of authority which takes 'kind' as a substantive and 'reply' as a verb here. The 'sportive kind' are therefore the insect youth on the wing, sporting with quick glance, the 'quivering *nations*' as Thomson calls them, whose murmur seems to the poet to shape itself in words. It is certainly better to suppose this to be the primary meaning than to say with Dr Bradshaw "sportive kind, men of the world, and gay friends of Gray's, whom he supposes to mockingly reply to his moralizing." Nevertheless this view is sanctioned by the author of the version in *Arundines Cami*, who writes:

"Forte (?) *aliquis* cui cura joci, cui ludere cordi est" &c.

where the Latinity and the interpretation are both questionable.

But the ear tempts us to give 'kind' the emphasis which would make it an adjective.—'Methinks I hear the reply sportive yet pitying conveyed in the murmurs around me.' Compare each corresponding line to this in the poem:

Fair Venus' traín, appear
A broader brówner shade
The panting hérds repose
Such is the ráce of man.

Gray is fond of two adjectives without a *copula*; 'headlong, impetuous'; 'longing, lingering'; 'unbless'd, unpitied'; 'fond, impious.' The same thing has a peculiar charm in Collins' *Evening*:

"Thy genial lóv'd return"

and

"The gradual dúsky veil."

But it will be replied that the epithets in all these instances are if not *cognate* at least not *contrasted*; and we must perhaps abandon the attempt to rescue Gray from the conventionalism 'the sportive kind.'

II. SONNET ON THE DEATH OF RICHARD WEST.

West was the dearest of Gray's Eton friends. He was the son of Richard West, who died Lord Chancellor of Ireland at the age of 35. The mother of Gray's Richard West was daughter of the historian

Bishop Burnet, and sister of Judge Burnet. When Gray was at Peterhouse, Cambridge, West was at Christchurch, Oxford, which he left early in 1738, intending (as Gray then intended) to devote himself to law; but he was disgusted with legal studies, became restless, and seems to have had some thoughts of entering the army. His health was bad, and was not improved by domestic troubles. For the circumstances of his death see Introduction to the preceding Ode, and references there; and for further particulars of life and literary remains *Gray and His Friends*, pp. 13—17 and 65—151. The text is given from Mr Gosse's reproduction of Gray's spelling, &c. in the Pembroke MS., dated by Gray "At Stoke, Aug. 1742." Gray invariably added 'ing' without change to a verb ending in **e**, *e.g.* smileing, writeing, &c. He had his theories of spelling, as had Milton; though I do not think Gray ever stated them; he certainly never enforced them upon his printers.

3. **amorous Descant.** Milton, *P. L.* IV. 602:

"...all but the wakeful nightingale,
She all night long her amorous descant sung."

Luke.

Descant means variation upon plain song in music; and as applied to the nightingale by Milton has a distinctive truth which is lost in Gray.

8. Rogers quotes Dryden (Ovid—an insufficient reference):

"And in my ear the imperfect accent dies,"

—not I suppose for the thought—but for the form of the line. Gray acknowledged his obligations to the numbers of Dryden, and no doubt moulded many of his lines on more or less conscious reminiscence. See *Progress of Poesy* ad fin. and notes there.

14. **And weep the more.**

"So must we weep, because we weep in vain,"

Cibber's alteration of Shakespeare's *Richard III.* II. 2. Solon, according to Diogenes Laertius, when he wept on his son's death, replied to one who told him 'weeping will not help' Δι' αὐτὸ δὲ τοῦτο δακρύω, ὅτι οὐδὲν ἀνύττω, I weep for that very cause, that weeping will not avail. The same is told of Augustus. See also Fitzgeffry's *Life and Death of Sir Francis Drake*, II. 99

"Oh! therefore do we plaine,
And therefore weepe, because we weepe in vaine."

From Mitford. Cf. Addison in *Spectator* no. 574.

III. ODE ON A DISTANT PROSPECT OF ETON COLLEGE.

Gray himself has given us in the Pembroke MS. the date of this Poem. He writes at the end of it "At Stoke Aug. 1742."

The personal element in this and the following Ode is of the strongest. West had been dead little more than two months when Gray wrote it. Our poet was still estranged from Walpole, from whom he had parted at Reggio, but he had written, on West's death, a letter to Ashton[1], couched in friendly terms, although there is little doubt that Ashton's mischief-making had brought about the famous quarrel and that Ashton was never really forgiven. Of the four members of the Quadruple Alliance, as they were called at Eton (Gray, Walpole, Ashton and West), West was the one friend who was left to Gray in '42; and when *he* died Gray must have felt very isolated. His life-long friendship with Wharton he contracted at Cambridge before his travels; yet, though he addressed him from Florence in 1740 as "My dear, dear Wharton, which is a dear more than I give anybody else," it is noticeable that there is no extant letter to Wharton between this and one in April 1744. Seeing how religiously Wharton treasured every memento of Gray, I am inclined to think that this friendship had been allowed to lapse during the temporary break up of Gray's association with Cambridge.

The sad circumstances of West's death must also be remembered, as bearing upon the profound melancholy of the Eton Ode; his end is said to have been accelerated by the painful discovery of the sin—some say the crime[2]—of a mother whom he tenderly loved. Both in his own family and in West's, Gray had already, at the age of twenty-six, sad experience of the workings of those fury Passions which he has vividly described.

When Gray writes "Ah, fields beloved in vain" he has in mind a friendship broken up, partly by estrangement, and partly by death; and when, in the succeeding Ode, written in the same month (Aug. 1742) he prays

"The gen'rous spark *extinct* revive
Teach me to love and to forgive,
Exact my own defects to scan,
What others are, to feel, and know myself a Man"

his yearning for the renewal of the broken tie with Walpole reveals itself. The train of reflection in these lines remained with him; it

[1] *Gray and His Friends*, p. 172.

[2] See *Gray and His Friends*, pp. 15—17.

prompts him to write to Chute, the common friend of Walpole and himself, in 1746, after his reconciliation with Walpole, "Our *imperfections* may at least excuse, and perhaps recommend us to one another; methinks I can readily pardon sickness, and age, and vexation, for all the depredations they make within and without, when I think they make us better friends, and better men, which I am persuaded is often the case."

That in July 1742 (the correct date of a letter hitherto assigned to 1745) Gray could write to Chute and Horace Mann who were in Italy an extremely festive letter adapted to their more frivolous temperaments, is only an evidence that he had two moods, the social and the serious, and did not wear his heart upon his sleeve. These 'Italianated' friends knew nothing of Gray's English ties and had met (I believe) none of the companions of his Eton days except Walpole.

"This is the first English production of Mr Gray which appeared in print," says Mason. It was printed in 1747 for Dodsley in a folio pamphlet of eight pages and sold for sixpence. Dodsley reprinted it in his *Miscellany* of 1748. When Walpole was discussing with Gray which poems of his should be included in the *Miscellany*, Gray replied "As to my Eton Ode, Mr Dodsley is *padrone*," meaning I think that he has a right to reprint it in the *Miscellany* if he chooses. (Nov. 1747.) In 1747 and 1748 the Poem was anonymous. The title in the Pembroke MS. is "Ode. on a distant Prospect of Windsor, & the adjacent Country," and, oddly enough, Eton is not mentioned in the title. The motto from Menander is there written along the right hand side of the fifth and sixth stanzas. It was added to the printed poem in 1768, together with Gray's notes. Gray does not, if I remember rightly, punctuate the passage in his marginal note. But it is probably rightly pointed, as we here give it, after Meineke, *Comicorum Graecorum Fragmenta*, vol. IV. (*Menandri Fabulae Incertae* CCLXIII.). Gray doubtless found it in Stobaeus, *Flor.* XCVIII. 7. Perhaps we may render 'I am a man; a sufficient excuse for being unhappy.' Meineke l.c. compares a fragment of Philemon, Menander's rival, which looks like a parody:

ἐμέθυον· ἱκανὴ πρόφασις εἰς θἀμαρτάνειν.

'I was in liquor:—a sufficient excuse for doing wrong.'

Gray very fitly linked his motto, in the first instance, to the lines which end "Ah, tell them they are men!"

Mason says that, about the same time as the publication in 1747, "at Mr Walpole's request, Mr Gray sat for his picture to Echart, in which, on a paper which he held in his hand, Mr Walpole wrote the title of this Ode, and to intimate his own high and just opinion of it, as a first production, added this line of Lucan by way of motto:

'Nec licuit populis parvum te, Nile, videre.'"

Pharsalia, lib. x. l. 296.

The full passage, part of a lengthy description of the Nile, runs

"Arcanum Natura caput non prodidit ulli,
(Nec licuit populis parvum te, Nile, videre,)
Amovitque sinus, *et gentes maluit ortus*
Mirari quam nosse tuos.

If this really was the date[1] of a portrait by Eckhardt to which Mason refers (a print of which is given in Cunningham's edition of Walpole's *Letters*, vol. IV. p. 465), it is clear that two years after their reconciliation, Walpole looked upon Gray, still unknown to fame, with the utmost pride and affection. The context of the line from Lucan shows Walpole's drift; in this ode, in which Gray appears for the first time to the world, he is a great and mature, but anonymous poet; just as the Nile, when it first visits the nations, is already a mighty flood, though its sources are unknown.

3. **Science.** Used by Gray for knowledge, or learning: as in the *Elegy* (Epitaph 119),

"Fair Science frowned not on his humble birth."

4. King Henry the Sixth, founder of the College. Gray. Cf. the *Bard*, l. 90, and his note there.

12. **in vain.** Here, says Mr Gosse, "Gray permits himself to refer to the constant pressure of regret for his lost friend; the fields are beloved in vain, and in Wordsworth's exquisite phrase he turns to share the rapture—ah! with whom?"

19. "'And bees their honey redolent of Spring.' Dryden's Fable on the Pythagorean System." Gray.

21. "His supplication to father *Thames*, to tell him who drives the hoop, or tosses the ball, is useless and puerile. Father *Thames* has no better means of knowing than himself."—Johnson. Frivolous as the objection is, it is not exactly countered by the passage from Johnson's *Rasselas* (Chapter xxv.) which Dr Bradshaw, after Lord Grenville, has had in mind in his note here:—

"As they were sitting together, the princess cast her eyes upon the river [Nile] that flowed before her. 'Answer' said she 'great father

[1] The companion picture of Walpole which hung with it in the Blue Bedchamber at Strawberry Hill is probably later by some years, for it has in the background the famous Gothicized building.

of waters, thou that rollest thy floods through eighty nations, to the invocations of the daughter of thy native King: tell me if thou waterest, through all thy course, a single habitation from which thou dost not hear the murmurs of complaint.'"

Johnson does not censure Gray for addressing Thames and attributing to him sight and speech, but for putting to him a question to which a better answer could be got by a visit to the playing-fields. Personification once admitted, the question of the princess is less exceptionable, and if father Nile could not answer it, no one else could.

Nevertheless Johnson's is the kind of criticism in which we ought not to indulge, except when we are spiteful. The invocation itself and the question are mere conventions; and the *poetic* truth in Gray seems to be, but is not, subordinate. As, for Johnson, the great river passes by myriad dwellings of the ever-lamenting, so for Gray it has witnessed generation after generation of the ever-glad. Father Thames, in fact, is supplied by Eton "with an unfailing succession of young friends," to quote the beautiful expression of Hawtrey, the genial Head Master of Eton, who said that on this account he "could not feel the sadness of growing old." (*Memoir* by F. St J. Thackeray p. 111.)

Matthew Green in the *Grotto*, a poem which, as we have seen, Gray knew and admired, has a 'Say, Father Thames':

"Say, father Thames, *whose gentle pace*
Gives leave to view what beauties grace
Your flowery banks, if you have seen
The much sung Grotto of the queen.
Contemplative, forget awhile
Oxonian towers &c."

where again the really *poetic* element is the picture of the gently-flowing river, and the stately buildings by which it passes.

23. **margent green**. Probably a reminiscence of Milton, *Comus* 232, "By slow Meander's margent green." 'Margent' is the invariable form for 'margin' in Shakespeare and Milton.

29. In the Pembroke MS. "**To chase the hoop's elusive speed.**" Dr Bradshaw notes that Gray uses the phrase in his fragmentary *Agrippina*:

"We could not have beguiled
With more *elusive speed* the dazzled sight
Of wakeful jealousy."

So speaks Otho eloping with Poppaea.

This is in the *second* scene of the play, of which we have only twelve lines. Gray had written the first scene as early as the end of March or beginning of April 1742, at which time he sent the last long speech in it to West. In April 1742 he wrote to West that *Agrippina* is "laid up to rest till next summer," and Mason says "he never afterwards awakened her." But I am inclined to think that this second scene was an unsuccessful attempt to 'awaken her.' In December 1746 (in a letter hitherto assigned to 1751) Gray sent to Walpole "a scene of a tragedy"—i.e. the first scene of *Agrippina*. He did not send the whole of the first scene, because he could not find it; but in January 1747 he *did* send the 'remainder' in "an outrageous long speech," the same which he had sent to West. If his statements are quite exact he must have written 'elusive speed' in *Agrippina* after this; and though he wrote to Walpole early in 1747 "*Agrippina* can stay very well, she thanks you, and be damned at leisure," I believe that these twelve lines were added about that time, under the short-lived *stimulus* of Walpole's praise. Was then 'elusive speed' first given to the hoop, or to the elopement? To the hoop, I think; and borrowed thence for the elopement. On the supposition that Gray was 'cocker'd up,' to use an expression of his own, to finish *Agrippina*, possibly for the stage, he would shrink from using exactly the same phrase in such different connections in the Ode, shortly to be published by Dodsley (albeit anonymously), and in a tragedy certain, however short lived, to be exposed to a fire of criticism; and if the play were successful, the authorship of the Ode would not long be a secret. 'The rolling circle's speed' is probably *not* the reading which Gray preferred, but is due to the poet's fear of being taxed with poverty of resource. I do not know when the Pembroke copy was made by Gray, but I am quite sure that if he had meant the printed reading to take the place of that which he records, he would have noted this in the margin. It was only under a sort of compulsion that Gray here joined the ranks of those who call a 'hat' a 'swart sombrero,' and a courageous editor will some day print 'the *hoop's* elusive speed' in his text. Supposing the expression occurred first in 1747 in *Agrippina*, and was afterwards adopted for the ode, the argument for it is still stronger.

32. **Their murm'ring labours.** They are supposed to be conning by heart and repeating aloud to themselves the tasks, 'saying lessons' &c. which they are to repeat in the 'graver hours,' i.e. when 'up' to their masters in school.

36. They go 'out of bounds.'

37. Mitford says, "This line is taken from Cowley, *Pindarique*

Ode to Hobbes, 'Till unknown regions it descries.'" The coincidence of expression, though complete, may be accidental.

45. "His epithet ***buxom health*** is not elegant; he seems not to understand the word."—Johnson. What sense Johnson would give it, I know not. But the word had already long ago lost its primary sense of 'obedient.' It is derived from A. S. *búgan* 'to bow.' Instances of the primary sense abound: e.g. *Piers Plowman* (1377), Passus III. l. 262:

"God hymself hoteth (biddeth)
The[e] be boxome at his biddynge."

But the idea of prompt, ready, and so brisk and lively, was derived from this; so Pistol in Shakespeare, *Henry V.* III. 6. 25:

"Bardolph, a soldier, firm and sound of heart,
And of *buxom* valour,"

though Pistol is not a model of 'elegance.'

The same sense is commonly given to the word in the Prologue to *Pericles*, l. 23 (whoever wrote this):

"...a female heir,
So buxom blithe and full of face
As heaven had lent her all his grace":

whence no doubt Milton took his

"So buxom blithe and debonair"

as a description of Euphrosyne or Mirth in *L' Allegro*, if Masson is right in supposing that *L' Allegro* as we have it now was written as early as 1632. But Randolph, as Masson tells us, had in 1635 used the very words "to make one *blithe, buxom and deboneer.*" Richardson (*Eng. Dict.* s.v.) quotes from the *Tatler* (but with the wrong reference) "The first I encounter'd were a parcel of *buxom* bonny dames, that were laughing, singing, dancing and as merry as the day was long." One would think that these instances justify 'buxom' as an epithet of Health. Perhaps *we* associate with it the notion of 'full of face' more closely than Gray did.

59. In the Pembroke MS. the reading is 'griesly,' and 'murtherous' is suggested in the margin.

61. **fury-passions.** The expression is from Pope's *Essay on Man.*

68. **Envy wan.** Milton, *Sonnet to H. Lawes* (XIII. 6), "With praise enough for *Envy* to look *wan.*" Wakefield.

faded Care. "care
Sat on his faded cheek."
Milton, *Par. Lost*, I. 601, 602. Luke.

69. Probably, as Todd seems to suggest, combined (in scarce

conscious reminiscence) from Shakespeare, *Rich. III.* I. I. 9, "*Grim-visaged* war," and *Comedy of Errors*, V. I. 80 [moody and dull melancholy], "Kinsman to grim and *comfortless* despair."

79. **moody Madness.** "Madness laughing in his ireful mood." Dryden's *Palamon and Arcite*, [ii. 581]. Gray.

83. **family of Death.** Dryden, *State of Innocence* V. I,

"With all the numerous family of Death."

Followed by Pope, *Essay on Man* II. 118,

"Hate, fear and grief, the family of pain."

In this connection 'family' is not used in the sense of 'progeny,' but of attendants, and ministers. The ministers of Fate (l. 56 sq.) vex the soul; if man escapes these, more inevitably the ministers of Death vex the body; and the frame *must* yield to 'slow-consuming Age,' which appropriately comes last.

But while including Poverty among physical evils, Gray cannot forget that she is also an evil to the mind—she 'numbs the *soul* with icy hand.' Cf. *Elegy*,

"Chill Penury repressed their noble rage
And froze the genial current of the soul."

95. Wakefield compares Milton, *Comus* 359 sq.

"Peace, brother: be not over-exquisite
To cast the fashion of uncertain evils,
For, grant they be so; whilst they rest unknown,
What need a man forestall his date of grief,
And run to meet what he would most avoid?"

98. Gray was a student of Sophocles and has left some MS. notes on him; but it is a coincidence only that this thought of ignorance of ill *as proper to childhood* is found in the *Ajax*; where Ajax recovered from his madness and meditating suicide, addresses his infant son Eurysakes: (555)

καίτοι σε καὶ νῦν τοῦτό γε ζηλοῦν ἔχω
ὀθούνεκ' οὐδὲν τῶνδ' ἐπαισθάνει κακῶν.
ἐν τῷ φρονεῖν γὰρ μηδὲν ἥδιστος βίος
ἕως τὸ χαίρειν καὶ τὸ λυπεῖσθαι μάθῃς.

......I could well envy you
Because you have no inkling of these troubles:
The happiest life consists in ignorance,
Before you learn to grieve and to rejoice.

(Sir G. Young.)

The sentiment, expressed in more general terms, is too common to be traced to one original. Luke quotes from Prior, *Epistle to Hon. C. Montague*:

"From ignorance our comfort flows,
The only wretched are the wise."

And Mitford from Davenant's *Just Italian*, "since knowledge is but sorrow's spy, it is not safe to know." It is noticeable that Richardson puts this quotation into a letter from his Pamela (jealous of her Mr B—), "But all this had been prevented, had not this nasty Mr Turner put into my head worse thoughts. For now I can say with the poet

'Since knowledge is but sorrow's spy,
'Twere better not to know.'" (Letter 72)

This is in the second part of *Pamela*, which was added in 1742; in what month published I do not know. Since in April 1742, as we see from a letter to West of that date, Gray had read *Joseph Andrews*, which was, *inter alia*, a burlesque of Pamela, we may suppose that he had read Pamela *so far* also; whether the continuation of Pamela had appeared before August, 1742, I cannot determine. I heard the late Professor H. A. J. Munro quote the passage above, in evidence that Gray had found in 'Pamela' the original of his own more famous lines. But long ago Montaigne had said (*Essais*, Livre I. c. xl.), "A quoy faire *la cognoissance des choses*, si nous en devenons plus lasches? *si nous en perdons le repos et la tranquillité où nous serions sans cela?*"

Gray has made the thought a 'household word.' His lines were at any rate known to Sterne when (1760 circ.) he wrote "'Gracious heavens!' cried my father, looking upwards and clasping his hands together—'there is a worth in thy honest ignorance, brother *Toby*—'twere almost a pity to exchange it for a knowledge.'" (*Tristram Shandy* III. chap. xviii.) But Sterne had read Montaigne as well as "all such reading as was never read."

IV. HYMN TO ADVERSITY.

In the Pembroke MS. this is called 'Ode' &c. When it was first published by Dodsley in 1753, among the 'Six Poems' with Bentley's designs, it was called 'Hymn,' and as Gray took a particular interest in this edition, we may conclude that he preferred this title; probably as befitting the praise of a goddess. Mason changed 'Hymn' to 'Ode' in his edition "for the sake of uniformity in the page"—adding "it is unquestionably as truly lyrical as any of his Odes." This we may admit, though it is not much to the purpose.

It appeared again as 'Hymn' in the 4th volume of Dodsley's *Miscellany*, which was published in 1755; and again in 1758.

The motto from Aeschylus was first printed in the edition of 1768 (in which the Poem is still a 'Hymn'); but is given also in the Pembroke MS. with the additional quotation

Ξυμφέρει
Σωφρονεῖν ὑπὸ στένει.
Id. *Eumenid.* 523.

Gray has further added the note "At Stoke, Aug. 1742."

The motto from the Agamemnon may be rendered 'Zeus who leads mortals in ways of wisdom by appointing to Suffering Instruction for her very own.' And that from the Eumenides 'It profiteth through sorrow to get discretion.'

Mitford says that this Ode was suggested by Dionysius' Ode to Nemesis. Of this I know nothing; but there is little reason to question Johnson's opinion that "the hint was at first taken from 'O Diva gratum quae regis Antium'"—if we bear in mind also, what Johnson did not much concern himself with, that it owes its more vital origin to the poet's own experience (cf. Introduction to preceding Ode). Horace's 'Diva' (Carm. I. 35) is Fortune; but he attributes to her terrors not unlike Gray's "iron scourge and torturing hour"; makes her feared by "purple tyrants"; and anticipates Gray's lesson of the uses of Adversity when he writes

Te Spes et albo rara Fides colit
Velata panno, nec comitem abnegat
Utcunque mutata potentes
Veste domos inimica linquis.
At volgus infidum et meretrix retro
Perjura cedit; diffugiunt cadis
Cum faece siccatis amici
Ferre jugum pariter dolosi.

Thee Hope, and white-robed Faith so seldom found
Attend to cheer; nor from thy presence fly,
When those proud halls, for splendour long-renowned
Thou leavest in angry haste and garb of poverty.

But that false crew which flatters to betray—
The perjured partner of Love's wanton bower—
Will drain the lowest dregs; then shrink away,
Nor bear the equal yoke in Friendship's trying hour.
(T. Bourne.)

Johnson says "Gray has excelled his original by the variety of his sentiments, and by their moral application. Of this piece, at once poetical and rational, I will not by slight objections violate the dignity." Himself schooled in adversity, the old critic was too sincere, spite of prejudice, to withhold a tribute, which his life's experience told him was deserved; and it should be remembered that Gray was but twenty-six when he wrote the poem which extorted this praise. Cento as it is (to some extent) it is such a cento as only a true poet could have made; and whether Johnson could have raised some 'slight objections' to it or not, it is perhaps the most *faultless* piece of work which Gray ever produced, though it does not give us the measure of his genius.

1. **Daughter of Jove.** Mitford seems inclined to identify Gray's Adversity with Ate, whom Homer calls (*Il.* XIX. 91 sq.)

πρέσβα Διὸς θυγάτηρ Ἄτη, ἣ πάντας ἀᾶται,

'Eldest of Zeus' daughters, Ate, who blindeth all.' (Way.)

But Ἄτη is better represented by Infatuation, Blind Folly, or even Sin, than by Adversity. She is an absolutely mischievous or vindictive Power, and in Homer's story, deceived Zeus himself; who therefore hurled her from Heaven, by no means as the 'nurse' of Virtue. But Mitford adds "Perhaps however Gray only alluded to the passage of Æschylus which he quoted, and which describes Affliction as sent by Jupiter for the benefit of man." Here second thoughts were best.

3. "Affliction's *iron* flail." Fletcher, *Purple Island* IX. 28. Mitford.

"...when the scourge
Inexorably, and the *torturing hour*
Calls us to penance."

Par. Lost, II. 90 sq. Mitford.

5. **adamantine chain.**

Ἀδαμαντίνων δεσμῶν ἐν ἀρρήκτοις πέδαις.

Aesch. *Prom. Vinct.* l. 6.

And Milton, *Par. Lost*, I. 48

"In adamantine chains and penal fire."

Mitford.

7. "Purpurei metuunt tyranni." Hor. *Carm.* I. 35. 12.

Pope, too boldly, in the first of his two choruses to the tragedy of *Brutus*:

"Till some new tyrant lifts his *purple* hand
And civil madness tears them from the land."

Luke also refers to Tasso, *Ger. Lib.* Canto VII. 52, who has "purpurei tiranni" after Horace, but in a passage which suggested nothing to Gray, but much to Milton, for it is the source of *Par. Lost* I. 598 ("with fear of change perplexes monarchs") and *P. L.* 12. 634.

8. "Strange horror seize thee, and *pangs unfelt before.*"

Par. Lost, II. 703. Mitford.

"In Pembroke MS. he first wrote '**and misery not their own**'; a line is drawn through these words and '**unpitied and alone**' written above" (Dr Bradshaw).

16. It is obvious, with Luke, to compare Dido's "non ignara mali, miseris succurrere disco" (*Aeneid* I. 630). Bradshaw compares Pope's Elegy [*to the Memory of an Unfortunate Lady*, ll. 45, 46],

"So perish all, whose breasts ne'er *learn'd* to glow
For others' good, or *melt at others' woe.*"

18. Milton, *Il Penseroso*, 1, 2,

"Hence, vain deluding joys,
The brood of Folly without father bred."

20. Mitford quotes from Cowley

"If we for happiness could leisure find,"

and still more appositely from Oldham

"And know I have not yet the leisure to be good"

(but with inadequate references).

22. **The summer Friend.** Whether Gray had read Herbert may be questioned. But the exact expression is traced to Herbert's 'The Answer,'

"...all the thoughts and ends
Which my fierce youth did bandie, fall and flow
Like leaves about me, or *like summer friends,*
Flies of estates and sunshine."

This is only coincidence. Gray was influenced by Shakespeare,

"For men, like butterflies,
Shew not their mealy wings, but to the *summer.*"

Troilus and Cressida, III. 3. 79, 80.

Cf. "summer flies," 3 *Henry VI.* II. 6. 17; "such summer-birds are men," *Timon of Athens*, III. 6. 34.

25. Wakefield comp. *Il Penseroso* 16 (of Melancholy's 'saintly visage'):

"O'erlaid with black, staid wisdom's hue."

28. Ib. (l. 43) of the eyes of Melancholy,

"till
With a sad *leaden* downward cast
Thou fix them on the earth as fast."

The form of Gray's phrase is after Dryden's *Cymon and Iphigenia*, l. 57, "And stupid eyes that ever *loved* the ground." Both in Dryden and Gray there is a reminiscence of the use of 'amare,' for to cling to, to be constantly fastened to, as in Horace's "amatque Janua limen."

32. Gray has written opposite this line in Pembroke MS. 'ἁ γλυκυδακρὺς' (sic), transferring, I think, to Pity, the epithet from Meleager's κηρύσσω τὸν Ἔρωτα (Lost! a boy called Love),

ἔστι δ' ὁ παῖς γλυκύδακρυς, ἀείλαλος, ὠκύς, ἀθαμβής.

"*Sweet in his tears* is the boy, ever prattling, nimble and fearless."

35. Milton, *Par. Lost*, II. 611,

"Medusa with *Gorgonian terror* guards
The ford."

According to Gray, Adversity is seen by the Impious, as the Eumenides (or Furies) were seen by Orestes after the murder of his mother,

Γοργόνων δίκην
φαιοχίτωνες καὶ πεπλεκτανημέναι
πυκνοῖς δράκουσι·

(Aeschylus, *Choephoroe* 1048 sq.)

"—*like Gorgons*,
In robes of black, with serpents in their hair
Coiling abundant."

36. **vengeful Band**. Perhaps Gray imagines Adversity as leader or directress of the Furies or Eumenides. These, as they were conceived of by the Greek Tragedians, were not limited in number (the *three*, Tisiphone, Alecto and Megaera, belong to a later poetry); Gray therefore names them at his pleasure Horror, Despair &c.

43. **philosophic Train** in contrast to the 'vengeful band' (l. 36). Therefore perhaps he has in mind Abstractions; such as Milton makes attendant on Melancholy (*Il Penseroso* 45—55); especially

"...calm Peace, and Quiet,
Spare Fast, that oft with gods doth diet";

and 'chiefest'—

"The Cherub Contemplation."

Gray may have felt that he had neither space nor inclination to personify further, where he has personified so much. Or we may suppose that by the 'philosophic train' he means the many philosophers, especially of the Stoic school, who have treated of the uses of Adversity.

45. **The gen'rous spark.** See Introduction to preceding Ode.

V. HYMN TO IGNORANCE.

On the 25th of March, 1742, West had asked Gray's opinion of the 4th Book of the *Dunciad* which had just appeared ("the New Dunciad: Qu'en pensez-vous?"). Gray between this date and April sent West a brief criticism of it. It was fresh in his mind when he wrote this fragment, obviously inspired by Pope; the new *Dunciad* gave him also in part the expression "the *silken son* of dalliance" in *Agrippina*, which he had in hand at the date of the above letters. In July 1742 (in a letter hitherto assigned to 1745), he wrote to Chute, "I am just going into the country for one easy fortnight, and then in earnest intend to go to Cambridge, to Trinity Hall"—(he in fact returned to Peterhouse, I believe as a fellow-commoner).

Gray had left Cambridge in September 1738. From the lines

"*Thrice* hath Hyperion roll'd his annual race,
Since weeping I forsook thy fond embrace,"

we may safely conclude that this 'Hymn' was written before September 1742. It is probable that it was written much earlier in that year; and the lines just quoted perhaps indicate that Gray had reluctantly made up his mind to return to Cambridge, even before the death of West. This Hymn forms a prelude—though a very sinister prelude—to his long residence at Cambridge, and the poems he there composed, and this seems the best place for it.

Perhaps also this may be the best place to point out a singular parallel between moments in the life-story of Milton and of Gray. If we combine this *Hymn to Ignorance* with the letters which Gray between his return from the Continent and his return to Cambridge wrote to West and Chute, we have a picture which corresponds detail for detail with the account which Milton gives in the first of his Latin elegies of *his* feeling towards Cambridge, and the way in which he spent his time during his supposed rustication from the University, to which like Gray he professes himself reluctant to go back, though he forces himself to do it:

"Stat quoque juncosas Cami remeare paludes
Atque iterum raucae murmur adire Scholae."

Eleg. I. 89, 90.

"And I will e'en repass Cam's reedy pools
To face once more the warfare of the Schools." (Cowper.)

It was to his father's house in London that Gray went when he came from abroad; and probably from the same house that his letters from town of this period were written, though his father died about two months after his return. Milton's father was a money-scrivener; so was Gray's; London was the native city of both poets. Milton writes (*Eleg.* I. 9, 10)

"Me tenet urbs refluâ quam Thamesis alluit undâ
Meque, nec invitum, patria dulcis habet,"

and implies that it was no banishment "patrios adiisse penates" (l. 17). Cambridge and its surroundings are uncongenial to a lover of the Muses:

"Nuda nec arva placent, umbrasque negantia molles:
Quam male Phoebicolis convenit ille locus!"
"Nor aught of pleasure in those fields have I,
That to the musing bard all shade deny." (Cowper.)

His life he says is pleasantly spent between his books, the public parks and gardens and the theatre (compare Gray's later letters to West and those to Chute of Sept. 7, 1741, and July 1742). The friendship between Milton and Charles Diodati, to whom this *Elegia* is written, has its exact counterpart in that between Gray and West. Milton and Diodati were schoolfellows at S. Paul's, as Gray and West were schoolfellows at Eton. In both instances the friends were separated by a different choice of University; Milton and Gray went to Cambridge: Diodati and West to Oxford. Both pairs of friends corresponded in much the same fashion; in particular they cheered and advised each other with much solicitude; the *Elegia* I. of Milton is called forth by a letter from Diodati, rebuking him for poring too much over his books, which exactly resembles extant letters from Gray to West, and West to Gray. The parallel extends yet further. Both Diodati and West died prematurely; Diodati while Milton was upon his foreign travels; West, not very long after Gray had returned from *his*. Diodati's death is the subject of the most beautiful of Milton's Latin poems, the *Epitaphium Damonis*; West's, of the sonnet we have annotated, and of the beautiful tribute which closes all that Gray has written of his "De Principiis Cogitandi."

1. From Satan's words in *Par. Lost*, I. 250,

"Hail, horrors! hail
Infernal world &c."

3. **Where rushy Camus'**—cf. passage from Milton's *Elegia* I. supr., and

"Jam nec arundiferum mihi cura revisere Camum."
(Ib. l. 11.)

"Nor zeal nor duty now my steps impel
To reedy Cam." (Cowper.)

In the *Installation Ode*, the words which Gray puts into Milton's mouth (ll. 27—29),

"Ye brown o'er-arching groves,
That Contemplation loves,
Where *willowy* Camus lingers with delight,"

are in quaint contrast with Milton's own complaint (quoted supra) that there were no shades about Cambridge at all, and that the place was therefore not congenial to 'Contemplation.' Perhaps the 'brown o'er-arching groves' have grown since Milton's time.

4. Undoubtedly from Milton (as Mitford suggests),

"Where rivers now
Stream and *perpetual draw their humid train*."
Par. Lost, VII. 306.

11. **Hyperion**—See Note on Progress of Poesy, l. 53.

14. **leaden ægis.** The ægis as understood by Herodotus was a goatskin (from *αἴξ*, goat), most commonly assigned to Pallas as a breastplate, and such is the ægis of ancient sculpture. Herodotus IV. 189 says 'The dress wherewith Athene's statues are adorned, and her ægis, were derived by the Greeks from the women of Libya...For the Libyan women wear over their dress goat-skins stript of the hair, fringed at their edges and coloured with vermilion' (Rawlinson's Tr.). According to legend, the skin was that of the goat Amalthea which suckled Jupiter, and in its centre was the head of the Gorgon Medusa, the sight of which struck the beholder into stone. When Pallas Athene moved through the air, she used the ægis as a sail (*πτερῶν ἄτερ ῥοιβδοῦσα κόλπον αἰγίδος*, 'rustling, without aid of pinions, my swelling ægis,' she is made to say of herself in the *Eumenides* of Aeschylus, l. 382).

But it is the Homeric (the earlier) conception of the ægis which most prevails in poetry. This was a ponderous shield

"Forged by Hephæstus for a gift to Zeus,
His buckler wherewithal to awe mankind."
Il. XV. 308—310 (Cordery's Tr.).

It had a hundred golden tassels, each the price of a hundred oxen, *Il.* II. 448—450. Like the other ægis it had the Gorgon's head, *Il.* V. 741. It was the instrument in the hands of Zeus, or Apollo, or Athene, of spreading panic and raising tempests. Homeric interpreters commonly trace this emblematic use of it to *αἰγίς* in the sense of 'storm.' Apollo spreads his ægis over the corpse of Hector (*Il.* XXIV. 20).

According to Horace, Pallas 'opposed' her 'sounding ægis' to the Giants when they attempted to scale Heaven (*Carm.* III. 4. 57).

Ib. "To hatch a new Saturnian age of lead."

Pope, *Dunciad* I. 28.

"And so in the speech of Ignorance in 'Henry and Minerva' by I. B. 1729 (one among the poetical pieces bound up by Pope in his library, and now in my possession):

'Myself behind this *ample shield of lead*
Will to the field my daring squadrons head.'" Mitford.

22. "Here *Ignorance* in steel was arm'd, and there,
Cloath'd in a cowl, dissembled fast and pray'r;
Against my sway her pious hand stretched out,
And *fenc'd* with *double fogs* her idiot rout."

Henry and Minerva.

And so in the *Dunciad* I. 80,

"All these and more the cloud-compelling queen
Beholds *thro' fogs* that magnify the scene."

Mitford.

37. **Sesostris.** Herodotus (II. 102—111), our oldest authority for the achievements of the Egyptian conqueror Sesostris, does not mention the legend of his yoking conquered monarchs to his car. Whether it is in Diodorus I know not. For modern poets I suppose the authority was Lucan, *Pharsalia* X. 276,

"Venit ad occasum mundique extrema Sesostris
Et Pharios currus regum cervicibus egit,"

possibly also Pliny, *Hist. Nat.* XXIII. 3.

It was probably a reminiscence of Lucan that suggested to Marlowe to transfer to his Tamburlaine the exploit of Sesostris, in the famous passage of which Pistol (2 *Henry IV.* II. 4. 178) makes mincemeat:

"Holla, ye pamper'd jades of Asia,
What! can ye draw but twenty miles a day?"

(Pt. 2 *Tamburlaine* IV. 4). The 'jades' are the vanquished kings.

Ib. "Sesostris-like such charioteers as these
May drive *six harness'd monarchs* if they please."

Young, *Love of Fame*, Sat. V.

"High on his car, Sesostris struck my view,
Whom sceptred slaves in golden harness drew."

Pope, *Temple of Fame.*

Luke.

Mitford adds J. Philips, *Blenheim* l. 16,

"As curst Sesostris, proud Egyptian king,
That *monarchs harness'd* to his chariots yok'd."

39. Dr Bradshaw notes that this line is in Pembroke MS. after the asterisks.

VI. ODE ON THE DEATH OF A FAVOURITE CAT.

Gray from Cambridge, March 1, 1747, in a letter to Walpole containing this Ode, writes "As one ought to be particularly careful to avoid blunders in a compliment of condolence, it would be a sensible satisfaction to me (before I testify my sorrow, and the sincere part I take in your misfortune) to know for certain, who it is I lament. I knew Zara and Selima (Selima was it? or Fatima?), or rather I knew them both together; for I cannot justly say which was which. Then as to your handsome cat, the name you distinguish her by, I am no less at a loss, as well knowing one's handsome cat is always the cat one likes best; or if one be alive and the other dead, it is usually the latter that is the handsomest. Besides, if the point were never so clear, I hope you do not think me so ill-bred or so imprudent as to forfeit all my interest in the survivor: oh no! I would rather seem to mistake, and imagine to be sure it must be the tabby one that had met with this sad accident. Till this affair is a little better determined, you will excuse me if I do not begin to cry.

'Tempus inane peto, requiem, spatiumque doloris.'"

He adds that he is "about to immortalize feuë Madame Selima for one week or fortnight" and then gives the poem.

Mystified himself, Gray has mystified his commentators. Yet it is clear, I think, that he believes that the deceased cat was not 'the tabby' —but the other, presumably a tortoise-shell; but he wishes to be in the good graces of the survivor; and therefore he will pretend that it is the 'tabby' whose death he is mourning; that the 'tabby' may be charmed with the fine things which the poet has said about her, under the impression that she is no more. Therefore to please her he writes

"Demurest of the *tabby* kind."

And, though he says also

"Her coat, that with the *tortoise* vies,"

that, to the 'tabby,' will mean that she was quite as beautiful as her deceased rival. If, as Gray rather anticipates, the victim of 'Malignant

Fate' was the tortoise-shell, then 'the tabby kind' is simply a synonym for 'cats,' and the other ambiguous line has its more obvious meaning. But this is the *exoteric* doctrine of the poem; the *esoteric* doctrine is for the private ear of the 'tabby.'

A little later Gray wrote to his friend Wharton a letter which Wharton has endorsed "Mr Gray, March 1747, Ode on the Cat." He says "the most noble of my Performances latterly is a Pôme on the uncommon Death of Mr W^{s}. Cat wch being of a proper Size and Subject for a Gentleman in your Condition to peruse (besides that I flatter myself Miss —— [the lady to whom Wharton was engaged] will give her Judgement upon it too, I herewith send you, it won't detain you long."

This copy is in the Wharton Correspondence of Gray in the British Museum. Gray there entitles it "On a favourite Cat, call'd Selima that fell into a China Tub with Gold-Fishes in it and was drown'd." I print it as it stands there, except where I indicate variations. There is another copy in Gray's hand at Pembroke, Cambridge, but this I have had no opportunity of working from. In the copy to Wharton Gray had already made some of the alterations which he adopted after the publication in Dodsley's *Miscellany* of 1748, in which the text was probably that of the copy which he sent to Walpole (March 1, 1747). The mishap occurred at Walpole's house in Arlington street, not long before Walpole purchased the little house at Twickenham which he converted into the famous Strawberry Hill. To Strawberry Hill the vase was ultimately transferred; Walpole wrote to Mason, July 29, 1773, "I have a pedestal making for the tub in which my cat was drowned; the first stanza of the Ode is to be written on it, beginning thus:

'Twas on this lofty vase's side, &c."

This tub was sold says Cunningham (in a note l. c.) at the Strawberry Hill sale in 1842 for £42, and is now at Knowsley, the seat of the Earl of Derby.

2. **Where China's gayest art** &c. Dr Bradshaw quotes from Lady Mary Wortley Montagu's *Town Eclogues*

"Where the tall jar erects its stately pride
With antic shapes in China's *azure* dyed."

Gray probably had read this, for most of these eclogues had been published before 1747, though his reference to them in his correspondence is of later date.

3. **The azure Flowers, that blow.** Johnson says "In the first

stanza *the azure flowers that blow*, shew how resolutely a rhyme is sometimes made when it cannot easily be found." It is certain that there is redundancy or some sort of weakness in the expression here. Those of Gray's apologists who admit redundancy, defend it by classical examples, some of which are not redundant at all. And how is Johnson answered by saying that ancient poets were sometimes guilty of redundancy? Again Gray is quoted in defence of himself. In the *Progress of Poesy* I. 1. 5, he has written "the laughing flowers that round them blow." But this is not redundant; Gray says that the 'thousand rills' of which he has just spoken are *engarlanded* with flowers which 'draw life and fragrance' from them; the added words 'round them' here make all the difference, especially in such a context.

On the other hand if Gray meant, as Dr Bradshaw says,—'so that we, as it were, see the flower in full blow'—if, that is, we are to understand that the flowers are represented vividly, and with truth to nature, Gray has expressed this feebly and inadequately.

4, 5. These lines are transposed in the edition of 1748.

13. **"gazed. but"** Wharton MS. A peculiarity of Gray's to begin a new sentence without a capital, if the first word of it is not a substantive.

14. **angel-Forms.** **"beauteous forms"** in 1748.

17, 18. Wakefield compares Virgil (*Georg.* IV. 274)

"Aureus ipse: sed in foliis, quae plurima circum
Funduntur, violae sublucet purpura nigrae."

Mitford adds from Pope

"His shining horns diffused a golden gleam."

(*Windsor Forest* 331), and *Temple of Fame* 253.

24. **"a foe to fish"** 1748.

25. **Looks.** **"Eyes"** Wharton MS.

31. **Eight Times.** "A cat has nine lives, as everybody knows." Phelps.

34. **No Dolphin came.** "Alluding to the well-known story of the dolphin's carrying Arion on his back to land. It is possible that the allusion in *Nereid* is to the story of Sabrina in *Comus*."

[The water-nymphs that in the bottom played,
Held up their pearled wrists, and took her in,
Bearing her straight to aged Nereus' hall.
ll. 833—835.] Phelps.

35. **Susan.** **"Harry"** Wharton MS.

36. **"What favourite has a friend?"** 1748.

40. **tempts.** "**strikes**" Wharton MS.

42. A proverb, of which it is enough here to say, that it was a proverb in the days of Chaucer, is used by Spenser, *F. Q.* II. 8. 14 ("Yet gold all is not that doth golden seem"), and by Shakespeare in the casket-scene in the *Merchant of Venice.*

"The last stanza ends in a pointed sentence of no relation to the purpose; if what *glistered* had been *gold*, the cat would not have gone into the water; and if she had, would not less have been drowned." Johnson. The logic is irresistible, but so was the temptation to defy it.

Walpole, Aug. 27, 1783, thought all his gold-fish were stolen. Next morning however he writes "In the mud of the troubled water I have found *all my gold*, as Dunning and Barré did last year [when they got pensions] and have taken out fifteen young fish for Lady Aylesbury and reserved them as an offering worthy of Amphitrite, in the cat's vase amidst 'the azure flowers that blow'."

VII. AGRIPPINA.

We place the fragmentary *Agrippina* here, because the few lines of the second scene are an attempt to complete it, made, as we believe, about the same time as the *Ode on the Cat* was written. (Cf. n. on the *Eton Ode* l. 29.) Gray communicated part of the first scene to Walpole in Dec. 1746 ("I send you a scene in a tragedy; if it don't make you cry it will make you laugh; and so it moves some passion, that I take to be enough"). In January 1747 he sent him the remainder of the scene, "that was lost in a wilderness of papers." Walpole had evidently complimented him on the portion already sent, and Gray says "Certainly you do her too much honour; she seemed to me to talk like an old boy, all in figures and mere poetry, instead of nature and the language of real passion. Do you remember 'Approchez-vous Néron'? Who would not rather have thought of that half line, than all Mr Rowe's flowers of eloquence?"

"Approchez-vous Néron" is from Racine's *Britannicus* (IV. ii. 1); it is thus that Racine's Agrippina re-asserts her authority over her son who has put her under arrest. Burrhus has just been urging her to remember in the coming interview that Nero is her emperor. (Compare the counsels of Gray's Aceronia.) A like master-stroke of Racine's is the "Tu peux sortir" with which Agrippina dismisses Nero after upbraiding him with the murder of Britannicus (V. vi. ad fin.).

Gray saw *Britannicus* in Paris on the 21st of May 1739, as he tells West next day; "all the characters, particularly Agrippina and Nero, done to perfection." Walpole was no doubt with him and would remember the effect given to these touches on the stage. Those who choose to compare the Argument of *Agrippina* with *Britannicus* will see that Racine is copied almost with a schoolboy's fidelity; the projected union of Junia and Britannicus, favoured by Agrippina, would have found its counterpart in that of Otho and Poppaea, favoured by the same person from analogous motives; the passion of Nero would again have been the obstacle; Nero was to have been in hiding once more to overhear a conversation; the part of Burrhus would have been played by Seneca; the pretended friend Narcissus would have reappeared in *Agrippina* in the person of Anicetus, captain of the guard; Agrippina's confidante Albina is replaced by Aceronia.

Gray is his own best critic on *Agrippina*, the interest of which lies mainly in the remarks to which it gave occasion. He returned from abroad with a vivid impression of the French classic stage,—of its constructive power, which he could only imitate with Chinese exactness,—and its dramatic *point*, which as he confesses, perhaps too humbly, he could not imitate at all. Johnson says "It was certainly no loss to the English stage that *Agrippina* was never completed." Nevertheless, if Gray *had* completed this effort of his 26th year, *Agrippina* would have compared favourably with anything which the English stage produced at the same epoch. If Gray had been prevailed upon by Walpole, it might have appeared about the same time as Johnson's own *Irene*, which was certainly no gain to our dramatic literature; and in structure (thanks to Racine), in diction, and above all in the management of tragic blank verse *Agrippina* would have much excelled Johnson's cumbrous performance. Or it might have been acted side by side with Thomson's posthumous *Coriolanus*, the last of those tragedies of his which Voltaire found 'frigid,'—an epithet with which we now conveniently damn almost all eighteenth century Tragedy, Voltaire's included; and it would at least have achieved that dignity of expression which Thomson in his plays only affected, whilst it would have been free from the vulgarisms of which he was often capable.

Gray tells Walpole (Jan. 1747) "Poor West put a stop to that tragic torrent he saw breaking in upon him"—but it does not seem that he acquiesced in the main article of West's criticism. West wrote (April 4, 1742) "The style appears to me too antiquated. Racine was of another opinion [he means to Gray]: he nowhere gives you the phrases of Ronsard. I should rather choose a style that bordered upon [Addison's] *Cato*, than upon Shakespeare. One may imitate (if one can) Shakespeare's manner, his surprising strokes of true nature, his expressive force in painting characters, and all his other beauties; preserving at the same time our own language. Were Shakespeare alive now, he would write in a different style from what he did."

Gray's reply has often been quoted, and has for us a wider scope than belongs to it as a defence of his *Agrippina*. "As to the matter of stile, I have this to say: The language of the age is never the language of poetry; except among the French, whose verse, where the thought or image does not support it, differs in nothing from prose. Our poetry, on the contrary, has a language peculiar to itself; to which almost every one, that has written, has added something by enriching it with foreign idioms and derivatives: nay sometimes words of their own composition or invention. Shakespeare and Milton have been great creators this way; and no one more licentious than Pope or Dryden, who perpetually borrow expressions from the former." Then he gives instances from Dryden, among which it is curious to note such words as 'mood,' 'smouldering,' 'beverage,' 'array,' and 'wayward' mentioned as having an antiquated sound; a fact which may teach us how much even the current language of our time owes to the principle for which Gray contends, and which he followed in his verse.

ACT I. SC. I.

Agrippina. Racine says in the preface to *Britannicus* that he has taken more pains to represent effectively Agrippina than any other character in his play, and that his subject is quite as much her downfall as the death of Britannicus. Gray's attempt is therefore just a second Part, with the disadvantage that the situations are too analogous, and the sentiments of the heroine, though expressed with more ornament and perhaps more vehemence, savour inevitably of repetition. But the original inspiration of both Gray and Racine is found in Tacitus. "J'avais copié," says Racine, "mes personnages d'après le plus grand Peintre de l'antiquité, je veux dire d'après Tacite. Et j'étais alors si rempli de la lecture de cet excellent historien, qu'il n'y a presque pas un trait éclatant dans ma Tragédie, dont il ne m'ait donné l'idée." Gray, as his correspondence with West shows, was steeped in Tacitus; *Agrippina* will show this too.

Aceronia. First mentioned by Tacitus in his vivid account of the attempt to drown Agrippina. She was lying over Agrippina's feet on the deck and speaking with joy of the reconciliation of mother and son, when the covering above them fell in; they escaped this destruction; after this Aceronia, when the vessel seemed sinking, not suspecting any criminal design, shouted that *she* was Agrippina, in hope that the sailors would rescue her,—whereupon they slew her with poles, oars etc.

Speaks...entering. If this stage direction is Gray's we must understand 'entering' of Agrippina, Anicetus being supposed to be outside the scene, while she comes in with her attendant. Gray probably intended to open with a strong stage effect. Those who have seen the Louis XI. of Irving will remember the king's first entrance upon the stage in a towering passion (Act II. Sc. vii. of the original play by Casimir Delavigne).

Anicetus. He was a freedman (once tutor of Nero), in command of the fleet at Misenum, when he undertook the murder of Agrippina, and suggested the original device for it. He was subsequently suborned by Nero to confess himself guilty with Octavia; then was banished to Sardinia, where, Tacitus adds suggestively, he found exile endurable, as he was very well off; and there he died.

5. Nero, on Agrippina's resentment at the murder of Britannicus, "Excubias militares, quae ut conjugi imperatoris olim, tum ut matri servabantur...digredi jubet," Tac. *Ann.* XIII. 18.

lictor. Among the honours paid to Agrippina on Nero's accession were two lictors to go before her. "Decreti et a senatu duo lictores," Tac. *Ann.* XIII. 2. Cf. Racine, *Britannicus* Act I. Sc. i. (Albine speaks):

"Néron devant sa mère a permis le premier
Qu'on portât les faisceaux couronnés de laurier."

6—8. Ironical, like what follows.

18, 19. Mitford quotes Racine, *Britannicus* IV. 2:

"Vous êtes un ingrat, vous le fûtes toujours.
Dès vos plus jeunes ans, mes soins et mes tendresses
N'ont arraché de vous que de feintes caresses."

But Racine in his preface acknowledges that he gets this from Tacitus' *factus naturâ velare odium fallacibus blanditiis.*

21. **th' unpledg'd bowl** &c. Evidence that Gray meant to carry on the story as told by *Racine*. For the allusion is, I think, to the death of Britannicus; and Tacitus (*Ann.* XIII. 16) says that Britannicus was wont to dine at a separate table with other noble children of his own age; that his meat and drink were tasted before they were set before him (as in our English 'assay of meats'); that on this occasion

he was supplied at first with drink, harmless, but very hot, and that when, as was expected, he rejected it, the poison was administered in the water poured in to cool it. But Racine invents a feast to celebrate the reconciliation of Nero and Britannicus, wherein Nero pledges Britannicus, and then:

> "Par les mêmes sermens Britannicus se lie.
> La coupe, dans ses mains, par Narcisse est remplie;
> *Mais ses lèvres à peine en ont touché les bords*—
> Le fer ne produit point de si puissans efforts."

29.

> "Haec (exclamat) mihi pro tanto
> Munere reddis præmia, gnate?
> Hac sum, fateor, digna carina,
> Quæ te genui, quæ tibi lucem
> Atque imperium, nomenque dedi
> Cæsaris amens."

Agrippina's Speech in Seneca's [?] *Octavia* v. 333.
Mitford.

38. So *Elegy* (Epitaph), "A youth to fortune and to fame unknown"; (Mitford). Cf. n. on *Eton Ode* l. 29; and l. 145 n. infra.

40. **Some edileship.** The ædiles had authority over the markets. Gray has Juvenal in mind, who, in speaking of the honours of Sejanus and his fall, and his body dragged to the scalæ Gemoniæ or the Tiber says (*Sat.* x. 99):

> "Hujus, qui trahitur, prætextam sumere mavis,
> An Fidenarum Gabiorumve esse potestas
> *Et de mensura jus dicere, vasa minora*
> *Frangere pannosus vacuis ædilis Ulubris?*"
> "Say, would'st thou rather don the stately robe
> He wore, thus dragged along; or be great man
> In some provincial market-town, *with power*
> *To judge of weights and measures*, and to smash—
> A shabby aedile—vessels undersized?"

Also Persius l. 129, 130:

> "Sese aliquem credens, Italo quod honore supinus
> Fregerit heminas Arreti ædilis iniquas."
> "Deeming himself a personage, because
> Erst at Arezzo short half-pints he smash'd
> With head well-back, in dignity provincial."

45. "Ce jour, ce triste jour, frappe encor ma mémoire,
Où Néron fut lui-même ébloui de sa gloire."
Racine, *Britannicus* I. i. (Mitford). Cf. l. 32 supr.

50. **Julian fire.** Agrippina was the grand-daughter of Julia the daughter of Augustus, and the mother of Augustus was the daughter of Julia, sister of the great Julius Cæsar. Agrippina was thus of the blood of the great Julian house.

64 sq. Tacitus (*Ann.* XIV. 9) "Hunc sui finem multos ante annos crediderat Agrippina contempseratque. Nam consulenti super Nerone responderunt Chaldaei fore ut imperaret matremque occideret; atque illa 'occidat' inquit 'dum imperet.'"

To this incident Agrippina refers more obscurely in *Britannicus:*

"Remords, crainte, périls, rien ne m'a retenue
J'ai vaincu ses mépris, j'ai détourné ma vue
Des malheurs qui dès lors me furent annoncés."

71. **whiter**, in the sense of more propitious, favourable. Thus lucky days were noted by the Romans with a white, and unlucky with a black mark.

72. **Think too.** Note the maturity of mind revealed in this reflection. Johnson, in his 42nd year, wrote in the *Rambler* (no. 87), "There are minds so impatient of inferiority, that their gratitude is a species of revenge, and they return benefits, not because recompense is a pleasure, but because obligation is a pain.' He even defended Reynolds for telling some ladies who were lamenting the death of a friend who had been kind to them, 'You have however the comfort of being relieved from a burthen of gratitude.'

82 to end of sc.] Gray thought this speech too long, and West agreed with him, but could offer no suggestion by way of retrenching it. Mason, who is unhappily our only authority for the text, was more enterprising, and his interpolations are quite the silliest of all his silly interferences with the poetic fragments of Gray. All these, but one, Dr Bradshaw has removed, but he has left the worst. Aceronia, as Gray reminds West, has been giving quiet counsels, yet Mason assigns to *her* all the strongest incitements by which Agrippina lashes herself to revolt, prefacing them with the ridiculous apology (inserted after 'house' l. 105):

"Did I not wish to check this dangerous passion,
I might remind my mistress" &c.

I can only be certain that the text as I try to restore it is much nearer to what Gray wrote than hitherto. It must be questionable whether ll. 105, 6 are *exactly* Gray's text; whether

"Ha! by Juno
It bears a noble semblance" (ll. 118, 119)

was written by him or by Mason; especially since 'on this base' will close l. 118; whether two lines (after l. 155)

"'Tis time to go, the sun is high advanc'd
And ere mid-day, Nero will come to Baiæ,"

are Mason's, or words of Gray's Agrippina transferred by Mason to Aceronia. The *length* of the speech is more after the French than the English model; the very speech of Agrippina in Racine, the exordium of which Gray so much approved, is longer than her speech in Gray; nor is the French *Romantic* drama prejudiced against long speeches, if we may judge by the very long soliloquy of Charles of Spain in Victor Hugo's *Hernani*, of which audiences are still more than patient.

88. **heed 'em.** On l. 55 of the *Eton Ode* ('*around 'em*') Dr Bradshaw notes, "This abbreviation of *them*, or perhaps a survival of the O. E. *eom*, is now a vulgarism or only used colloquially, but Gray printed it thus to avoid the unmusical sound of the *d* and *th*; and he has it in *Agrippina*: 'He perchance may heed 'em.'"

What is there so unmusical in 'around them' and 'heed them'? The fact is that 'heed 'em' &c. was an ugly affectation to which Gray's ear was not sensitive, because it was fashionable (as the dropping of final *g* is now); Swift, in the *Tatler*, no. 230 (Sept. 28, 1710), says, "I should be glad you would bestow some advice upon several young readers in our churches, who, coming up from the universities *full fraught with admiration of our town politeness*, will needs correct the stile of their Prayer-books. In reading the Absolution they are very careful to say Pardons and Absolves; and in the Prayer for the Royal Family it must be *endue 'um, enrich 'um, prosper 'um, and bring 'um.*"

98. "I guess the most faulty expressions may be these—*silken* son of *dalliance*—*drowsier* pretensions—wrinkled *beldams*—*arched* the hearer's brow and *riveted* his eyes in fearful *exstasie.*" Gray to West (April, 1742).

Gray compounds "silken son of dalliance" out of the "New" *Dunciad* which West had not seen:

"To where the Seine, obsequious as she runs,
Pours at great Bourbon's feet her *silken sons.*"
Dunciad, Bk IV.

and Shakespeare, *H. V.* ii. chorus l. 2:

"And *silken dalliance* in the wardrobe lies."

99. **Rubellius.** Gaius Rubellius Plancus was the son of Julia, daughter of Drusus the son of Tiberius; and thus boasted the genuine blood of the imperial house. Gray, in his Argument, postdates for dramatic purposes the fact that Agrippina was accused of inciting Rubellius to assert his claims against Nero's. This was four years before the date of the 'action.' Though Agrippina then triumphed over her accusers, in A.D. 60, the year after her death, the appearance of a comet ('with fear of change perplexing monarchs,' as Milton has it) set people thinking, and Nero banished Rubellius to Asia, where, two years later, he had him murdered.

100. **Sylla.** Faustus Cornelius Sulla was son-in-law of Claudius, the late emperor. There was a plot, real or supposed, to put him on the throne, soon after Nero's accession;—Nero became jealous of him, though the accusation failed; a fresh plot was invented as a plea for his banishment. He was sent to Massilia, A.D. 59, the year with which this tragedy is connected; and put to death there, A.D. 63.

104. **Drowsier.** See n. on l. 98.

110. **Corbulo,** A.D. 58, fought successfully against Tiridates, brother of Vologeses, for the control of Armenia. Corbulo, had he chosen to be faithless to Nero, might have subverted him. Hence in A.D. 67 Nero invited him to meet him at Cenchreæ (the port of Corinth), and there ordered his execution. Corbulo plunged a sword into his own breast, exclaiming "Well deserved."

113. **the Masians.** Who were these, and what had they to do with Germanicus? I cannot help suspecting that Gray wrote the *Asians.* Agrippina is speaking of the *legions*; 'those of Egypt' of course means the legions in Egypt; and the Asians might well mean the legions in Asia. When he was recalled from his triumphs in Germany, all the Eastern provinces were assigned to Germanicus, except that Piso was set to check him in Syria; and he visited Egypt, ostensibly in an official capacity. Moreover he died at Antioch, 'ingenti provinciæ luctu' says Tacitus. Mason's sight was bad; he either misread Gray (though Gray's writing can scarcely be misread), or not understanding him, substituted, or allowed the printer to substitute, something quite unintelligible[1].

115. **the Prætorian camp.** "Tiberius concentrated the cohorts previously scattered up and down the city (Tac. *Ann.* IV. 2) and

[1] There was a river Masius in Egypt, but if Gray had been thinking of that, he would never have written 'the Masians *and those of Egypt.*'

established them outside the Colline gate at the North-east of the city in a permanent camp, whose ramparts can be traced at the present day, being embedded in the later walls of Aurelian." (Lightfoot, detached note on *Philippians* i. 13). Here were placed the Prætorians, the imperial body-guard on whose voices the election to the empire got more and more to depend.

116. Racine, *Britannicus* II. ii.:

"Et moi, qui sur le trône ai suivi mes ancêtres,
Moi, fille, femme, sœur, et mère de vos maîtres."

Mitford.

But both Gray and Racine draw from Tacitus, who states that it was a fact of which history up to his time had no other example, 'imperatore genitam, sororem ejus qui rerum potitus sit, et conjugem et matrem fuisse' (*Ann.* XII. 42). Agrippina was daughter of Germanicus, in the military and proper sense 'imperator,' sister of the emperor Caligula, wife of the emperor Claudius, mother of the emperor Nero.

117. Gray or Mason makes the imperial Agrippina swear by Juno the queen of heaven.

122. **spirit-stirring**. Ll. 94—96 will remind us of *Othello*, III. iii. 351 sq.

"The shrill trump
The *spirit-stirring* drum, the ear-piercing fife,
The royal banner, and all quality,
Pride, pomp and circumstance of glorious war."

And perhaps this epithet here shows that Shakespeare was lurking in Gray's mind.

Soranus. Barea Soranus; it was later than A.D. 60 that Barea was proconsul of Asia; and Gray has warrant for assuming that he was at this time at Rome and in the Senate. He was subsequently accused for aiming at a revolution in his proconsular capacity; and for his intimacy with Rubellius. The Stoic P. Egnatius Celer was the chief witness against him and his daughter, whom Egnatius himself had encouraged in the magic arts she was charged with practising; and both victims were condemned to death. To this Juvenal refers in a famous passage (*Sat.* III. 116):

"Stoicus occidit Baream, delator amicum,
Discipulamque senex."

"The Stoic, turn'd informer, kill'd his friend,
The greybeard kill'd the girl who was his pupil."

123. **Cassius**. Gaius Cassius, consul A.D. 30, proconsul of Syria

A.D. 48, was a distinguished jurist, and a strict advocate of the discipline both military and civil of republican days. Tacitus (*Ann.* XIV. 43) makes him speak of his 'amor antiqui moris'; he opposed (A.D. 58) the extravagant rejoicings over a victory in Armenia; was banished to Sardinia A.D. 65, accused (*inter alia*) of having the bust of his ancestor, the murderer of Cæsar, in honour; was recalled by Vespasian, and soon afterwards died.

Vetus. Lucius Antistius Vetus was consul with Nero in the first year of his reign (A.D. 55), commanded (A.D. 58) a Roman army in Germany, and employed it in joining the Moselle and Saône by a canal, by way of connecting the Mediterranean and the Northern Ocean; was father-in-law to Rubellius (l. 99 n.); together with his mother-in-law and daughter anticipated Nero's sentence by opening his own veins (A.D. 65).

Thrasea. Thrasea Pætus married Arria, daughter of that famous Arria, who under Claudius set her husband Cæcina Pætus the example of suicide, stabbing herself and handing him the dagger saying, 'Pætus, it does not hurt' (amplified by Martial, *Ep.* I. 14). Thrasea was a Stoic, admired the younger Cato, and wrote his life. When Nero had murdered Agrippina, and the servile senate voted him honours in consequence, Thrasea walked out. In A.D. 62 he even carried a majority of the senate with him in resisting the proposal to put to death the prætor Antistius to please Nero. In A.D. 63 he was condemned by the extorted sentence of the senate, and committed suicide.

132. **Wrinkled beldams.** See n. l. 98.

145. **The gilded swarm &c.** 'The swarm that in thy noontide beam were born.' *Bard* (l. 69)—Mitford. Cf. l. 38 n.; *Eton Ode* l. 29 n.

146 sq. **Seneca be there &c.** Of this long speech (ll. 82 to end of sc.) Gray wrote to West (April, 1742), 'The first ten or twelve lines are, I believe, the best, and as for the rest, I was betrayed into a good deal of it by Tacitus; only what he has said in five words, I imagine I have said in fifty lines.' To this West replied, 'You think the ten or twelve first lines the best, now I am for the fourteen last; add, that they contain not one word of Ancientry.'

What Gray here says of Tacitus and himself is only a slight exaggeration; as will be seen if we compare with ll. 146—151, and ll. 157 to end of sc., twenty-eight lines in all, the one place of the *Annals* which supplied their substance. Agrippina after the degradation of Pallas (A.D. 55) is made to say, 'Non abnuere se, quin cuncta infelicis domus mala patefierent.' She would go to the camp with Britannicus—

'Audiretur hinc Germanici filia, inde vilis [?] rursus Burrus et exul Seneca, truncâ scilicet manu et professoriâ linguâ [Gray's 'laboured eloquence'] generis humani regimen expostulantes. Simul intendere manus, aggerere probra, consecratum Claudium ['enshrined Claudius'] infernos Silanorum manes ['ghosts of the Syllani'] invocare, et tot inrita facinora' ['fruitless crimes'] *Ann.* XIII. 14. Cf. Racine, *Britannicus* III. iii.

"J'ai choisi Burrhus pour opposer un honnête homme à cette peste de Cour [Narcisse]. Et je l'ai choisi plutôt que Sénèque. (See introductory note.) En voici la raison. Ils étaient tous deux gouverneurs de la jeunesse de Néron, l'un pour les armes, et l'autre pour les lettres. Et ils étaient fameux, Burrhus pour son expérience dans les armes et pour la sévérité de ses mœurs, *militaribus curis et severitate morum* (Tac.); Sénèque pour son éloquence, et le tour agréable de son esprit, *Seneca praeceptis eloquentiae et comitate honestâ.* Burrhus après sa mort fut extrêmement regretté à cause de sa vertu: *civitati grande desiderium ejus mansit per memoriam virtutis,*" Racine (Preface to *Britannicus*). Gray would have assigned to Seneca a less important part than Burrhus plays in Racine (see Argument).

148. "Je répondrai, Madame, avec la liberté
D'un soldat qui sait mal farder la vérité."

And again:

"Burrhus pour le mensonge eut toujours trop d'honneur."
Burrhus in Racine, *Britannicus* I. ii. Mitford.

164. See n. on l. 98. Did Gray anticipate Mark Pattison's criticism? Pope had written (Ep. to Arbuthnot, 1735, a passage which Gray certainly had not forgotten):

"Whom have I hurt? has poet yet, or peer
Lost the *arch'd eyebrow* or Parnassian sneer?"

"The 'arched eyebrow,'" says Pattison, "expresses derision. Less properly, Gray has made it expressive of horror." In Shakespeare 'the right arched beauty of the brow' is not a transient but a fixed character of the face.

166. "J'avouerai les rumeurs les plus injurieuses,
Je confesserai tout, exils, assassinats,
Poison même." *Britannicus* III. iii. Mitford.

171. **Syllani.** So probably in the text of Tacitus which Gray used. The form now preferred is Silani. They belonged to the Junia gens; they were two brothers and on the maternal side great-great-grandsons of Augustus; who lived to see the elder (born A.D. 14). The younger

Silanus was betrothed to Octavia, daughter of Claudius, but Agrippina, wishing to marry her to Nero, brought a false charge against Silanus, who was in consequence ejected from the senate and his prætorship, and, on the marriage of Octavia, destroyed himself. The elder brother was the first victim under Nero. Agrippina, without Nero's knowledge, caused him to be poisoned, when he was proconsul of Asia, by two persons of his household. She feared that he might avenge his brother; and he was formidable because of his descent from Augustus, though inert (Claudius called him 'pecus aurea') and unambitious.

SC. II.

Otho, &c. M. Salvius Otho, Emperor after Galba. He was one of Nero's boon companions. Of his connection with Poppæa, Tacitus gives two different accounts. In the *Histories* (I. 13) he says that Nero had put his mistress Poppæa under the charge of Otho, till he could get Octavia out of the way; and then suspecting Otho about Poppæa, banished him, under the pretence of putting him in command there, to Lusitania. In the *Annals* (XIII. 45, 46), Otho is represented as having enticed Poppæa from her husband Rufius (*sic*, *ap.* Ritter) Crispinus, and married her; and as having made Nero his rival by praising her beauty. Suetonius (*Otho*, 3) says that she was taken from her husband and married to Otho, but only to serve Nero's wicked purposes; that Otho was too much attached to her, and hence was sent to Lusitania. This exile began A.D. 58; Gray therefore postdates as well as modifies the story.

For the main fact (see Argument) that Poppæa instigated Nero to the murder of Agrippina, Gray had the authority of Tacitus (*Ann.* XIV. 1). She afterwards induced Nero to divorce Octavia (A.D. 62); married him a few days later; and made him slay Octavia the same year. She died of a kick which Nero gave her (A.D. 65).

186. **elusive speed.** See n. on *Eton Ode* l. 29.

190. For this poetic commonplace Mitford gives several classical parallels, one of which is certainly not to the point, for it turns out to be part of a description of the constellation Draco (!) out of Cicero's translation of Aratus. Curious and a little more apposite is a quotation he adds from Constantinus Manasses (a writer in the 12th century A.D. who compiled Σύνοψις ἱστορική, a sort of rhythmic history from the creation), who rationalizes the legend of Helen's birth by the swan, by tracing it to her long white neck:

"Δειρὴ μακρὰ κατάλευκος, ὅθεν ἐμυθουργήθη
Κυκνογενῆ τὴν εὔοπτον Ἑλένην χρηματίζειν."

Of course the resemblance to Akenside, *Pleasures of the Imagination*, Bk. I.:

> "That soft cheek springing to the *marble neck*
> Which *bends aside* in vain,"

is fortuitous, even if we are right in supposing that this scene was added in 1747. Akenside's poem appeared anonymously in January 1744, when he was in his 23rd year; he is the 'young friend' of Wharton's to whom Gray refers in a letter of April of that year, in which he says that he has rather 'turned over than read' the thing, which seemed to him 'above the middleing.'

192. "Yielded with coy submission, *modest* pride,
And sweet *reluctant* amorous delay."
Milton, *Par. Lost*, IV. 310. Luke.

VIII. ALLIANCE OF EDUCATION AND GOVERNMENT.

Gray wrote to Wharton from Stoke, Aug. 19, 1748, "I fill up with the Beginning of a Sort of Essay. What name to give it I know not, but the Subject is, the Alliance of Education and Government; I mean to shew that they must necessarily concur to produce great and useful Men. I desire your Judgement upon so far, before I proceed any farther...Pray shew it to no one (as it is a Fragment) except it be St[r] [Stonhewer], who has seen most of it already I think."

Here followed the first part of the poem down to the words "vintage as it grows." The rest of the transcript of this fragment in the Egerton MSS. in the British Museum is in Wharton's handwriting. But the whole fragment is in Gray's handwriting in the Pembroke MSS. With a single exception Mason's printed text corresponds with the Pembroke MS. word for word. He has been unjustly suspected of making these variations between his text and that in the British Museum, as thinking them improvements. But they are made by Gray, and *are* improvements. The point is of importance as bearing on the date at which the Pembroke transcripts were made; they sometimes certainly give us Gray's *ultima manus*. See *Eton College Ode* l. 29 *n*.

On March 9, 1749 Gray tells Wharton of the work of "the President Montesquieu, the Labour of Twenty Years. it is called L'Esprit des Loix, 2 v. 4to. printed at Geneva. he lays down the Principles on w[ch] are founded the three sorts of Government, Despotism, the limited Monarchic, & the Republican, & shews how from thence are deducted the Laws & Customs, by which they are guided and maintained : *the Education proper to each Form, the influences of Climate, Situation, Religion, &c., on the Minds of particular Nations, & on their Policy.* the Subject (you see) is as extensive as Mankind, &c."

It is probable that Gray had not seen *L'Esprit des Lois* until he had written all that we possess of his fragment. But I think it likely that he had read Montesquieu's *Considerations sur les Causes de la Grandeur des Romains, et de leur Décadence*, which was published in 1739. One point of contact certainly is to be found between Gray's opinions and this work of Montesquieu, in the 'detached sentiment' which Mason reasonably supposes was a note for this poem. Gray's words will be found on p. 29 of the text : 'The doctrine of Epicurus is ever ruinous to society,' &c. Compare the whole passage with this from c. x. of the *Grandeur et Décadence* :

'Je crois que la secte d'Epicure, qui s'introduisit à Rome sur la fin de la république contribua beaucoup à gâter le cœur et l'esprit des Romains. Les Grecs en avaient été infatués avant eux ; aussi avaient-ils été plus tôt corrompus,' &c.

It was the theory that the gods were indifferent to human affairs,—a practical atheism—which made Epicureanism so pernicious in the judgment of Montesquieu, as will be seen by further reference to this Chapter X. With all his aversion to dogmatic theology Gray's was essentially a *religious* mind ; this would prejudice him in favour of Montesquieu's view, which perhaps confuses cause and effect, even if it does not imply the popular misconception of the real character of the tenets of Epicurus himself.

We cannot be certain that Gray had not received and read *L'Esprit des Lois*, before he carried the poem further than that portion of it which he sent to Wharton; therefore the discrepancy which Mason finds between Gray's views and those of Montesquieu in his 14th Book if it exists, may be intentional. But I question its existence, and at any rate Mason has not defined or indicated it properly. Montesquieu in this book, whilst he insists strongly upon climatic influences, points out that the best laws are those which are designed to correct those influences, and, *inter alia*, instances—strangely enough for readers of to-day—China as an example of good, and Japan of bad legislation in this respect. Gray's haste to suggest the remedial aspects of this question (ll. 64—84), which are really his theme, is due to his aversion to everything that savoured of the doctrines of necessity and materialism, believing as he did that these have a pernicious effect upon conduct. About ten years after the date of this poem he wrote to Stonhewer, his *confidant* perhaps on such topics, "That we are indeed mechanical and dependent beings, I need no other proof than my own feelings; and from my own feelings I learn, with equal conviction, that we are not *merely* such: that there is a power within that struggles against the force and bias of that mechanism, commands its action, and, by frequent practice, reduces it to that ready obedience which we call *habit*; and all this in conformity to a preconceived opinion, (no matter whether right or wrong,) to that least material of agents, a thought. I have known many...who, while they thought they were conquering an old prejudice, did not perceive that they were under the influence of one far more dangerous; one that furnishes us with a ready apology for all our worst actions," &c.

Mason tells us that on reading *L'Esprit des Lois* Gray said 'the Baron had forestalled some of his best thoughts.' 'Some time after,' adds Mason, 'he had thoughts of resuming his plan, and of dedicating it, by an introductory Ode to M. de Montesquieu; but that great man's death, which happened in 1755, made him drop his design finally."

Gibbon (*Decline and Fall* c. XXXI. *n.* 127) has written, "Instead of compiling tables of chronology and natural history, why did not Mr Gray apply the powers of his genius to finish the philosophic poem of which he has left such an exquisite specimen?" We do not answer this question by lamenting, with Mitford, 'the situation in which Gray was placed, which was not favourable to the cultivation of poetry.' If he could write the *Progress of Poesy, the Bard, the Installation Ode*, and over a hundred lines of this fragment at Cambridge, it is hard to see why he could not have finished it there. He lived at Cambridge by his own choice; what could have kept him there but a strong inclination for those studies which the place is supposed to have forced upon him? Mitford confuses cause and effect. Gray's propensity was towards research. Walpole says that when they were abroad "Gray was all for antiquities," &c. The passion for minute inquiries is not often combined with a great poetic gift; when these are found together in a man of leisure, not at all solicitous of money, and very little solicitous of fame, poetry is likely to take the second place; especially when tasks of the first kind come easily, and verse involves considerable mental strain. No poetry is less spontaneous than Gray's; of *him* it is emphatically true that there is 'not a line of his, but he could tell us very well how it came there.'

In this connection the motto which Gray has adopted for the poem has great significance. By it the poet lashes himself to exertion. It means, as Lang renders it, "Begin, my friend, for be sure thou canst in no wise carry thy song with thee to Hades, that puts all things out of mind."

2. **barren.** **flinty** Egerton MS.

9. **vital airs**, a classicism : vitales auras, *Aen.* I. 387.

14. "And lavish *nature* laughs and throws her *stores* around." Dryden Virg. [Luke, ap. Mitford, but with quite useless reference].

17, 18. Cf. *Elegy* l. 63 and note there.

21. **blooming.** **vernal** Egerton MS.

45. "Diffusing *languor* in the panting *gales.*" Pope, *Dunciad* IV. 300.

47. [Si] *bellica nubes* [Ingrueret], Claudian, *Laus Serenæ Reginæ*, l. 196. Luke.

48. **sweepy sway.** An expression of Dryden's of which Mitford on l. 75 of the *Bard* gives three examples from his translations. Here he quotes an odd application of the expression from Pope, *Odyssey* V. 303

"And next a *wedge* to drive with *sweepy sway.*"

One would suspect the hand of Broome or Fenton here, but Courthope says that this 5th book was *really* translated by Pope.

51. **blue-eyed.** 'Caerula quis stupuit Germani lumina?' asks Juvenal (*Sat.* XIII. 164), implying that all Germans had blue eyes. Tacitus, *Germania* 4, attributes to them '*truces* et *caerulei* oculi,' and Plutarch (*Marius* II.) a *χαροπότης τῶν ὀμμάτων*. Now the adjective *χαροπός*, whether it strictly means 'glad-eyed' or not, is invariably used of 'sparkling' eyes, and, again, was closely connected with the colour of gray or light-blue. The connotation 'fierce' also belongs to it; cf. *χαροποὶ λέοντες*, *Odyssey* II. 611. 'Cæruleus' as applied to eyes does not quite escape this connotation, as we see from Tacitus *supra* and from Horace, *Epodes* XVI. 7, speaking of Rome, which 'Nec *fera caeruleâ* domuit Germania *pube*.'

54—57. Gibbon, in the note above cited, quotes these lines in illustration of his own words: "These delights [of the Goths] were enhanced by the memory of past hardships: the comparison of their native soil, the bleak and barren hills of Scythia, and the frozen banks of the Elbe and Danube, added new charms to the felicity of the Italian climate."

55. **Heav'ns.** **Skies** Egerton MS.

56. **Scent.** **Catch** Egerton MS.

57. A great temptation, according to Claudian. 'Quid palmitis uber Etrusci...Semper in ore geris?—'Why prating ever the exuberance Of the Etruscan vine'? he makes (*de Bello Getico* l. 504) an old Getic warrior say to Alaric, in dissuading him from pushing further into Italy.

58, 59. Gray is thinking partly of the empire of Turkey in Asia but also of the progress of Mahommedan despotism further east, and notably in India. Aurungzebe, the Charlemagne of the East, died only in 1707, little more than 40 years therefore before these lines were written; and one mark of the interest which his career excited in Europe is the fact that Dryden (1676) wrote a tragedy about him while he was alive: 'In the same month in which Oliver Cromwell died, he assumed the magnificent title of Conqueror of the World, and was the sovereign of a larger territory than had obeyed any of his predecessors' (Macaulay, *Hist. Eng.* III. chap. 18). Gray probably knew that this great fabric was unstable; Nadir Shah of Persia had defeated the Great Mogul at Delhi (bearing away with him the famous Koh-i-Noor) about ten years before the date of this poem and Gray jocularly refers 'to the peace between Adil Shah (nephew of Nadir) and the Great Mogol,' at that time Mohammed Shah, in a letter to Wharton of March 9, 1749. But he also knew that whatever the vicissitudes of empire in the East, there

> "An Amurath an Amurath succeeds
> Not Harry, Harry,"

and none surely have been more 'pliant to the rod' than the natives of Bengal. What Gray did not know was that in two years' time the foundation of a more solid rule in Asia would be laid in Clive's capture and defence of Arcot.

60—63. The word 'still' shows what is in Gray's mind. He is thinking of the Turks in Europe, who had not ceased to be a danger, though their repulse from before Vienna by John Sobieski in 1683 may be regarded as the final turning of the tide. But there was still flow as well as ebb. Thus by the peace of Carlowitz in 1699, the Venetians obtained the Morea and some places in Dalmatia. But the Morea was again overrun by the Turks, who retained it by the peace of Passarowitz in 1718 though they had to surrender Belgrade. In 1739 Belgrade and the Austrian part of Servia were ceded to Turkey, which on the other hand lost Azoff to the Russians. Perhaps on the whole we need not stumble at applying 'her lessening lands' to 'European freedom'; but we have the extremely awkward alternative of making the 'her' of l. 61 refer to Asia, while the 'her' of l. 63 refers to Europe.

63. The dominions of Turkey in Europe, and those in Asia and Africa which once acknowledged European rule, whether that of Macedonian sovereigns, of Rome, or of the Byzantine Empire.

66. "...as those nightly tapers disappear
When day's bright lord ascends our hemisphere,
So pale grows reason at religion's sight," &c.
Dryden, *Religio Laici* [8—11]. Rogers.

But Dryden's 'tapers' are the stars which do indeed disappear from sight, but do not expire. In fact Gray sanctions a popular domestic fallacy that the sun puts the fire out.

91. **side-long.** 'The suffix *-ling* or *-long* is adverbial, as in headlong. Hence *sidelong*, adj.' Skeat. The common plough turns the soil to one side called the furrow-side, the other, where a straight cut is made is called the land-side. Cf. (with Luke,) Thomson, *Spring*, 40—43:

"...incumbent o'er the shining share
The Master leans, removes the obstructing clay,
Winds the whole work, and *sidelong lays the glebe.*"

91—93. The resemblance, pointed by Mitford, between these lines and Goldsmith's *Traveller*, (198—200) of the Swiss mountaineer:

"Or drives his venturous *ploughshare to the steep;*
Or seeks the den where snow-tracks mark the way,
And drags the struggling *savage* into day"—

is coincidence merely. Goldsmith is little likely to have seen this fragment; his *Traveller* was published in December 1764, and these lines first saw the light in Mason's *Memoirs* in 1775. Nevertheless Matthew Arnold states that in *The Alliance of Education and Government* Gray gave Goldsmith hints for the *Traveller* which he used. The simple truth is that Goldsmith drew from *L'Esprit des Lois*, to which Gray's fragment has some analogy, 'Savage' for 'wild-beast' with no previous intimation that man was *not* meant, perhaps was justified to Gray and Goldsmith by the Latin 'fera.' Pope is more cautious:

"The *lion* thus, with dreadful anguish stung,
Roams through the desert, and demands his young:
When the grim *savage*, to his rifled den
Too late returning, snuffs the track of men," &c.
Iliad XVIII. (318—322 in the Greek).

101. **his summer-bed.** "I was particularly anxious to learn from the priests why the Nile, at the commencement of the *summer* solstice, begins to rise, and continues to increase for a hundred days; and why, as soon as that number is past, it forthwith returns and contracts its stream, continuing low during the whole of the winter until the summer solstice comes round again." Herodotus II. 19 (Rawlinson's Tr.).

103. Wakefield compares Denham, Cooper's Hill, of the Thames:

"...survey his shore,
O'er which he kindly *spreads his spacious wing*,
And hatches plenty for th' ensuing spring."

104—107. No doubt suggested by Virgil, *Georg.* IV. 287 sq.:

"...qua Pellaei gens fortunata Canopi
Accolit effuso stagnantem flumine Nilum
Et circum pictis vehitur sua rura phaselis."

'Where the favoured race of Macedonian Canopus dwell by the still broad overflow of Nile and ride round their own farms in painted boats.' Mackail.

104, 105. "Learn of the little nautilus to sail
Spread the thin oar and catch the driving gale."

Pope, *Essay on Man* III. 177, 178. The passage was about 15 years old, and Gray had it more or less in memory as he wrote.

105. **dusky.** Gray has in mind the epithet 'fuscus' so frequently applied by the Latin poets to the Egyptians. Dryden writes 'the sunburnt people' in his translation of Virgil l. c. supra.

106. **frail floats.** So Lucan, *Pharsalia* IV. 135 sq., describing a boat made of willow overstretched with oxhide, compares it to the 'frail floats' used by the Veneti on the Po, or to the British coracle, and adds

"Sic, cum tenet omnia Nilus,
Conseritur bibulâ Memphitis cymba papyro,"

'bibulâ' implying that the papyrus-boat was likely to be leaky. Juvenal too *Sat.* XV. 126 sq. speaks of the Egyptians as an unprofitable rabble paddling about in painted earthenware.

distant, Pembroke and Egerton MS. Mason prints **neighb'ring.**

108, 109. "I find also among his papers a single couplet much too beautiful to be lost, though the place where he meant to introduce it cannot be ascertained; it must, however, have made a part of some description of the effect which the reformation had on our national manners." Mason.

Dryden, *Hind and Panther* III. 203—205, makes the Panther (the Church of England) say:

"Thus our eighth Henry's marriage they defame;
They say the schism of beds began the game,
Divorcing from the Church to wed the dame."

This is perhaps the source of Gray's much praised conceit, the second line of which is detestable,—hyperbole pushed to profanity. Horace Walpole probably knew Gray's lines when in 1771 he wrote for a cross to be erected at Ampthill 'the mournful refuge of the injured queen' Katharine, the lines:

"Yet Freedom hence her radiant banners waved
And love avenged a realm by priests enslaved.
From Catherine's wrongs a nation's bliss was spread
And Luther's light from Henry's lawless bed."

These lack, says Mitford, the 'metaphorical beauty' of Gray's couplet. The less of such 'metaphorical beauty' the better.

IX. THE ELEGY.

In August 1746 Gray writes to Wharton from Stoke, "The Muse, I doubt, is gone, and has left me in far worse company; if she returns, you will hear of her." And from the same place to the same correspondent, on the following Sept. 11 (after the account of Aristotle quoted by Matthew Arnold in his Essay on Gray): "This and *a few autumnal Verses* are my Entertainments dureing the Fall of the Leaf." I know of no poem but the *Elegy* to which these fitful efforts of the 'Muse' are likely to belong.

Once more from Stoke, on June 12, 1750, Gray writes to Walpole, "I have been here a few days (where I shall continue a good part of the summer) and having put an end to a thing, whose beginning you have seen long ago, I immediately send it to you. You will I hope look upon it in the light of a thing with an end to it; a merit which most of my writings have wanted, and are likely to want."

That this 'thing' was the *Elegy* there can be no doubt. Walpole could not have seen the 'beginning' of it at an earlier date than Nov. 1745,—the date, as I have shown (*Gray and His Friends*, p. 7), of his reconciliation with Gray,—except we adopt the extremely bold hypothesis that the *Elegy* was begun before the quarrel, that is to say before, as far as can be ascertained, Gray had written a line of original English verse.

Mason, in his *Memoirs of Gray*, speaking of the date August 1742, that month of exceptional efflorescence in Gray, says, "I am inclined to believe that the *Elegy in a Country Churchyard* was begun, if not concluded, at this time also. Though I am aware that, as it stands at present, the conclusion is of a later date; how that was originally, I have shown in my notes on the poem." (The four stanzas which, according to Mason, originally ended the poem will be found *infra*, n. on l. 72.)

Of the MS. of the *Elegy* in which these four stanzas occur, called by Dr Bradshaw the 'Original,' by Mr Gosse the 'Mason,' and by Mr Rolfe the 'Fraser' MS. 100 copies were printed in 1884. The MS. does *not* end with these four stanzas, but contains them *with* the conclusion as we now read the poem[1]. Gray added his after-thoughts without effacing the lines for which he meant to substitute them: this is characteristic of him, for he had a great aversion to erasure. That he could not have intended the *second* and *fourth* of these stanzas to remain is clear, because they are remodelled in ll. 73—76, and ll. 93—96; but the four stanzas, however beautiful, are abrupt, considered as the last lines of the poem. When Gray sent the poem to Walpole in 1750, he could congratulate himself that the 'thing' had really an *end* to it, both as compared with its previous state and with the fragmentary *Agrippina*.

Walpole did not at first accept the account of the date of the poem, submitted to him by Mason before the Memoirs of Gray went to press. He writes, Dec. 1, 1773:

"The 'Churchyard' was, I am persuaded, posterior to West's death [1742] at least three or four years. At least I am sure that I had the twelve or more first lines from himself above three years after that period, and it was long before he finished it."

And yet Mason appears to have satisfied Walpole that the opinion expressed in the Memoirs was correct, for Walpole writes to him Dec. 14, 1773, that his account of the *Elegy* puts an end to his criticism on the subject.

[1] Mason says, 'In the first manuscript copy of this exquisite poem I find the conclusion different from that which he afterwards composed.' He has only inferred that the four stanzas were the original *conclusion* and endeavours thus to force this inference upon his readers.

Walpole was surely *complaisant*, if Mason induced him, against his better memory, to admit that the *Elegy* could have been concluded, in any sense, in 1742. What evidence could Mason have adduced that it was even begun in that year? Not certainly the testimony of Gray himself, for if Mason could have relied upon that he would have let us know it. He must, I think, have persuaded Walpole that the three or four opening stanzas were not, as Walpole supposed, written shortly before he saw them, but, like the fragment of *Agrippina*, had long been laid aside. But would not Gray have told Walpole this, and would not Walpole, whose own impressions receive much confirmation from Gray's hints to Wharton in 1746, have recollected it?

If, as seems probable, Gray gave Walpole these opening stanzas not by letter, but when the reconciled friends were together, whether in '45 or in the summer of '46, when he was at Stoke and 'seeing Walpole a great deal' (to Wharton Aug. [13] 1746), Walpole would have no *documentary* evidence to oppose to Mason's representations whatever they may have been, and might easily have been induced by a man more conceited and obstinate than himself to mistrust his memory of what had happened twenty-seven years before. And that Mason's notions of the date of the *Elegy* were in no way modified by what Walpole told him, leads one to mistrust those notions altogether. However this may be, there can be no doubt that a goodly part of the *Elegy* was composed at intervals between August 13, 1746, and June 12, 1750. That the death of Gray's maiden aunt, Mrs Mary Antrobus, at Stoke, on Nov. 5, 1749, stimulated Gray to resume the poem may be true, and is more probable than that the death of his uncle Rogers in October 1742 prompted him to begin it.

Lastly, Gray's heading to the Pembroke MS. is 'Elegy written in a Country Churchyard 1750.' He has given in the same MS. minute details as to the editions of the *Elegy*; if he had written a substantial part of it as early as 1742 (a year so memorable to him), he might have been expected to record this.

Of the *Elegy* there are three copies in Gray's handwriting extant; the one mentioned already, which may be considered as the rough draft; this was purchased in 1875 by Sir Wm. Fraser. It will be referred to in these notes, after Mr Rolfe, as the Fraser MS. Another copy was in Wharton's possession, and accordingly is in the Egerton MSS. in the British Museum. I have never seen it, for when I consulted the Wharton Letters there, the *Elegy* had been taken out for exhibition. Of the third, the MS. at Pembroke College, Cambridge, I made such memoranda as a brief opportunity admitted. Many therefore of the Various Readings here recorded are given on the faith of previous editors.

Walpole was so delighted with the *Elegy* that he showed it about in manuscript with the result that it got into the hands of the enterprising publisher. Accordingly Gray wrote to Walpole from Cambridge, Feb. 11, 1751:

"As you have brought me into a little sort of distress, you must assist me, I believe, to get out of it as well as I can. Yesterday I had the misfortune of receiving a letter from certain gentlemen (as their bookseller expresses it) who have taken the Magazine of Magazines into their hands. They tell me that an *ingenious* Poem called Reflections in a Country Churchyard has been communicated to them, which they are printing forthwith; that they are informed that the *excellent* author of it is I by name, and that they beg not only his *indulgence*, but the *honour* of his correspondence, &c. As I am not at all disposed to be either so indulgent, or so correspondent, as they desire, I have but one bad way left to escape the honour they would inflict upon me; and therefore am obliged to desire you would make Dodsley print it immediately (which may be done in less than a week's time) from your copy, but without my name, in what form is most convenient for him, but on his best paper and character; he must correct the press himself, and print it without any interval between the stanzas, because the sense is in some places continued beyond them; and the title must be,—Elegy, written in a Country Churchyard. If he would add a line or two to say it came into his hands by accident, I should like it better. If you behold the Magazine of Magazines in the light that I do, you will not refuse to give yourself this trouble on my account, which you have taken of your own accord before now. If Dodsley do not do this immediately, he may as well let it alone."

The *Elegy* appeared on the 16th of February 1751 in a quarto pamphlet with the following Title-page.

"An Elegy wrote in a Country
Church Yard

London: Printed for R. Dodsley in Pall-Mall; And sold by M. Cooper in Pater-noster-Row. 1751. [Price Sixpence.]

Advertisement. The following Poem came into my hands by Accident, if the general Approbation with which this little Piece has spread, may be call'd by so slight a Term as Accident. It is this

Approbation which makes it unnecessary for me to make any Apology but to the Author: As he cannot but feel some Satisfaction in having pleas'd so many Readers already, I flatter myself he will forgive my communicating that Pleasure to many more. The Editor."

The Editor is Walpole, as will be seen by Gray's letter *infra*. He pretends to have been one of many readers into whose hands the poem *accidentally* fell, and to have taken the same unwarrantable liberty with it, which had in fact been taken by the Magazine of Magazines. The plain truth might easily have been told as to the circumstances which led to its publication by Dodsley, without any sacrifice of the *anonymity* which Gray desired. And how does a poet indifferent to fame and money prevent the surreptitious publication of his works, by making the public believe that the offence has been *twice* committed with no remonstrance on his part? His real injury is the issue of a bad text; his only remedy the issue of a text revised by himself. Such remedy Macaulay took when an unauthorized edition of his speeches, deformed by ridiculous blunders, was published by Vizetelly. Such remedy Gray did *not* take; with a consequence of which he could not reasonably complain. He writes to Walpole from Cambridge on Ash Wednesday, 1751:

"You have indeed conducted with great decency my little *misfortune;* you have taken a paternal care of it, and expressed much more kindness than could have been expressed [? expected] from so near a relation. But we are all frail; and I hope to do as much for you another time.

Nurse Dodsley has given it a pinch or two in the cradle, that (I doubt) it will bear the marks of as long as it lives. But no matter; we have ourselves suffered under her hands before now; and besides, it will only look the more careless and by *accident* as it were. I thank you for your advertisement, which saves my honour, and in a manner *bien flatteuse pour moi*, who should be put to it even to make myself a compliment in good English."

It is hard to understand why Gray's honour needed saving, or how by this expedient it was saved. But the worst of an affectation pushed as far as he pushed it, is that it leads to much bewilderment, and a good deal of superfluous lying.

The 'pinches' were more severe than I supposed. See Gray to Walpole, Mar. 3, 1751, and notes in my edition of the letters; the punctuation is perhaps not quite exact; and in stanza 7, l. 3, the word 'they' is twice repeated. There is no interval between the stanzas, but the first line of every stanza is *indented*. Gray took ample pains in the long run that the world should know what he had really written.

To the title of the Pembroke MS. he has appended a note:

"Published in Febry. 1751, by Dodsley: and went thro four Editions; in two months; and afterwards a fifth, 6th, 7th, and 8th, 9th, and 10th, and 11th. Printed also in 1753 with Mr Bentley's Designs, of whch there is a 2nd Edition and again by Dodsley in his Miscellany, Vol. 7th, and in a Scotch Collection called *The Union*, translated into Latin by Chr. Anstey Esq., and the Revd Mr Roberts, and publish'd in 1762; and again the same year by Robert Lloyd, M.A."

The text with the exception of the bracketed stanzas, is given, upon the faith of Mr Gosse, from the edition of Gray's Poems published by Dodsley in 1768.

Mason states that Gray originally gave the poem only "the simple title of 'Stanzas written in a Country Church-yard.' I persuaded him first to call it an Elegy, because the subject authorized him so to do; and the alternate measure, in which it was written, seemed peculiarly fit for that species of composition. I imagined too that so capital a Poem, written in this measure, would as it were appropriate it in future to writings of this sort; and the number of imitations which have since been made of it (even to satiety) seem to prove that my notion was well founded."

Mason delighted to *pose* as Gray's literary *confrère* and adviser; and when we remember that he was capable of inserting in his version of Gray's letters compliments to himself which never came from Gray, we must accept such statements of his, particularly those which refer to this early stage of the friendship between the two men, with great caution.

Johnson was thinking of this sentence of Mason's when (in the Life of Hammond) he said, "Why Hammond *or other writers* have thought the quatrain of ten syllables elegiac it is difficult to tell. The character of the *Elegy* is gentleness and tenuity; but this stanza has been pronounced by Dryden, whose knowledge of English verse was not inconsiderable, to be the most magnificent of all the measures which our language affords.'

Since the name was invented there have been elegies and elegies; but the *residuum* of truth in Johnson's remark is that this measure, because of its stateliness, at once betrays, by mere force of contrast, 'tenuity' of thought. Take one of the three stanzas of Hammond which Johnson derides:

"Panchaia's odours be their costly feast,
And all the pride of Asia's fragrant year,
Give them the treasures of the farthest East,
And what is still more precious, give thy tear."

Even the few weak places of Dryden's *Annus Mirabilis* become through this mould the more obvious. It cannot therefore be successfully employed on trivial themes. It was used *inter alios* by Davenant for his heroic poem of Gondibert; by Hobbes for his curious translation of Homer; by Dryden for his *Annus Mirabilis*. The suggestion that the posthumous publication of Hammond's Love Elegies in 1745 had anything to do with Gray's choice of this measure may be dismissed; it comes oddly from those who affirm that the *Elegy* was begun in 1742.

The Curfew. The evening bell still conventionally called curfew, though the law of the Conqueror, which gave it the name, had long been a dead letter. In Shakespeare the sound of the Curfew is the signal to the spirit-world to be at large. Edgar in *Lear* feigns to recognize 'the foul fiend Flibbertigibbet: he begins at curfew and walks till the first cock' (III. 4. 103); and in *The Tempest*, V. 1. 40, the elves 'rejoice to hear the solemn curfew.' The mood of the *Elegy* is that of *Il Penseroso* and the scene in both poems is viewed in the evening twilight:

"Oft on a plat of rising ground
I hear the far-off curfew sound,
Over some wide-watered shore,
Swinging slow with sullen roar."

Milton, *Il Penseroso*, 72—75.

Milton's '*far-off* curfew' reminds us of the squilla *di lontano* of Dante, which Gray quotes for the first line of the *Elegy*. I supply in brackets the rest of the passage; *Purgatorio*, VIII. 1—6.

[Era gia l' ora, che volge 'l disio
A' naviganti, e 'nteneresce 'l cuore
Lo dì ch' han detto a' dolci amici addio:
E che lo nuovo peregrin d' amore
Punge, se ode] squilla *di lontano*
Che paia 'l giorno pianger, che si muore.

[Now was the hour that wakens fond desire
In men at sea, and melts their thoughtful heart
Who in the morn have bid sweet friends farewell,
And pilgrim, newly on his road, with love
Thrills, if he hear] the vesper bell from far
That seems to mourn for the expiring day. Cary.

The curfew tolls from Great S. Mary's, at Cambridge, at 9, from the Curfew Tower of Windsor Castle (nearer the scene of the *Elegy*) at 8, in the evening.

Warton, *Notes on Pope*, vol. I. p. 82, reads:

"The curfew tolls!—the knell of parting day."

But we know exactly what Gray wrote, and what he meant us to read.

2. **wind.** Not *winds*, as so commonly printed.

"'Wind' has a more poetical connotation, for it suggests a long slowly-moving line of cattle rather than a closely packed herd." Phelps.

Add that of Gray's cattle some are returning from the pasture, but others from the plough. Of the innumerable passages that might be quoted in illustration of this line, perhaps that given by Mitford from Petrarch [Pte I. Canzone IV.] is nearest to Gray's picture:

"Veggio, la sera, *i buoi* tornare *sciolti*
Dalle campagne e da' *solcati colli;*"

which, again, is very like Milton's

"what time the labour'd ox
In his loose traces from the furrow came."

Comus, 291, 2.

Cf. also Homer, *Odyssey*, IX. 58:

Ημος δ' ἠέλιος μετενίσσετο βουλυτόνδε.

(when the sun was passing over toward the hour of loosing the oxen).

And Horace's

"Sol ubi montium
mutaret umbras, et juga demeret
bobus fatigatis..." (*Odes*, III. 6. 42.)

(what time the sun shifted the shadows of the hills and took the yoke from off the laboured oxen).

A scholar-poet could scarcely mention the 'lowing herd' and the 'plowman' without some reminiscence of this old-world note of time.

Cf. also, after Phelps, Ambrose Philips, Pastoral II. *ad fin.*

"And *unyoked* heifers, pacing homeward, low."

4. Cf. after Mitford, Petrarch [Sonetto CLXVIII.]

"Quando 'l sol bagna in mar l' aurato carro
E l' aer nostro e la mia mente imbruna."

"What time the sun
In ocean bathes his golden car and leaves
Over our air—and on my soul—a shade."

Gray's words are more suggestive. In broad daylight the scene belongs to the toiler; when he withdraws, he resigns it to the solitary poet, and to the shadows congenial to *his* spirit. Munro renders this line:

"Cunctaque dat tenebris, dat potiunda mihi."

6. **And all. And now**—Fraser MS.

Ib. 'Stillness' is here the nominative; 'air' the objective case.

"aeriumque *tenent otia dia* polum." Munro.

7. **the beetle.** A sinister note of approaching darkness in *Macbeth*, III. 2, 42.

"ere, to black Hecate's summons,
The *shard-borne beetle with his drowsy hum*
Hath rung night's yawning peal, there shall be done
A deed of dreadful note."

Dryden (*Absalom and Achitophel*, Pt. I. ll. 301, 2) employs the beetle to crush

"such *beetle* things
As only buzz to heaven with *evening* wings."

In December 1746 Collins published among other poems his *Ode to Evening*, and Joseph Warton's volume including, I believe, *his* 'Evening' appeared in the same month and year. Collins writes:

"Now air is hushed save [where the weak-eyed bat
With short shrill shriek flits by on leathern wing
Or] where the beetle winds
His small but sullen horn
As oft he rises 'midst the twilight path
Against the pilgrim borne in heedless hum."

And here may be the best place to note after Dr Phelps that the 'whole atmosphere of Collins's *Ode* is similar to that of the *Elegy*. Cf. especially stanza 10,

"And hamlets brown, and dim-discovered spires,
And hears their simple bell, and marks o'er all
Thy dewy fingers draw
The gradual dusky veil."'

Dr Phelps notes also that Joseph Warton's verses contain some of Gray's pictures, and something of the same train of thought: *e.g.*:

"Hail, meek-eyed maiden, clad in sober grey,
Whose soft approach the *weary* woodman loves,
As homeward bent to *kiss his prattling babes*
Jocund he whistles through the twilight groves."

add:

"Now every Passion sleeps; desponding Love,
And pining Envy, ever-restless Pride;
A holy calm creeps o'er my peaceful soul,
Anger and mad Ambition's storms subside."

The latter stanza might well be the form in embryo of the four rejected stanzas quoted *infra*, n. on l. 72. Dr Phelps remarks that "the scenery as well as the meditations of the *Elegy* were by no means original: they simply established more firmly literary fashions which were already becoming familiar."

And certainly if the opening stanzas of the *Elegy* as we now have them were written as early as 1742, their composition was in no way affected by the poems of Warton and Collins; the same must be said even if the 'autumnal verses' of the letter of Sept. 11, 1746, were the *Elegy*. The spirit of gentle melancholy was in the air; and in 1746 and 1747 found in three young poets, Collins, Joseph Warton and Thomas Warton, that voice to the world at large which is found again in Gray in 1750. For in 1747 Thomas Warton published anonymously these lines, which he had written in his 17th year (1745):

"Beneath yon ruin'd abbey's moss-grown pile
Oft let me sit, at twilight hour of eve
Where thro' some western window the pale moon
Pours her long-levell'd rule of streaming light;
While sullen *sacred silence* reigns around,
Save the lone screech-owl's note, who builds his bow'r
Amid the mould'ring caverns dark and damp,
Or the calm breeze, that rustles in the leaves
Of flaunting ivy, that with mantle green
Invests some wasted tow'r:"

where resemblance to the *Elegy* is closest of all.

Between these three poets communication of ideas was probable; but at this date even Thomas Warton, with whom he afterwards corresponded, was an absolute stranger to Gray. And Gray is so far from feeling that in any of these there were 'kindred spirits' who might 'enquire his fate' that he writes, Dec. 27, 1746:

'Have you seen the Works of two young Authors, a Mr Warton and a Mr Collins, both Writers of Odes? it is odd enough, but each is the half of a considerable Man, and one the counterpart of the other. The first has but little invention, very poetical choice of Expression, and a good Ear, the second a fine fancy, model'd upon the Antique, a bad Ear, great variety of Words, and Images with no choice at all. They both deserve to last some Years, but will not.'

So little are men conscious of that 'stream of tendency' on which they themselves are borne.

8. **And.** **Or** Fraser and Pembroke MSS.; perhaps also Egerton MS.

9. **ivy-mantled tow'r.** The church at Stoke Pogis is undoubtedly most in Gray's mind in the *Elegy*, but we need not suppose that he reproduces his scene like a photographer. If he needed to see an 'ivy-mantled' tower in order to imagine it he would find one at Upton old church, not far from Stoke, but nearer to Slough and Eton.

10. It seems unnecessary to quote from the literature of all ages in illustration of this and like commonplaces of poetry. The skill of Gray lies in the perfect combination of such details;—Thomson and Mallet, almost simultaneously, were enlisting the 'owl'; cf. also Thomas Warton in preceding note. Gray may have remembered the 'ignavus bubo' of Ovid, *Metamorphoses*, v. 550; but we will credit him with sufficient observation to have discovered independently that the owl 'mopes.'

In this picture it is noteworthy that we have a deeper shade of growing nightfall than in the preceding.

11, 12. Over **wand'ring** Fraser MS. gives **stray too.**

11. **bow'r.** The proper sense of bower is any place to be or dwell in; often used in poetry for 'my lady's chamber.' Gray no doubt used the word in its root-sense, but surely with some connotation of 'arbour'; which again is really 'harbour' and has nothing to do with 'arbor,' tree, although the sense '*a bower made of branches of trees*' points to that as the accepted derivation of the word. Similarly the etymologist Junius thought 'bower' was so called from being made of boughs; a fancy which has no doubt affected the sense of the word.

12. **Molest her ancient.** **& pry into** (over) Fraser MS.

13. **That yew-tree's shade.** The yew-tree of Gray's time still exists in Stoke Church-yard, according to Dr Bradshaw; 'it is on the south side of the church, its branches spread over a large circumference, and under it, as well as under its shade, there are several graves.'

16. **rude.** Of course in the sense of simple and unlettered.

'The poor people were always buried in the church-yard, the rich inside the church.' Phelps. **Village** struck through by Gray and **Hamlet** written over it in Fraser MS.

17, 18. **For ever sleep: the breezy Call of Morn**
Or &c. Fraser MS.

"...Whenas sacred light began to dawn
In Eden, on the humid flowers, that breathed
Their morning incense."

Par. Lost, IX. 193. Wakefield.

19. **Or Chaunticleer so shrill or echoing Horn** Fraser MS.

"...The crested cock, whose *clarion* sounds
The silent hours." *Par. Lost*, VII. 442. Wakefield.

"When chanticleer with *clarion shrill* recalls
The tardy day." J. Philips, *Cyder*, I. 753. Mitford.

Cyder was published in 1708, the year of the death of J. Philips. Philips in the *Splendid Shilling* parodied, and in *Cyder* imitated, Milton. Gray knew his verse well, and perhaps (*Gray and His Friends*, p. 298) at an early date attempted to translate a part of the *Splendid Shilling* into Latin Hexameters.

But here again, if there is imitation at all on Gray's part, it is to be found in the same *combination* of cockcrow and the hunter's horn which Milton had already given in his picture of Morning in *L'Allegro*, l. 49 sq.

"While the cock, with lively din,
Scatters the rear of darkness thin.

. . . .

Oft listening how the hounds and horn
Cheerly rouse the slumbering morn."

20. **lowly bed.** "Lloyd," says Dr Bradshaw, "in his Latin translation strangely mistook 'lowly bed' for the grave."

Dr Phelps on the other hand says, 'This probably refers to the humble couch on which they have spent the night; but it is meant to suggest the grave as well.' This seems probable.

21. **For them** etc.

"Jam jam non domus accipiet te laeta, neque uxor
optima, nec dulces occurrent oscula nati
praeripere et tacita pectus dulcedine tangent."

Lucretius, III. 894—896.

"Now no more shall thy house admit thee with glad welcome, nor a most virtuous wife and sweet children run to be the first to snatch kisses and touch thy heart with a silent joy." (Munro.)

Though Lucretius is only mentioning these common regrets of mankind in order to show their unreasonableness, there is no doubt that Gray had this passage well in his mind here. Feeling this, Munro renders it in quite Lucretian phraseology: *e.g.*

"*Jam jam* non erit his rutilans focus igne:

and

non reditum balbe current patris *hiscere* nati."

But Gray adds also an Horatian touch, as Mitford points out:

"Quodsi pudica mulier in partem juvet
domum atque dulces liberos

. . . .

sacrum vetustis excitet lignis focum
lassi sub adventum viri," &c. Hor. *Epode*, II. 39 sq.

["But if a chaste and pleasing wife
To ease the business of his life
Divides with him his household care

. . . .

Will fire for winter nights provide,
And without noise will oversee
His children and his family
And order all things till he come
Weary and over-laboured home" &c. Dryden.]

Thomson in his *Winter*, 1726, had written of the shepherd overwhelmed in the snow-storm:

"In vain for him the officious wife prepares
The fire fair-blazing, and the vestment warm;
In vain his little children, peeping out
Into the mingling rack, demand their sire
With tears of artless innocence." (ll. 311—315.)

24. **Or.** **Nor,** Fraser MS.

envied. The Fraser MS. has **coming**, with **envied** written above it, and **doubtful** in the margin. Gray happily decided upon 'envied,' for 'coming' is a weak word; and 'doubtful' would have been ambiguous to any but a classical reader,—who alone would feel sure that the meaning was, it was uncertain to whom the privilege of the first kiss would fall. Cf. the 'praeripere' of Lucretius *supra*[1].

Cf. Virgil, *Georg.* II. 523 (describing the joys of the husbandman):

"Interea dulces pendent circum oscula nati."

[Meanwhile sweet children cling round his kisses. Mackail.]

[1] Add Dryden, as quoted by Mitford, (from ed. Warton, vol. ii. p. 565, a futile reference)

"Whose little arms around thy legs are cast,
And climbing for a kiss *prevent* their mother's haste."

25. **sickle. Sickles** Egerton MS.

26. **the stubborn glebe.** Luke quotes from Gay's *Fables*, Vol. II. Fable XV. l. 89:

"'Tis mine to tame the stubborn *glebe*."

—What Gay really writes is:

"'Tis mine to tame the stubborn *plain*,
Break the stiff soil, and house the grain."

This is a curious example of the way in which a perfectly needless parallel 'may be made when it cannot be found.'

27. **afield**, to the field. 'We drove afield,' Milton, *Lycidas*, l. 27; this is probably Gray's warrant for the word. Whether we refer the prefix 'a' to 'on' or to 'at' here, the secondary notion of 'motion towards' is easily attached to it; *e.g.* in Shakespeare 'away' [on way] sometimes means 'hither': and for 'at' in the sense of 'to' cf. '*at* him again!' Instances of 'sturdy stroke' are quoted from Spenser, *Shepherd's Calendar*, February [ll. 201, 202] and, Dryden, *Georgics*, III. 639.

29. **useful.** Fraser MS. suggests in margin **homely**; and for **homely** of next line gives **rustic.**

29—32. "The rimes in this stanza are scarcely exact": says Dr Phelps. That they were at one time exact is certain; and they were probably exact to Gray's time. The wearisome frequency of the rhyme 'join' with such words as 'combine,' 'sign,' 'line,' in Dryden, Pope, &c. establishes the pronunciation of 'join' as 'jine' over a long period up to the middle of the 18th century; in Dryden we have 'spoil' rhyming with 'guile' and 'awhile'; 'boil' rhyming with 'pile,' and in Pope, *Odyssey*, b. I.:

"Your widow'd heart, apart, with female *toil*
And various labours of the loom *beguile*."

The very rhyme of the text is doubtless frequent; I find it casually in Johnson's London (1738):

"On all thy hours security shall *smile*,
And bless thine evening walk, and morning *toil*."

It is on record as an instance of Gray's pronunciation that he would say, 'What *naise* is that?' instead of 'noise.' The sound here indicated must be approximately that of the last syllable of 'recognize'; and analogously it seems probable that Gray himself said 'tile' for 'toil.'

Now for the rhyme of 'obscure' with 'poor.' If Gray pronounced 'scure' much as we pronounce 'skewer,' the rhyme is not quite exact;

but it is more probable, if only from a certain Gallicizing tendency of his, that the sound for him was rather like the French 'obscur.' Dryden's rhyme for 'poor' is most frequently with 'more,' 'store,' &c., from which I infer, doubtfully, that *he* pronounced poor as 'pore.' Pope, makes 'poor' rhyme with 'door' which of itself determines nothing; but he also makes it rhyme with 'cure,' 'endure' and 'sure'; (which is like Gray); and further with 'store' and 'yore' (which is like Dryden). Thus in the famous story of Sir Balaam, with an interval of only two lines we have:

... "his gains were *sure*,
His givings rare, save farthings to the *poor*.

and

"Satan now is wiser than of *yore*,
And tempts by making rich, not making *poor*."

On the whole we may conclude that Gray pronounced 'poor' much as we do, and 'obscure' so as to rhyme with it.

When such rhymes as this stanza offers became merely conventional it would be harder to determine.

32. *Annals of the Poor*, a pretty book by Leigh Richmond, author also of the *Dairyman's Daughter*, takes its title and motto from this line and stanza, as Dr Bradshaw reminds us.

33—36. Cowley had written:

"*Beauty* and strength, and wit, and *wealth*, and *power*,
Have their short flourishing hour;
And love to see themselves, and smile
And joy in their pre-eminence awhile:
E'en so in the same land
Poor weeds, rich corn, gay flowers together stand.
Alas! Death mows down all with an impartial hand."

A passage no doubt known to West, when he wrote, Dec. 1737, in his Monody on the death of Queen Caroline [*Gray and His Friends*, pp. 108, 110—114],

"Ah me! what boots us all our boasted power,
Our golden treasure, and our purpled state?
They cannot ward th' inevitable hour,
Nor stay the fearful violence of Fate."

lines which Gray undoubtedly remembers and improves upon here.

35. **Awaits.** The reading 'Await' has no MS. authority; according to Dr Bradshaw it first appeared in Dodsley's Collection, Vol. IV. published in 1755; but in editions of 1753 and 1768, for the text of

which Gray has some responsibility, we have 'awaits,' as well as in every copy in his handwriting. That 'hour' is the nominative the slightest reflection should show us. We pursue our several ambitions as if unconscious of our doom, it is the hour that awaits *us*; if *we* awaited the hour we should be less absorbed in our aims. The sentiment of the stanza is Horatian; omnes una manet nox—one night awaits us all, says Horace in the 28th Ode of the 1st Book; he has spoken of philosophers, Archytas, Pythagoras; heroes, Tantalus, Tithonus, Minos, Euphorbus, and proceeds to tell us how the warrior perishes in battle, and the sailor in the sea:

"Dant alios Furiae torvo spectacula Marti:
Exitio est avidum mare nautis," &c.

Conington translates, unluckily perpetuating the misreading in the *Elegy*, but acknowledging the identity of thought:

"Yes, all 'await the inevitable hour';
The downward journey all one day must tread,
Some bleed to glut the war-god's savage eyes;
Fate meets the sailor from the hungry brine;
Youth jostles age in funeral obsequies;
Each brow in turn is touched by Proserpine."

The paths. Here again there is the frequent misquotation 'The path of glory *leads*,' &c. Gray means, after Horace, that whatever way to fame we select, the end is the same. Accordingly Munro renders this line:

"metaque mors, *quoquo* gloria flectit iter."

36. In Kippis, *Biographia Britannica*, Vol. IV. p. 429, in the *Life of Crashaw*, written by Hayley, it is said that this line is "literally translated from the Latin prose of Bartholinus in his Danish Antiquities." Mitford.

Nothing accessible to me shows that Gray was at all acquainted with Bartholin at the date of the completed *Elegy* (see introduction and notes to *Norse Odes*, *infra*).

37. **Forgive ye proud th' involuntary Fault**
If Memory to these &c.

Fraser and according to Bradshaw all MSS. Bradshaw adds 'The present reading is written in the margin'; but I did not find this so in Fraser MS.

39. **isle.** Spelt **Ile** by Gray, in Fraser MS. The word is from French *aile*, a wing, and the s, says Skeat, is a meaningless insertion.

fretted. A fret is defined by Parker, *Glossary of Architecture*, 'an ornament used in Classical architecture, formed by small fillets intersecting each other at right angles'; a fillet, again, is a narrow band used principally between mouldings, both in Classical and Gothic architecture. It is Gothic architecture that Gray has in his mind's eye; the lines that go to make the fanshaped roof of King's College Chapel or of S. George's, Windsor, for example.

The derivation of 'fret,' 'fretted,' in this technical sense is uncertain. Skeat hesitates between tracing it to an A.-S. word meaning to 'adorn,' or through French and Low-Latin to 'ferrum.' In Heraldry fret means 'a bearing composed of bars crossed and interlaced,' and for this sense of the word Skeat suggests the latter, not the A.-S. derivation. Littré, however, traces the heraldic term to the same origin as *flèche*, an arrow.

It seems probable that the architectural and heraldic word, representing much the same sort of device, are one and the same, and have a common origin, whatever that may be.

Note Shakespeare's use of the word:

> *Dec.* Here lies the east: doth not the day break here?
> *Casca.* No.
> *Cinna.* O pardon, sir, it doth; and yon grey lines
> That *fret the clouds* are messengers of day.
>
> *Jul. Caes.* (II. 1, 104).

—lines of light that shoot athwart the clouds and intersect them.

But *Hamlet*, II. 2, 313, 'this majestical roof fretted with golden fire' is less clear. For these frets may be 'Hyperion's *shafts*' or 'fretted' may mean 'studded' or 'embossed' with stars, the 'stellèd fires' of which he speaks in *Lear*. The word proper to the long lines that mark out the roof may be applied to the ornaments in which such lines might terminate or be concentred,—so in *Cymbeline*, II. 4. 88:

> "The roof o' the chamber
> With *golden cherubins* is *fretted*."

Perhaps Munro would interpret Gray's 'fretted' in the sense of 'embossed' for he renders this line:

> "longus ubi alarum ductus, *crustataque* fornix"

where, I think, by 'crustata' he means set with decorations moulded in plaster or the like pliable material.

vault. 'The high embowèd roof' of Milton, *Il Penseroso*, 157.

41. An urn with an inscription on it, a common form of funereal monument in imitation more or less of the antique[1]. The 'pictured urn'

[1] See additional note, p. 291.

of *Progress of Poesy*, l. 109, which Dr Bradshaw here compares is quite a different thing.

Animated bust. Cf. Pope, *Temple of Fame*, ll. 73, 74:

"Heroes in animated marble frown,
And legislators seem to think in stone."

But the original both for Gray and Pope is Virgil, *Aen.* VI. 848, 849:

"Excudent alii *spirantia* mollius aera,
Credo equidem; *vivos* ducent de *marmore vultus*."

'Others shall beat out the breathing bronze to softer lines; I believe it well; shall draw *living* lineaments from the marble.' (Mackail.)

Cf. *Georg.* III. 34:

"Stabunt et Parii lapides, *spirantia* signa."

['There too shall stand *breathing* images in Parian stone.' *Id.*]

The expression is rescued from the charge of imitation or conventionalism by the thought which it is made to serve, that all the skill of the artist in simulating the breath of life cannot bring it 'back to its mansion.'

43. **provoke.** Call to life, rouse to action, a classical use of the word, as in Pope, *Ode on St Cecilia's Day*, III.

"But when our country's cause *provokes* to arms."

In Fraser MS. Gray writes '**awake**' in the text, suggesting '**provoke**' in the margin. The alteration is a clue to the meaning he attaches 'to honour's voice,' which Dr Bradshaw interprets to be 'words or speeches in honour of the dead.' This does not give the right significance to 'honour' here. Among the 'paths of glory,' lineage, statecraft, beauty, wealth, are named (33—36); it would be strange if the poet made no reference to the calling with which 'glory' is most associated. He has the 'brave' here specially in mind; of whose tombs Collins writes:

"There *honour* comes, a pilgrim gray,
To bless the turf that wraps their clay."

Honour, whose servants they were, may bless or praise them: but they can no longer rise at that voice which in life they were so eager to obey. To this effect Munro's version:

"Voce valet cinerem succendere *gloria* mutum."

44. **dull, cold.** They compare Wolsey, in *Henry VIII.* III. 2. 434:

"And when I am forgotten, as I shall be,
And sleep in *dull cold* marble."

46. **pregnant...fire]** Cowper has the expression in *Boadicea*:

"Such the bard's prophetic words,
Pregnant with celestial fire,
Bending as he swept the chords
Of his sweet but awful lyre." Bradshaw.

47. Mitford quotes Ovid [*Heroides*] Ep. v. l. 86 [Œnone Paridi.]

"Sunt mihi quas possint sceptra decere manus."

Fraser MS. reads '**reins** of empire' here. Dr Bradshaw suggests that Gray made the alteration because Tickell (cited by Mitford) had written, *Poem to Earl of Warwick*, l. 37:

"Proud names that once *the reins of empire* held."

48. **Wake to ecstasy.** Cf. *Progress of Poetry*, l. 2. Mitford quotes from Cowley [*Resurrection* st. 2, l. 1]:

"Begin the song and strike *the living lyre*."

Pope no doubt had this line in mind when he wrote in *Windsor Forest*, l. 281 (cited by Mitford):

"Who now shall charm the shades, where Cowley strung
His *living harp*, and lofty Denham sung?"

49. The germ of the four following stanzas is probably to be found in these lines of Waller (to Zelinda):

"Great Julius on the mountains bred,
A flock perhaps or herd had led,
He that the world subdued had been
But the best wrestler on the green.
'Tis art and knowledge which draw forth
The hidden seeds of native worth;
They blow those sparks and make them rise
Into such flames as touch the skies."

Gray possessed and had studied Waller; he has transferred this thought from a trivial setting, and placed it where it fitly exemplifies the pathos of human life. Cf. Addison, *Spectator*, 215.

It should be noted that Gray's Cromwell was originally Caesar, Waller's 'Great Julius.'

49. **Rich with the spoils of time.** Mitford compares Sir T. Browne, *Religio Medici* [Pt. I. Sect. XIII. where he breaks into verse],

"And then at last, when homeward I shall drive,
Rich with the spoils of nature, to my hive,
There will I sit, like that industrious fly
Buzzing thy praises" &c.

Whether Gray needed this quaint original to inspire him may be questioned.

unroll. The word, as Bradshaw points out, is suggested by the primary meaning of *volumen* when used of a book, i.e. a scroll, unrolled in order to be read.

51. **rage**, ardent ambition. Gray is thinking of possible statesmen and warriors, as well as poets; although it is of poetic inspiration that the word was commonly used in a good sense. Mitford quotes Pope to Jervas (the painter), l. 12:

> "Like them [Dryden and Fresnoy] to shine through long succeeding age,
> So just thy skill, so *regular my rage*,"

where the epithet 'regular,' so singularly inept for that which is by its very nature without restraint, shows that this conventional use of 'rage' is really a misuse of it. It is employed, oddly enough, in connection with a reed, by Collins (1746) of Music in *Ode on the Passions* (quoted by Bradshaw):

> "'Tis said, and I believe the tale,
> Thy humblest *reed* could more prevail,
> Had more of strength, diviner *rage*,
> Than all which charms this laggard age."

But the word scarcely in this use of it belongs to our best poetic diction, for example Shakespeare employs it thus only once, and then with a clear notion of exaggeration (Sonnet XVII. 11);

> "The age to come would say, 'This poet lies':
> So should my papers, yellowed with their age,
> Be scorn'd, like old men of less truth than tongue,
> And your true rights be termed a poet's *rage*
> And stretchèd metre of an antique song."

The word indeed belongs to what Burke calls 'the contortions of the Sibyll':

> "et *rabie* fera corda tument." *Aen.* VI. 49,

from which, and the kindred inspiration of the Pythoness, the expression has been transferred to a milder enthusiasm; Shakespeare is nearest to adopting it when he speaks of 'the poet's eye in a fine *frenzy* rolling.' Milton never uses it in this way at all.

Had **damp'd** with **depress'd: repress'd** written over, Fraser MS.

52. **genial.** The word connotes at once cheering and fertilising; the fervour and the creative power of genius. Its two senses in Latin are 'belonging to generation or birth' and 'belonging to enjoyment,

jovial.' Gray has used it in the double sense of 'kindly' and 'productive' in *Alliance of Education and Government*, l. 3:

"Nor *genial* warmth, nor *genial* juice retains,
Their roots to feed, and fill their verdant veins."

Ib. Cf. Scott's *Old Mortality*, chap. XIII. where with obvious reminiscence of this stanza, it is said of Henry Morton, 'the *current of his soul was frozen* by a sense of dependence—of *poverty*—above all, *of an imperfect and limited education*.'

53, 54. Mitford cites Milton, *Comus*, 22:

"That like to rich and various gems inlay
The unadornèd bosom of the deep;"

but, very inappositely, since the 'sea-girt isles' to which the simile refers are conspicuous and on the surface, whilst it is of the essence of Gray's thought that the gems are invisible and at the bottom. Milton's thought is in fact Shakespeare's (*Rich. II.* II. 1. 46):

"This precious stone, set in the silver sea."

The quotation from Bishop Hall's *Contemplations*, VI. 872, is better: "There is many a rich stone laid up in the bowells of the earth, many a fair *pearle in the bosome of the sea*, that never was seene nor never shall bee." Noteworthy perhaps as a coincidence is the line Mitford quotes from the Greek of an Italian poet (I think), of the *Renaissance:*

Μάργαρα πολλὰ βαθὺς συγκρύπτει κύμασι πόντος,
[Many a pearl far under the waves lies hidden of Ocean.]

55. Mitford gives these parallels (the exact references are due to Dr Phelps):

William Chamberlayne, *Pharonnida* (London, 1659, Book IV. canto 5, p. 94):

"Like beauteous flowers which vainly waste the scent
Of odors in unhaunted deserts."

From Ambrose Philips (1671—1749] *The Fable of Thule:*

"Like beauteous flowers, which paint the desert glades,
And waste their sweets in unfrequented shades."

From Young, *Universal Passion* [1725], Sat. V. ll. 229—232:

"In distant wilds, by human eyes unseen
She rears her flow'rs, and spreads her velvet green.
Pure gurgling rills the lonely desert trace
And waste their music on the savage race."

Mr Yardley in *Notes and Queries* (Sept. 1, 1894) suggests that Gray imitated Waller's 'Go, lovely Rose':

"Tell her that's young
And shuns to have her graces spied
That, hadst thou sprung
In deserts where no men abide,
Thou must have uncommended died."

Perhaps this is the starting-point in the line of succession of the poetical idea for Gray: but it passes through Pope and comes nearer in the form:

"There kept my charms concealed from mortal eye,
Like roses that in deserts bloom and die."

Rape of the Lock, IV. 157, 158.

This idea Pope cherished, for he gave it, in an improved form, to Thomson for the *Seasons*: the lines in the episode of Lavinia, Autumn, 209—214,

"As in the hollow breast of Apennine,
Beneath the shelter of encircling hills,
A myrtle rises, far from human eye,
And breathes its balmy fragrance o'er the hills,
So flourished blooming, and unseen by all,
The sweet Lavinia."

are to be seen, in a handwriting, probably Pope's, in an interleaved copy of the *Seasons* (ed. 1738) in the British Museum [C 28 E.] Whether Gray had seen these lines, not published until 1744, will depend upon the date we assign to this portion of the *Elegy*.[1]

56. **desert air.** Wakefield compares Pindar, *Ol.* I. 10, ἐρήμας δι' αἰθέρος; and Rogers, *Macbeth*, IV. 3. 194,

"I have words
That would be howl'd out into the *desert air*."

This line, as the present editor pointed out to Dr Bradshaw, soon became proverbial. It is found in Churchill's *Gotham*, 1764:

"So that they neither give a tawdry glare
Nor 'waste their sweetness on the desert air.'"

57 sq. **Hampden,** &c. The line in Fraser MS. stands thus:

Some village Cato with dauntless Breast.

the missing word is, I suppose, either now invisible or was never written. (I have only seen the facsimile.)[1]

Why did Gray select *Cato?* I think (and this tends to confirm my notion that his original was Waller) it was because in the order of his thoughts, though not of his setting of them, he began with Caesar. This suggests Cato of Utica, and his resistance to Caesar's

[1] See additional note, p. 292.

tyranny. Otherwise the withstander of the 'tyrant of the fields' might well have found his greater counterpart in Gracchus, as the champion of the fast dwindling class of small landed proprietors against the large landowners of Italy. It is both for this reason, and because Cato, a true oligarch and the opponent of the popular party in Rome, was no fitting analogue to Hampden that Munro in translating this line, instead of reverting to Gray's original hero, writes:

> "forsitan hic olim intrepido qui pectore ruris
> restiterat parvo *Graccus agrestis* ero
> vel mutus sine honore Maro, vel Julius alter
> immunis patrii sanguinis ille, cubet."

Of course Virgil was inevitable as the counterpart to Milton. But note that both in Gray's first conception and in his second his types are all contemporary; Caesar, Cato, Cicero suggested one another irresistibly to his student-mind, and it must not be forgotten that the debates on the Catilinarian conspiracy bring precisely these three names into prominence in the pages of Sallust. When he changed his *terrain* Gray again sought and found contemporaries; with the additional link in common that Hampden, Milton, Cromwell, were all associated in the same cause, and all, in some sense, champions of liberty.

By a happy coincidence the English examples which Gray substituted for the Roman had all some connection with the neighbourhood of Gray's churchyard. It was at Horton, which is at no great distance from Stoke Pogis, that Milton in his younger days composed *L'Allegro*, *Il Penseroso*, *Arcades*, *Comus*, *Lycidas;* it was to Chalfont St Giles within a few miles of the churchyard that in his old age he retired from the Great Plague of London with the finished MS. of *Paradise Lost*. Hampden was a Buckinghamshire squire, his family seat was Great Hampden, in the hundred of Aylesbury, he represented first Wendover, and then the county in Parliament. Cromwell was his cousin, and often visited both Hampden and his sister, Mrs Waller (the mother of the poet), who lived at Beaconsfield[1].

[1] "Waller's mother, though related to Cromwell and Hampden, was zealous for the royal cause, and when Cromwell visited her used to reproach him; he in return would throw a napkin at her, and say he would not dispute with his aunt [i.e. cousin]: but finding in time that she acted for the king as well as talked he made her a prisoner to her own daughter, in her own house." Johnson's Waller in *Lives of the Poets*.

Mitford records a line of Gray's in pencil:

The rude Columbus of an infant world.

This is possibly an afterthought for another stanza (of which it might have formed the first line), pointing to other lines of enterprise in embryo.

We lack a context by which to determine the sense of 'an *infant* world,' which may be used much as Berkeley writes of 'happy climes the seat of innocence,' or of 'Time's noblest *offspring*' as 'the *last*.' But on more general grounds we may safely conjecture that Gray had some thought of developing amid humbler scenes the picture sketched in the Eton Ode of those 'bold adventurers'

"who disdain
The limits of their little reign
And unknown regions dare descry."

One thinks of Wordsworth's *Blind Highland Boy*, who had heard how, in a tortoise-shell,

"An English boy, oh thought of bliss!
Had stoutly launch'd from shore,"

and was tempted to follow his example.

58. **fields.** **lands** erased in Pembroke MS.

59. **Milton.** **Tully** Fraser M.

60. **Cromwell.** **Caesar** Fraser MS. "See Cromwell damned to everlasting fame," Pope, *Essay on Man*, IV. 284. Mark Pattison observes of Pope, that 'in estimating historical characters he seems to have been without any proper standard, and wholly at the mercy of prevailing social prejudices.' But the prejudice against Cromwell in the eighteenth century was shared by men of very various opinions; literature in the *seventeenth* century was, on its lower levels, more vituperative, but on its higher, more appreciative and generous; the tributes of Milton and Marvell to Cromwell were of course spontaneous, but even those of Waller and Dryden were not altogether forced; they have a certain ring of sincerity about them. It is in the main Carlyle who has *rehabilitated* Cromwell in the popular mind.

61. Pope, *Moral Essays*, I. 184 (speaking of Wharton). 'Though wondering senates hung on all he spoke.' Mitford.

62. As Sir Thomas More, Sir John Eliot, Hampden, Algernon Sidney, Lord William Russell—heroes commemorated in Thomson's *Summer*, ll. 1488—1530; More as a 'dauntless soul erect, who smiled on death,' and Sidney as the British Cassius who 'fearless bled.'

63. Bradshaw compares *Education and Government*, ll. 17, 18, where it is the attribute of Justice to

> "Scatter with a free, though frugal, hand
> Light golden showers of plenty o'er the land."

65. **lot.** **Fate** in Fraser MS. with **lot** written over it.

65, 66. 'circumscrib'd' and 'confin'd' are finite verbs, the nominative being 'lot.'

66. **growing.** **struggling** in Fraser MS. with **growing** written over it.

67. Wakefield compares Pope's *Temple of Fame*, l. 347, where heroes addressing the goddess say:

> "[For thee...amidst alarms and strife
> We sailed in tempests down the stream of life;]
> For thee whole nations fill'd with flames and blood,
> And swam to empire through the purple flood."

68. **And.** **Or** Egerton MS.

Henry V. III. 3. 10. 'The gates of mercy shall be all shut up.' Mitford.

69—72. The general sense of the stanza seems to be: Their lot forbade them to be eminent persecutors (l. 69), unscrupulous place-hunters, or ministers to vice in high places (l. 70), or courtly and venal poets (ll. 71, 72).

69. **The struggleing~~s~~ pangs,** &c. Fraser MS. showing that Gray had some thought of making 'struggleing' a trisyllabic substantive, and changed his mind. He spells the same word without e in l. 66 (note) when it is a dissyllable.

71, 72. Thus in Fraser MS:

crown
And at the Shrine of Luxury and Pride
With by
~~Burn~~ Incense hallowd in the Muse's Flame.
kindled at

71. **Shrine.** **Shrines** Egerton MS.

72. After this follows in Fraser MS.,

"The thoughtless World to Majesty may bow
Exalt the brave, and idolize Success
But more to Innocence their Safety owe
Than Power and Genius e'er conspired to bless
And thou, who mindful of the unhonour'd Dead
eir
Dost in these Notes thy artless Tale relate

By Night and lonely Contemplation led
To linger in the gloomy walks of Fate
Hark how the sacred Calm, that broods around
Bids ev'ry fierce tumultuous Passion cease
In still small Accents whisp'ring from the Ground
A grateful Earnest of eternal Peace[1]
No more with Reason and thyself at Strife
Give anxious Cares and endless Wishes room
But thro the cool sequester'd Vale of Life
Pursue the silent Tenour of thy Doom"

"And here," says Mason, "the poem was originally intended to conclude, before the happy idea of 'the hoary-headed Swain &c.' suggested itself to him."

Mason perhaps converted Walpole by a reference to the state of this MS., which no doubt establishes an interval between the first and second half of the poem. But he ante-dated, it may be suspected, the composition of the first half.

The Fraser MS. (to judge from the facsimile) has a line drawn along the side of the last three, and possibly meant (as Sir W. Fraser's reprint interprets it) to include the first also of these four, stanzas.

The stanzas which follow these four are:

Far from the madding crowd's &c.

as in the received text (with minor variations to be noted), down to 'fires,' l. 92.

All the MS. to the end of the four rejected Stanzas is in a much more faded character; and Mason must be at least so far right that the Poem from 'Far from the madding &c.' was resumed after a considerable interval.

But we have only Mason's authority for the statement that the *Elegy* was ever meant to end with these four stanzas, and it is very questionable. We may be biased by the completeness of the poem in its published form,—but surely without this contrast to assist our judgment it would have seemed to us to finish baldly and abruptly with

"Pursue the silent Tenour of thy Doom."

And if this ending would not satisfy us it could not have satisfied Gray. Again, it is probable from the MS. that down to 'Doom' the *Elegy* was all written much about the same time, or as the Germans say, *in einem Guss*. Suppose then it had reached that point in 1742, and this is probably what Mason means when he suggests that it may have been concluded then; is it conceivable that Gray, who had

[1] See additional note, p. 292.

communicated to Walpole other completed poems of that date, and even the fragmentary *Agrippina*, would have kept back the *Elegy*, which *ex hypothesi* he must have regarded as finished? Yet Walpole, as we have seen, is certain that Gray sent him only the first three stanzas, two or three years after the year 1742. Surely either these twelve lines were all that Gray had then written, or they were a specimen only of the unfinished poem.

73. **Far from the madding Crowd's ignoble strife;**

In Fraser MS., the punctuation showing that it was the poet's first intention to make the line part of the *apostrophe* to himself. It echoes the sentiment of Gray's beautiful Alcaic Ode written in the album of the Grande Chartreuse Aug. 1741, as he was returning from his sojourn in Italy, in which he says,—if he cannot have the silence of the cloistered cell:—

Saltem remoto des, Pater, angulo
Horas senectae ducere liberas
Tutumque *vulgari tumultu*
Surripias, *hominumque curis.*

At least, O Father, ere the close of life
Vouchsafe, I pray thee, some sequestered glen,
And there seclude me, rescued from the strife
Of vulgar tumults and the cares of men.

[R. E. Warburton in *Notes and Queries*, June 9, 1883.]

Mason is perhaps so far right that it was with this *wish* that the Elegy, like the Alcaic Ode was meant to end; we may admit this without supposing that it was intended to close with 'Doom.'

But whilst it is probable, from the punctuation of 'strife,' that Gray meant through this and possibly other stanzas to end the *Elegy* after the manner of the Alcaic Ode, it is quite clear that he soon abandoned that intention; for 'strife' here necessitated in the ending of the first line of previous stanza:

'No more with reason and thyself at *strife*,'—

and in the corresponding rhyme, some alteration which he never took the trouble to make, preferring to give his thoughts a more general scope and to use the four stanzas above cited as far only as they could be set in a natural sequence on this new model. This is the explanation of his side line. He in fact could avail himself only of two stanzas, the second and the fourth; the first 'The thoughtless World' &c. has in either sequence a little too much the character of a detached sentiment to please him, and, upon the altered plan, it was, for the same reason, difficult to introduce the third. We may well regret this, for Mason is right in saying that it is equal to any in the whole *Elegy*.

'Far from the Madding Crowd' is the title of one of Thomas Hardy's best novels, in which every one of the characters is drawn from humble life.

madding. 'Far from the madding worldling's harsh discords' Drummond, cited by Rogers. Once, as Bradshaw notes, in Milton, *P. L.* VI. 210:

"[arms on armour clashing brayed
Horrible discord, and] the madding wheels
Of brazen chariots raged."

Gray himself in *Agrippina*, l. 83: 'the madding ear of rage.'

It may be questioned whether either Drummond or Gray used the word exactly in the sense of 'maddening.' It seems with them to mean 'frenzied.'

'If there were no comma after "strife," the sense of this couplet would be precisely the opposite of what Gray intended.' Phelps.

Even with the comma, there is some carelessness in employing the word 'stray' so close upon 'far from' &c. &c. with which there is a natural temptation to connect it. It is not in perfect lucidity of expression that Gray shines. It may be that he was disposed to retain the semicolon after 'strife' (vide *supra*) as avoiding the ambiguity, which is traceable in part to Gray's change of mind.

76. **noiseless.** '**silent**' in Fraser MS., with '**noiseless**' written over it.

77 sq. "The four stanzas, beginning 'Yet even these bones,' are to me original: I have never seen the notions in any other place: yet he that reads them here persuades himself that he has always felt them." Johnson (cf. Boswell's *Johnson*, 1775, ætat. 66).

Johnson's comment well illustrates Pope's line in the *Essay on Criticism*:

'What oft was thought but ne'er so well expressed'

which gives us briefly the aim and achievement of the best 18th century poetry.

78. **still.** Both Dr Bradshaw and Dr Phelps explain 'still' as 'always,' Dr Phelps adds 'as commonly in Shakespeare.' I question this explanation, which is only encouraged by the absence of the comma, and I cannot agree with Dr Phelps that Gray was particular about his punctuation; from my experience of his otherwise most carefully written MSS., I should say that he sometimes errs by excess

and sometimes by defect in this. It is surely more natural to suppose that he means 'though they have no stately tombs, and though their lives were most obscure, there remains some frail memorial of them still, in the gravestones around, to plead that they may not be quite forgotten.' Is it true that every grave in a country churchyard has had its stone and its inscription at some time or other?

81. **spelt...muse.** 'Under the yew tree [in the churchyard at Stoke] there is a tombstone with several words wrongly spelt, and some letters ill-formed, and even in the inscription which Gray composed for his aunt's tomb, the word "resurrection" is spelt incorrectly by the unlettered stone-cutter.' Bradshaw.

82. **elegy.** **epitaph** Fraser MS. The change is a distinct improvement, for the rustic inscriptions *are* epitaphs, however rude.

84. **That teach.** Mitford writes in second *Life of Gray*, "As this construction is not, as it now stands, correct, I think that Gray originally wrote '*to teach*' but altered it afterwards, *euphoniae gratia*, and made the grammar give way to the sound." That euphony was Gray's motive is probable, but the Fraser MS. shows that it was his motive from the first; there is no such *alteration* there, as Mitford supposes.

83 sq. Here again want of lucidity is the one defect in a beautiful stanza. Gray *seems* to mean 'who ever was so much a prey to dumb Forgetfulness as to resign life and its possibilities of joy and sorrow without some regret?' But not only is it patent that millions have been so much a prey to the 'second childishness and mere oblivion' of age that they have passed away without the power to feel regret, but the whole sequence of thought shows that this cannot be Gray's meaning. He uses 'prey' in a prospective sense, the *destined* prey; accordingly Munro translates

Quis *subiturus* enim Lethaea silentia &c.

It is perhaps Gray's classicism which betrays him here, for Horace, who has sometimes the same sort of obscurity due to condensation, has just this anticipatory use when he says (*Odes*, II. 3. 21 sq.) that it makes no difference whether as rich and high-born or poor and low-born you linger out life's little day, *the victim of merciless Orcus*; i.e. certain in either case to become so at last.

Again, Gray seems to be shaping anew the question in *Paradise Lost* (II. 146 sq.):

"For who would lose,
Though full of pain, this intellectual being,

These thoughts that wander through eternity,
To perish rather, swallowed up and lost
In the wide womb of uncreated Night,
Devoid of sense and motion?"

and when he speaks of 'this pleasing anxious being' and 'the warm precincts of the cheerful day,' he may be supposed to express the same horror of the annihilation of thought, the same dread of eternal darkness. Yet, in the main, the terror of which Gray speaks is the forgetfulness of the dead by the living. In this and the following stanza the true significance of the 'frail memorials' is explained. Though men are destined to oblivion they crave to be remembered, as they have craved for human support and affection in their last hours; it is thus that 'even from the tomb the voice of nature cries.' In fact whilst we find the form and some of the accessories of Gray's thought in Milton, we find the substance of it rather in Homer, Virgil and Dante, who give us the same voice of nature as heard from the further shore; as when the spirits say to Dante, *Inferno*, XVI. 85 sq.:

"if thou escape this darksome clime
Returning to behold the radiant stars,
See that of us thou speak amongst mankind."

84. **pleasing anxious.** Milton's 'intellectual being,' delightful in spite of pain and trouble. Grammarians call this figure *oxymoron*, something which is the more pointed because it seems paradoxical. It abounds in Shakespeare. Munro here renders

"*dulce*
tormentum hanc animam &c."

85. Correspondingly, in Homer, Virgil, Dante, the *desiderium* of the departed is for the *light* of the upper air.

precincts. Gray probably took this expression from *Paradise Lost*, III. 88, the only place in Milton's poems where 'precincts' occurs:

'Not far off Heaven in the precincts of light.' Bradshaw.

Note that Milton accentuates the word on the last syllable, Gray, in modern fashion, on the first.

89. So Drayton in his *Moses*, p. 1564, vol. IV. ed. 1753:

"It is some comfort to a wretch to die,
(If there be comfort in the way of death)
To have some friend, or kind alliance by
To be officious at the parting breath." Mitford.

'It has been suggested that the first line of Gray's stanza seems to regard the near approach of death; the second its actual advent; the third, the time immediately succeeding its advent; the fourth, a time still later.' Bradshaw.

For a like sequence of moments cf. n. on the third stanza.

91. Some lines in the *Anthologia Latina*, p. 680, Ep. CLIII. have a strong resemblance to those in the text:

"Crede mihi, vires aliquas natura sepulchris
Adtribuit, tumulos vindicat umbra suos."

See also Ausonius (*Parentalia*), ed. Tollii, p. 109:

"Gaudent compositi cineres sua nomina dici." Mitford.

(The quotation from Ausonius may illustrate also v. 81.)

92. Gray himself quotes here in illustration:

"Ch'i veggio nel pensier, dolce mio fuoco,
Fredda una lingua, e due begli occhi chiusi
Rimaner dopo noi pien di faville."

Petrarch, *Son.* CLXIX. CLI.

He had already, I believe, made the translation of this sonnet, which is preserved among his Latin poems; perhaps even the turn which he has given to it in the lines

"Nos duo cumque erimus parvus uterque cinis,"

and

"Ardebitque urnâ multa favilla meâ,"

may have set him on embodying in this place of the *Elegy* the passage quoted. Petrarch's words serve Gray's purpose best if severed from their context. In this sonnet the poet plays with the image of *flame.* He is burning; all believe this, save her whom alone he wishes to believe it; his ardour, of which she makes no account, and the glory he has given her in his rhyme, may yet inflame a thousand others:

"For in my thought I see,—sweet fire of mine!—
A tongue though chilled, and two fair eyes, though sealed,
Fraught with immortal sparks, survive us still."

Mitford quotes Chaucer, *Cant. Tales*, Reeve's prologue (3880):

"Yet in our ashen cold is fire yreken."

But the Reeve is speaking of the passions of youth surviving in old age.

And buried Ashes glow with Social Fires. Fraser MS.

And in our Ashes glow their wonted Fires. Egerton and Pembroke MS.

Awake and faithful to her wonted Fires. 1st and 2nd editions.

93. **For thee.** In Fraser MS. Gray thus writes:

'**For Thee, who mindful** &c.: as above.'

He meant to bring in the second of the four rejected stanzas, followed by this, (Frazer MS.):

If chance that e'er some pensive Spirit more,
By sympathetic Musings here delay'd
With vain, tho' kind, Enquiry shall explore
Thy once-loved Haunt, this long-deserted Shade.
Haply &c.

95. **If chance.** Shakespeare certainly seems to use 'chance' as a verb in such instances as 'How *chance* thou art returned so soon?' (*Com. of Errors* I. 2. 42), and *Lear* II. 3. 62 'How chance the King comes with so small a train?' Yet it is probable that 'if chance' is 'if perchance,' the substantive used adverbially. Cf. the similar use of 'if case.' ('Case' is not, I think, found as a verb.) 'If case some one of you would fly from us' (3 *Henry* VI. V. 4. 34; and ('to a Painted Lady' a poem doubtfully attributed to Donne), 'But case there be a difference in the mould' &c. (*in* case, probably).

97. **may. shall** Fraser MS.

98. Bradshaw compares Milton, *Comus* 138 sq.:

"Ere the blabbing eastern scout
The nice Morn, on the Indian steep
From her cabined loophole *peep*."

And in the *Installation Ode* (where the words are assigned to Milton, with the same rhyme as here):

"Oft at the blush of dawn
I trod your level lawn." ll. 30, 31.

99, 100. Milton's words again:

"...though from off the boughs each morn
We brush mellifluous dews."

Par. Lost V. 428, 429.

"Together both, ere the high *lawns* appeared
Under the opening eyelids of the morn
We drove afield." *Lycidas* 25–27. Bradshaw.

With hasty Footsteps brush the Dews away
On the high Brow of yonder hanging Lawn.

Fraser MS.

100. Gray, as Mitford suggests, may be influenced by the phrase 'incontro al sol' as used by Petrarch and Tasso in a similar connection.

101–104. "I rather wonder that he rejected this stanza, as it not only has the same sort of Doric delicacy, which charms us peculiarly in this part of the Poem, but also compleats the account of his whole day: whereas, this Evening scene being omitted, we have only his Morning walk, and his Noon-tide repose." Mason.

The stanza is here replaced in brackets, although it is conceivable that Gray may have rejected it, because, though the day is completed by it, it is not completed in sequence. But he might easily have achieved the exact sequence if he had written the rejected lines after ll. 105–108 instead of before them. As Dr Bradshaw points out, in ll. 113, 114, the custom'd *hill*, the *heath*, and *his fav'rite tree*, have obvious reference to the *three* scenes which the youth was known to haunt; so again have the *rill*, the *lawn* and the *wood* on ll. 115, 116. But, if the bracket should be removed, it is indispensable that we should return to the reading 'With gestures quaint' (l. 109) of Fraser MS. For it is obvious that Gray wrote 'Hard by yon wood' instead of it, when he had made up his mind to excise this stanza, yet saw that ll. 115, 116 implied a previous mention of three scenes.

103. Cf. the impromptu couplet preserved by Norton Nicholls, p. 75 *supra*.

104. **Whistful** *sic* in Fraser MS. It is possible that this spelling represents some vague etymological notion on Gray's part (though he could scarcely have connected the word with 'whist' in the sense of silent), and shows at any rate that he did not derive it from 'wist' in the sense either of 'knew' or 'known'—which derivation, says Skeat, 'is stark nonsense.' Skeat believes that *wistful* stands for *wishful*, the change in form being due to confusion with *wistly*, which was itself a corruption of the Middle-English *wisly*, certainly, verily, exactly. The sense which 'wistly' bears in two passages of Shakespeare (in whom alone and in the *Passionate Pilgrim* the word has been found) is 'attentively,' 'with scrutiny,' and this sense Skeat thinks may have arisen out of that of *wisly*. But in *Richard II*. v. 4. 7:

> ...speaking it, he wistly [Q. 2, wishtly] looked on me
> As who should say 'I would thou wert the man' &c.;

and in *Passionate Pilgrim* VI. 12 the sense is more probably *wishfully, longingly*.

105. **There.** **Oft** Fraser MS.

nodding. **hoary**, Fraser MS., with **spreading** and **nodding** superscribed.

Gray wrote from Burnham to Walpole, Sept. 1737, a description of the now much frequented Burnham Beeches:

'I have at the distance of half-a-mile, through a green lane, a forest (the vulgar call it a common) all my own, at least as good as so, for I spy no human thing in it but myself. It is a little chaos of mountains and precipices; mountains, it is true, that do not ascend much above the clouds, nor are the declivities quite so amazing as Dover cliff; but just such hills as people who love their necks as well as I do may venture to climb, and craggs that give the eye as much pleasure as if they were dangerous: Both vale and hill are covered with most venerable beeches, and other very reverend vegetables, that, like most other ancient people, are always dreaming out their old stories to the winds:

> And as they bow their hoary tops relate,
> In murmuring sounds, the dark decrees of fate;
> While visions, as poetic eyes avow,
> Cling to each leaf, and swarm on every bough.

At the foot of one of these squats me I (il penseroso) and there grow to a trunk the whole morning.'

It was amid the same scenes that he wrote in 1742, *Ode on Spring* (13-15):

> "Where'er the rude and moss-grown beech
> O'ercanopies the glade
> Beside some water's rushy brink" &c.

which anticipate this place in the *Elegy*.

If the four verses in the letter to Walpole are not Gray's, I am unable to trace them. The first line illustrates the '*nodding* beech' of the *Elegy*. Cf. the Var. Lect. of Fraser MS. here.

106. Nowhere do beeches assume more 'fantastic' forms than at Burnham.

Luke compares Spenser, *Ruines of Rome*, stanza XXVIII, which combines Gray's scattered details, in the picture of an aged tree,

> "Lifting to heaven her aged *hoarie* head,
> Whose foot in ground hath left but feeble holde,
> But halfe disbowel'd lies above the ground,
> Showing her *wreathed* rootes" &c.

107, 108. "He lay along
> Under an oak, whose *antique root peep'd out*
> Upon the *brook* that brawls along this wood."
>
> *As You Like It* II. I. 30-32.

This is said of the melancholy Jaques, between whom and himself the melancholy and self-conscious Gray could scarcely fail, in a similar scene, to make a fugitive comparison. But, as he himself suggests to Walpole, his nearer *analogue* in character is Milton's *Il Penseroso*:

'in close covert by some brook' &c.

babbles. Cf. (after Mitford) the 'loquaces lymphae' of Horace, *Carm.* III. 13, 15.

109. **With gestures quaint now smileing** &c. Fraser MS.

'Smiling as in scorn' is certainly much like Jaques.

wayward fancies ~~loved~~ would he

110. **Mutt'ring his fond conceits he ~~wont to~~ rove:**

Fraser MS.

would he, Egerton and Pembroke MSS.

drooping,

111. **Now woeful wan, ~~he droop'd~~, as one forlorn.**

Fraser MS.

I have printed 'woeful-wan' (with a hyphen) on the faith of Mr Gosse, who professes to print from the edition of 1768. But Dr Bradshaw affirms that there is no hyphen in the printed copies published in Gray's lifetime. *Non nostrum inter vos* &c. The hyphen is a mere convention, and it is admitted that it is found in the Pembroke MS. here. Dr Bradshaw says "woful-wan means sad and pale, not 'wofully pale'." The second interpretation being just that which the hyphen precludes, the hyphen is better retained.

113. **I. we** Fraser MS.

Along the

114. **By the Heath-~~side~~ and at his fav'rite Tree.**

Fraser MS.

116. **at. by** is written over this word in Fraser MS.

After 116 Gray began to write in Fraser MS.:

There scattered oft the earliest,

but struck it through.

117. **due. meet,** Fraser MS.

118. **thro** has **by** written over it in Fraser MS.

the church-way path] Wakefield compares

"the graves all gaping wide
Every one lets forth his sprite
In *the church-way paths* to glide."

Shakespeare, *Mids. Night's Dream*, V. I. 389.

Shakespeare's paths may be *in* the church-yard; the church-way paths at Stoke Pogis are, as is common in country churches, paths from the high-road to the churchyard, as Bradshaw notes.

119. **Approach and read, for thou canst read the Lay** Fraser

MS.; Gray's first meaning probably was only 'the Lay is there for any one to read.' But by bracketing 'for thou canst read' he has given the words more significance. As Professor Hales says "reading was not such a common accomplishment that it could be taken for granted." The 'hoary headed swain' is perhaps himself 'no scholar' (as he would put it), but presumes that the enquirer is more accomplished.

The change has the further advantage that Gray thus adopts a poetic device, such as Pope's

"Tell (for you can) what is it to be wise."

Pope, *Essay on Man*, IV. 260.

Or Young (quoted by Mitford without ref.):

"And steal (for you can steal) celestial fire."

120. **Grav'd. Wrote** Fraser MS. with **Graved** and **carved** written over it.

that Fraser MS. with **yon** written over it.

121–124. That Gray was inclined to retain this stanza is probable because he has written over it in Pembroke MS. 'Insert.' And the stanza itself as it there appears is obviously written much later than the rest of the MS. for the ink is much darker. Gray has noted also "Omitted 1753." Dr Bradshaw has ascertained that it was first printed in the *third* edition of the *Elegy*, March 1751. Mason says it was omitted because Gray thought that it was "too long a parenthesis in this place." Dr Bradshaw adds "he may have noted the resemblance it bears to some expressions and lines in Collins' *Dirge in Cymbeline*, published 1747[1]":

"To fair Fidele's grassy tomb
Soft maids and village hinds shall bring
Each opening sweet of earliest bloom,
And rifle all the breathing spring.

....

The redbreast oft, at evening hours,
Shall kindly lend his little aid,
With hoary moss, and gathered flowers
To deck the ground where thou art laid."

That Gray had read these stanzas on their first appearance is perfectly certain, and the resemblance between the two pictures can scarcely be accidental. But, as usual, he condenses; and in describing his own grave, he has a modest regard for probability. The

[1] Really 1746, but dated 1747.

redbreast of Collins is the sympathetic bird of those "Babes in the Wood," who received no burial

"Till Robin-red-breast piously
Did cover them with leaves,"

which "little poetical ornament," says Addison in the *Spectator* (no. 85), "shews the genius of the author amidst all his simplicity, being just the same kind of fiction which Horace has made use of upon a parallel occasion in that passage where he describes himself, when he was a child, fallen asleep in a desert wood, and covered with leaves by the doves that took pity on him" (*Od.* III. 4. 959).

121. **Spring**, Fraser MS. with **Year** written above.

122. **frequent**, Fraser MS. with **Showers of** superscribed.

Vi'lets, Fraser MS.

123. **Robin**, Fraser MS. **Redbreast** superscribed.

125. The Epitaph, which is not so headed in Fraser MS., is there written along the side of the page.

Ib. "how glad would lay me down
As in my mother's lap."

Par. Lost x. 777.
Mitford.

126. 'he lived unknown
To fame or fortune.' *Agrippina*, ll. 39, 40.

127, 8. **Science**. See note on *Eton Ode* l. 3.

To these two lines it has been objected that they are obscurely expressed, and seem to combine a blessing and a curse as if they were cognate ideas. But Gray defines his melancholy to West, May 27, 1742 'Mine, you are to know, is a white Melancholy, or rather Leucocholy for the most part, which though it seldom laughs or dances, nor ever amounts to what one calls Joy, or Pleasure, yet is a good easy sort of state' &c. His melancholy was closely connected with his studious retirement, and its nature is exactly fixed in these two lines. Milton's *Il Penseroso* is Gray all over, and it is noteworthy that whereas Milton is certainly indebted to the verses prefixed to Burton's *Anatomy of Melancholy* for his two companion poems, Burton has given to *his* melancholy man some of the pleasures which Milton has transferred to *L'Allegro*. Gray might say with La Fontaine:

J'aime...les livres, la musique
La ville et la campagne, enfin tout; il n'est rien,
Qui ne me soit souverain bien,
Jusqu'aux sombres plaisirs d'un cœur mélancolique.

127. **frown'd not**] Wakefield compares Horace IV 3. 1, 2:

"Quem tu Melpomene semel
Nascentem placido lumine videris" &c.
[He on whose birth the lyric Queen
Of numbers smiled &c. Atterbury.]

129 sq. Very possibly, as Mitford seems to think, suggested by Cowley's lines on the death of Mr William Hervey (*Golden Treasury* CXXXVII.):

"Large was his soul; as large a soul as e'er
Submitted to inform a body here,
High as the place 'twas shortly in Heaven to have
But low and humble as his grave;
So high that all the virtues there did come.
....
So low that for me too it made a room."

It is the same man, as described by himself and by 'the friend.'

soul. **Heart,** Fraser MS.

131, 132. "Much as I admire Gray, one feels I think, in reading his poetry never quite secure against the false poetical style of the eighteenth century. It is always near at hand, sometimes it breaks in; and the sense of this prevents the security one enjoys with truly classic work...

'Thy joys no glittering female meets—'
[*Ode on Spring* l. 45.]

or even things in the *Elegy*:

'He gave to misery all he had—a tear;
He gain'd from Heaven ('twas all he wish'd) a friend—'

are instances of the sort of drawback I mean." Matthew Arnold.

What Arnold notes is the affected antithesis and consequent exaggeration in 'all he had' and ''twas all he wished.' Add the straining after *point*. If his bounty was large, how comes it, the average reader asks, that he has only a tear to give to misery? If Heaven gave a large recompense, how came it that it gave him only one friend? The answer is that 'a tear' *is* 'large bounty,' and that 'a friend' *is* 'a large recompense.' And the retort is that, if this is the point, it is badly made and is not worth making.

We ought not, perhaps, to seek too close a correspondence between the poet's circumstances and the epitaph. It is a coincidence which we must not press, that he was temporarily inconvenienced during the time when he was fitfully engaged upon the second half of the *Elegy* by the loss of a house (insured) in Cornhill; at no time in his life was he really embarrassed. During the same period also he had more than one true friend besides Wharton. One cannot however help suspecting either that this epitaph was the one part of the *Elegy* written in 1742, although undoubtedly not entered in the oldest extant MS. until the completion of the Poem, or that it is retrospective, and recalls the regrets of that melancholy year, when West was dead and Gray, then really solitary, may have longed to be with him (see *Odes* II. and III. Introductory notes). Both here and in the *Progress of Poesy* the 'personal note' with which a very general theme is made to end is distinctly *not* effective. Whether consciously or not, Gray in this imitates West, whose 'Muse as yet unheeded and unknown' winds up 'the monody on the Death of Queen Caroline' with a self-reference, the feebleness of which Gray would have recognised in the case of any other friend[1].

131. **all he had, a tear]** Gray here translates himself; the tribute to West's memory

has lacrymas, memori quas ictus amore
Fundo, *quod possum* &c.

(*'tis all I can*) in *De Principiis Cogitandi*, Lib. ii. 27, 28, written as he himself records in Pembroke MS., at Stoke, June, 1742; this tends to confirm the notion that to this date belongs at any rate the *inspiration* of the Epitaph. It is a tribute to the Lucretianism of Gray's Latin lines that Mitford here attributes them to Lucretius.

134, 135. **Nor** think **seek to draw them from their dread abode**
(His Frailties there in trembling Hope repose)
Fraser MS.

135. —paventosa speme.
Petrarch, *Son.* 114, Gray.

The Sonnet is No. 97 in ed. Giacomo Leopardi, Florence 1847, l. 12 'freddo foco e *paventosa speme*,' said by Petrarch of his love kept in check by Laura. Gray might have found the same expression nearer home in a more apposite context, e.g. Hooker, *Ecclesiastical Polity* B. I. xi. [6] where it is said that Hope's highest object is 'that everlasting Goodness which in Christ doth quicken the dead,' and that she 'begins here with a *trembling expectation* of things far removed and as yet but only heard of' &c.

There is, however, surely a boldness the reverse of happy as well as some confusion of thought in speaking of a man's frailties as reposing in

[1] See *Gray and His Friends*, pp. 14, 114.

trembling hope on the bosom of God. The words of Gray himself to Mason recur to the mind 'all I can say is that your elegy should not end with the worst line in it.'

X. LONG STORY.

Mason writes that whilst Walpole was circulating the Elegy in MS. "among the rest of the fashionable world, for to these only it was at present communicated, Lady Cobham, who now lived at the mansion-house at Stoke Pogis, had read and admired it. She wished to be acquainted with the author; accordingly her relation Miss Speed and Lady Schaub, then at her house, undertook to bring this about by making him the first visit. He happened to be from home, when the Ladies arrived at his Aunt's solitary mansion; and when he returned was surprised to find, written on one of his papers in the parlour where he usually read, the following note: 'Lady Schaub's compliments to Mr Gray; she is sorry not to have found him at home, to tell him that Lady Brown is very well.' This necessarily obliged him to return the visit, and soon after induced him to compose a ludicrous account of this little adventure for the amusement of the Ladies in question."

Lady Cobham was at this time a widow, her husband, Field-Marshal Richard Temple, Viscount Cobham, having died in 1749. She was the daughter of Edmund Halsey, the predecessor of Thrale's father in the brewery now known by the name of Barclay and Perkins. She died in 1760.

Lady Schaub was the wife of Sir Luke Schaub, whom Cunningham describes as 'a kind of Will Chiffinch[1] to George I. and much in the favour of George II. He had several pensions from both kings for confidential services abroad and at home.' Horace Walpole in 1741 describes Lady Schaub as a pretty woman, 'a foreigner, who as Sir Luke says, *would* have him.' She was French, see l. 25. Her husband died in 1758, and she in 1793.

The Lady Brown who served as an excuse for the visit to the poet was the grand-daughter of the third Earl of Salisbury, and wife of Sir Robert Brown, Baronet, a merchant at Venice. Her 'Sunday nights' are described by Walpole (to Mann, Feb. 13, 1743) as 'the great mart

[1] See Scott's *Peveril of the Peak*, *passim*, for the character (in fact or libel) of this hero.

for all travelling and travelled calves.' It was probably as a 'travelled' man, through Walpole or perhaps earlier through John Chute, that Gray made her acquaintance.

Miss Henrietta Jane Speed was the daughter of Colonel Speed, the friend of Viscount Cobham. Cole the antiquary has stated that upon her father's decease she was brought up in the family of Lord Cobham and treated by him with paternal care and tenderness. Gray relates with manifest pleasure that she used to say φωνᾶντα συνετοῖσι in so many words to those who could not understand his Odes. Walpole says she was a niece of Lady Cobham. As a young girl at Stowe, the seat of Viscount Cobham, she met Pope, and probably Thomson, who celebrated Stowe and its Cobham in verse; the company of men of genius was therefore no new thing to her. At the date of the Long Story she was about 27 years old. Her 'pretty delicate features,' as Mr Gosse puts it, are represented in the 'Designs for Six Poems' by Richard Bentley (1753), where both 'the Amazon ladies are seen flying through the air, seeking for their victim the poet,' whilst 'the Rev. Mr Purt is represented as blowing the trumpet of Fame.'

Miss Speed's graceful letter of acknowledgement of the Long Story, ending with a fresh invitation to dinner, is given in *Gray and His Friends*, p. 197. The acquaintance ripened, not without some suggestion, at least on the part of gossiping friends, of matrimony. But Gray, though in the fashion of the time he might write complimentary verses to her (poems xxii., xxiii.), seems to have been heart-whole. She writes to Gray in August 1759 a letter inviting him to Stoke, which shows that they had been in correspondence, and she says, 'You can easily conceive me vain of the Partiality you show me'—and 'if you are at present an invalide, let that prompt you to come, for from the *affected Creature* you knew me I am nothing now but a comfortable nurse.' The letter shows her to be a clever, sprightly woman, with that indifference to spelling (she cannot even spell the poet's name) which was characteristic of her generation. Lady Cobham died in 1760, leaving Miss Speed 'at least £30,000, with a house in town, plate, jewels, china and old japan infinite,' says Gray to Wharton (July 1760); the affairs of 'Madam Speed, as she says, or her vagaries, as I say, have obliged her to alter her mind ten times within three weeks'; during which time the poet had been staying in town, expecting to go with the lady into Oxfordshire; with such a fortune,' he says, 'it would be ridiculous for her to know her own mind,—I who know mine, do intend to go to Cambridge,' &c. To the same correspondent he writes (Oct. 21, 1760) that he never had any expectations from Lady Cobham, though 'the world said, before her death, that Mrs Speed and I had shut ourselves up with her in order to make her will, and that afterwards we were to be married.' In Jan. 1762 to the same he writes that his 'old friend Miss Speed has done what the world calls a very foolish thing. She has married the Baron de la Peyriere, son to the Sardinian minister, the Comte de Viry. He is about 28 years old (ten years younger than herself) but looks nearer 40; he is good-natured and honest and no conjurer' (for which expression *cf.* l. 128, n. *infra*). 'The castle of Viry is in Savoy, a few miles from Geneva, commanding a fine view of the Lake. What she has done with her money I know not; but (I suspect) kept it to herself. Her religion she need not change, but she must never expect to be well received at that court till she does: and I do not think she will make quite a *Julie* in the country' (an allusion to the heroine of Rousseau's Nouvelle Héloïse). In 1766 Gray saw her once more; her husband was then Sardinian minister in London; 'she was a prodigious fine lady, and a Catholick, and fatter than she was: she had a cage of foreign birds and a piping bullfinch at her elbow, two little dogs on a cushion in her lap, a cockatoo on her shoulder, and a suspicion of rouge on her cheeks.'

When next we hear of her, Gray has been dead four years. Her husband's father being dead too, she is the Countess Viry, and Walpole describes her (Aug. and Sept. 1775) as having completed the conquest of France by her behaviour and the *fêtes* she gave in honour of the wedding of Madame Clotilde (sister of Louis XVI.) to the Prince of Piedmont. She has developed since Bentley pictured her (unless he flattered), for Walpole talks of her 'large cheeks.' Her husband was ambassador in France, but had in 1777 a 'sad fall,'—he was 'arrested at Susa and ordered to present himself twice a day to the governor. 'Madame has leave to go where she pleases,' says Walpole, but notes that 'she was supposed to be the cause of her husband's disgrace, as very intriguing,'—inducing him to try to make himself prime minister. 'Lord Shelburne, who was her friend, prevailed on the king to obtain their pardon in 1783, about which time she died suddenly'—in fact, just as she was about to come to England again, early in that year.

Mr Gosse says that Lady Cobham 'was unaware that Gray and she had lived together in the same country parish for several years.' She may well have been unaware of it, for it was probably not the case. Up to the time of her husband's death in 1749 she may be supposed to have lived at Stowe, and to have retired to Stoke Pogis because the house there was her own, her father having purchased it in 1720. Stowe passed into other hands on her husband's decease. At Stoke Pogis Lady Cobham was, I take it, a new-comer, and doubtless consulted 'Fame, in the shape of Mr Purt' about persons worth knowing in the neighbourhood. 'Stoke-house and the manor were sold by her heirs to William Penn, Esq., chief proprietor of Pensylvania.......It was pulled down in 1789 by Mr Penn, who has built an elegant modern mansion not far from its site from a design by Mr Wyatt.' (Lysons, *Magna Britannia*, I. p. 637).

The same Mr Penn erected the monument to Gray which stands in the field by the churchyard of Stoke Pogis.

3. **Huntingdons and Hattons.** 'Henry Hastings, Earl of Huntingdon, rebuilt the manor-house in the reign of Elizabeth. The estate was soon afterwards seized by the Crown for a debt. King James the First, about the year 1621, granted the manor in fee to Lord Chief Justice Coke, who appears to have held it many years before as lessee under the Crown. In 1601, being then Attorney-General, he entertained Queen Elizabeth very sumptuously at this place, and presented her Majesty with jewels to the value of £1000 or £1200....Sir Edward Coke died at Stoke Pogis. The house it appears was settled on his lady, who was relict of Sir William Hatton (nephew of the Lord Chancellor Hatton).' Lysons, *Magna Britannia*, I. pp. 635, 636.

It would seem that Gray's references to the Hattons are justified, if at all, by the fact that the house was settled on Lady Coke, and that at some entertainment given there 'my grave Lord Keeper' might possibly have led the brawls. Lysons tells us also that 'the "dim windows that excluded the light" were filled with the arms of the family of Hastings and its alliances, those of Sir Edward Coke, and many of his great contemporaries in the law.' That the Hattons had anything to do with building the pile does not appear. 'The chimneys of the ancient house still remain, to mark the locality; a column, on which is fixed a statue of Coke erected by Mr Penn, consecrates the former abode of its illustrious inhabitant.' (D'Israeli, *Curiosities of Literature*, p. 365, one vol. edit. of 1854.)

4. **Fairy hands.** A fancy more suited to the Arthurian legend than to the days of the Huntingdons and Hattons. But Gray feels bound to idealize the past as well as the present story of the house, where 'the power of magic was no fable.'

5. **fretted.** See n. on *Elegy*, l. 39.

6. **achievements.** Escutcheons, most commonly (in the form

'hatchments') used of the coat-of-arms of a newly-deceased person, publicly displayed. So Dryden uses 'achievements' (in the funeral of Arcite), *Palamon and Arcite*, l. 932,

"The steed, that bore him living to the fight,
Was cover'd with the *achievements* of the knight."

10. **fifty winters.** At the time of his great exploit as Lord Chancellor he was 49, according to Dr Phelps.

11. **My grave** &c. Hatton, prefer'd by Queen Elizabeth for his graceful Person and fine Dancing. Gray.

Cf. Sir Robert Naunton's sketch (cited by Phelps): "*Sir Christopher Hatton* came into the Court as his opposite, *Sir John Perrot*, was wont to say by the Galliard, for he came thither as a Private Gentleman of the Innes of Court in a Mask; and for his activity and person, which was tall and proportionable, taken into favour; he was first made Vice-Chamberlain, and shortly afterward advanced to the place of Lord Chancellor: a Gentleman, that besides the graces of his person, and dancing, had also the adjectaments of a strong and subtill capacity, one that could soon learn the discipline and garb both of the times and Court; the truth is, he had a large proportion of gifts and endowments, but too much of the season of envy; and he was a meer vegetable of the Court, that sprung up at night, and sunk again at his noon." (*Fragmenta Regalia*, ed. Arber, p. 44.)

The famous incident of Hatton's dancing when Lord Chancellor is derived from a letter from Captain Francis Allen to Anthony Bacon, 17 August, 1589, 'My Lord Chancellor's heir, Sir William Hatton, hath married Judge Gowdy's daughter and heir; and my Lord Chancellor danced the measures at the solemnity. He left the gown in the chair, saying "Lie thou there, Chancellor." Phelps.

Brawls. 'A kind of French dance resembling a cotillon.' Murray. Cf. 'a French brawl,' *Love's Labour's Lost*, III. 9, followed by a play on the word as meaning 'quarrel.' The word here is a corruption of the French *bransle* (now branle), the first meaning of which is 'a swinging from side to side,' 'cloches en branle,' for example, are bells at full swing, 'donner le branle' is to set a thing in movement. According to Littré all dances may be so called in which one or two dancers lead the rest, who repeat 'ce qu'ont fait les premiers.' He instances 'le grand-père' and 'le cotillon.' Phelps points out that the Lord Chancellor is said to have danced '*in the measures*, slow, sedate dances, minuets.' But Littré tells us, 'Il y a, ou plutôt il y avait, *des branles sérieux*; ceux qu'on donnait aux bals de Louis XIV, et qui sont décrits dans le *Maître à danser* du sieur Rameau, étaient *fort graves*. The Lord Keeper may possibly have 'led the brawls' and yet 'kept his gravity,' as he would need to do, if instead of putting aside the signs of office, as history affirms, he had the officials who bore the Great Seal and the Maces dancing before him (l. 12).

25. **The first.** Lady Schaub, a Frenchwoman. (See Introd. note.) 'Cap-a-pee' perhaps implies also that she was dressed in the height of French fashion.

29. **The other.** Miss Speed. (See Introd. note.)

30. **satire.** Note the rhyme with 'nature.' It is Dryden's also, e.g.

> "And wish for your own sakes, without a *satire*
> You'd less good breeding, or had more good *nature*."
> Prologue to *Arviragus &c.* (1690).

It is possible that Gray wrote 'satyr,' for that was the commonest spelling of 'satire' in his day; the Pembroke MS. would show whether this is so or not. The pronunciation is no doubt *sāter* and *nāter*.

31. **Cobham.** Lady Cobham. (See Introd. note.)

35. **'nom de guerre.'** 'nom que chaque soldat prenait autrefois en s'enrôlant, par exemple, La Tulipe, Sans-Quartier.' Littré. Hence for a name fancifully assumed. It was the fashion with sentimental ladies of fashion to correspond with their friends or admirers under some such name—after the manner of Thackeray's Lady Lyndon. Miss Speed probably followed this fashion, unless, which is less likely, she owes her name to Gray. It is perhaps needless to assume that Lady Schaub and Miss Speed had never met Gray before. They may have met, for instance, at Lady Brown's.

37. **capucine.** A cloak with a hood, like that worn by the Capuchins, of the order of St Francis, who were so called from wearing it. The word in this form seems to be unknown in French for an article of dress; the word for the friar's cloak is *capuchon*, for the lady's, after the same pattern, *capote* and *capeline*.

41. 'Mr Robert Purt was Fellow of King's College, Cambridge, 1738; A.B. 1742, A.M. 1746; was an assistant at Eton school, tutor to Lord Baltimore's son there, and afterwards to the Duke of Bridgewater; in 1749 he was presented to the living of Settrington, in Yorkshire, which he held with Dorrington in the same county. He died in April 1752 of the small-pox.' Isaac Reed.

From these dates it seems that he may have been about thirty-two or thirty-three at his death, two years after the Long Story was written.

'It has been said that this gentleman, a neighbour and acquaintance of Gray's in the country, was much displeased with the liberty here taken with his name: yet surely without any great reason.' Mason.

Gray printed 'Mr P—t,' and further disguised the name by a very bad rhyme. Poor Purt might have been more vexed still if he had lived to see himself figured by Bentley in 1753 as 'Fame blowing a trumpet.'

51. After the manner of Henry IVth's edict against the Welsh bards, issued in the 4th year of his reign, a re-enactment of Edward the First's proceedings against them. According to this 'Rymours, Ministralx ne Vacabundez' are not to be 'sustenuz en la terre de Galez.' 'Vagabond,' says Ritson, 'was a title to which the profession had long been accustomed:

> "Beggars they are with one consent
> And rogues by act of parliament."'
>
> Pref. to *Anc. Songs*, p. 11.

There are still stronger Scotch statutes against them, some condemning them and 'such like fules' to lose their ears, and others their lives. By a law of Elizabeth the English minstrels were pronounced 'rogues, vagabonds, and sturdy beggars,' 39 Eliz. c. 4, s. 2. See Ritson's *Eng. Songs*, I. liii. Barrington on the *Statutes*, p. 360. Dodsley, *Old Plays*, XII. p. 361. Strutt, *Sports and Pastimes*, pp. 182—196. Puttenham, *Art of Engl. Poesie* (1569), lib. ii. c. 9. Mitford.

54. Pronounce *venter'd*, and cf. Goldsmith to Mrs Bunbury (Aldine edition, p. 165),

> "All smirking and pleasant and big with *adventure*,
> And ogling the stake which is placed in the *centre*"

(written in 1774).

59. **his aunt.** Mrs Rogers, the widow of Jonathan Rogers; Gray's mother lived with her at this time.

65. There is a very great similarity between the style of part of this poem and Prior's Tale of 'The Dove': as for instance in the following stanzas, which Gray, I think, must have had in his mind at the time:

> "With one great peal they rap the door
> Like footmen on a visiting day:
> Folks at her house at such an hour,
> Lord, what will all the neighbours say?
>
> * * * * * *

Her keys he takes, her door unlocks,
Thro' wardrobe, and thro' closet bounces,
Peeps into every chest and box,
Turns all her furbelows and flounces.
* * * * * *

'I marvel much,' she smiling said,
'Your poultry cannot yet be found:
Lies he in yonder slipper dead,
Or maybe in the tea-pot drown'd?'" Mitford.

79. **whisk**, interjectional, like 'sweep,' l. 102;—a verb in Pope, *Dunciad*, II. 116:

"Songs, sonnets, epigrams the winds uplift,
And *whisk* 'em back to Evans, Young, and Swift."

103. **Styack**. The housekeeper. Gray.

In the elegant little edition of Gray's poems published by Sharpe, with illustrations by Westall, in 1826, this name is printed Tyacke in the text, and there is the following footnote,—'Her name which has hitherto, in all editions of Gray's Poems, been written Styack, is corrected from her gravestone in the churchyard and the accounts of contemporary persons in the parish. Housekeepers are usually styled Mrs; the final *s* doubtless caused the name to be misapprehended and misspelt.' There is a similar manuscript note in Upcott's edition, 1800, in the British Museum, signed 'P.' Bradshaw.

Gray probably added detail to the Long Story, after he became acquainted with the *ménage* of the Great House. His date Aug. 1750, though affixed to the poem as we have it, may be really the date of the earlier sketch.

115. **Squib**. Groom of the chambers. Gray.

'James Squibb was the son of Dr Arthur Squibb, the descendant of an ancient and respectable family, whose pedigree is traced in the herald's visitations of Dorsetshire to John Squibb of Whitechurch, in that county, in the 17th Edw. IV., 1477. Dr Squibb matriculated at Oxford in 1656, took his degree of M.A. in November, 1662, was chaplain to Colonel Bellasis's regiment about 1685, and died in 1697. As he was in distressed circumstances towards the end of his life, his son, James Squibb, was left almost destitute, and was consequently apprenticed to an upholder in 1712. In that situation he attracted the notice of Lord Cobham, in whose service he continued for many years, and died at Stowe, in June, 1762. His son, James Squibb, who settled in Savile Row, London, was grandfather of George James Squibb, Esq.

of Orchard Street, Portman Square, who is the present representative of the family.' Nicolas (*apud* Mitford.) The note is worth preserving, as showing the eminent respectability of the upper servants in great families in Gray's time. I conjecture from it that, on Lady Cobham's death in 1759, James Squibb returned to Stowe, to a house of his own there, and lived on his *peculium*.

116. **Groom.** The steward. Gray.

120. **Macleane.** A famous highwayman hanged the week before. Gray.

Before, that is, Gray's visit to the mansion-house. Macleane was *hanged* on the 3rd of October, 1750. But he was before the 'justice' at the end of July. It was however in September that when called to receive sentence, he only said, 'My Lord, I cannot speak.' If Gray has this in mind, his reference to Macleane in text and note is a poetic fiction, inserted in a second draft of the poem, unless his date 'Aug. 1750' is altogether a mistake of memory.

Macleane's story is a strange one, in some respects not unlike that of the notorious *Peace* of our own time.

"One night," says Walpole, "in the beginning of November, 1749, as I was returning from Holland House by moonlight, about ten at night, I was attacked by two highwaymen (M'Lean and Plunket) in Hyde Park, and the pistol of one of them going off accidentally, razed the skin under my eye, left some marks of shot on my face, and stunned me. The ball went through the top of the chariot, and if I had sat an inch nearer to the left side, must have gone through my head." (Short Notes of My Life.) This incident Walpole improved in the *World* (No. 103, Dec. 19, 1754), declaring that the whole affair was conducted with the greatest good-breeding on both sides; that the accomplished Mr M'Lean who had only taken a purse because he had that morning been disappointed of marrying a great fortune, no sooner returned to his lodgings, than he sent the gentleman two letters of excuses, which with less wit than the epistles of Voiture, had ten times more natural and easy politeness in the turn of their expression. In the postscript, he appointed a meeting at Tyburn at twelve at night, where the gentleman might *purchase again* any trifles he had lost; and my friend has been blamed for not accepting the rendezvous, as it seemed liable to be construed by ill-natured people into a doubt of the *honour* of a man' &c.

Walpole tells Mann, Aug. 2, 1750, that this fashionable highwayman is just taken; is little of a hero, cries and begs, and impeaches his accomplice Plunket. 'His father was an Irish Dean; his brother is a Calvinist minister in great esteem at the Hague. He himself was a grocer (in Welbeck Street), but losing a wife that he loved extremely about two years ago, and by whom he has one little girl, he quitted his business with two hundred pounds in his pocket, which he soon spent, and then took to the road with only one companion, Plunket, a journeyman apothecary, my other friend.... McLean had a lodging in St James' Street, over against White's, and another at Chelsea; Plunket one in Jermyn Street; and their faces are as known about St James' as any gentleman who lives in that quarter. McLean had a quarrel at Putney bowling-green two months ago with an officer, whom he challenged for disputing his rank; but the captain declined till McLean should produce a certificate of his nobility, which he has just received. Lord Mountford, at the head of half White's went the first day to see him; but the chief personages who have been to comfort and weep over this fallen hero are Lady Caroline Petersham and Miss Ashe: I call them Polly and Lucy, and asked them if he did not sing

"Thus I stand like the Turk with my doxies around,"

[Last song of Macheath in the *Beggars' Opera.*]

128. With a play on the sense 'not over wise'. Gray says to Wharton (Sept. 18, 1754) that Akenside is 'no conjurer' in architecture, and as we have seen *supra*, he uses the same phrase of Miss Speed's future husband.

129. **hagged.** 'i.e. the face of a witch or hag; the epithet Hagard has been sometimes mistaken, as conveying the same idęa; but it means a very different thing, viz. wild and *farouche*, and is taken from an unreclaimed hawk, called an Hagard; in which, its proper sense, the Poet uses it finely on a sublime occasion:

"Cloath'd in the sable garb of woe,
With hagard eyes the Poet stood."'

Bard, ll. 17, 18.

So Mason taught by Gray, see note on Bard *l.c.*; but Skeat says that 'haggard' is a corruption of haggèd, confused in spelling by the influence of haggard as a term for a hawk; though both words may be from the same root.

133. 'The exclamation of the Ghosts which follows is characteristic of the Spanish manners of the age when they are supposed to have lived; and the 500 stanzas, said to be lost, may be imagined to contain the remainder of their long-winded expostulation.' Mason.

The exclamation is characteristic of the 'drawing room of fierce *Queen Mary*.' An old songster (Dowland's second book of songs,

1600) marks the change of times from the ascendency of Roman Catholicism by suggesting *Vivat Eliza* for an *Ave Mary*.

140. **'five hundred.'** Miss Speed (*Gray and His Friends*) speaks of 'the loss of the 400 stanzas'; so perhaps in first draft.

It is affirmed both by Mr Gosse and Dr Bradshaw that *A Long Story* was only once printed in Gray's lifetime, viz. in the edition with Bentley's designs in 1753. Dr Phelps points out that it was published in a Dublin edition of Gray's poetry in 1768. Professor Dowden has kindly given me an account of this edition, which had the Rev. Mr Lloyd's Latin version of the *Elegy*, and another by 'an anonymous person,' while preceding the Elegy are some hexameters Ad Poetam. Parodies close the volume; 'Ode to Ranelagh,' 'An Evening Contemplation in a College,' and 'The Bard, a burlesque Ode by A. Lloyd and G. Colman.' The frontispiece is the Bard precipitating himself, and the last page represents the rider of Pegasus tumbling from the cliffs and following his wig into mid-air.

Further, Professor Dowden has an Edition of 1768 of Gray's poems printed at Cork, and dedicated to a Mrs Elizabeth Gray, as a chief 'Promoter of It.' This *also* contains *A Long Story*. In it the *Progress of Poesy* is called in the table of Contents *Ode to his Lyre*, and the *Bard*, 'Ode on Edward I. putting the Bards to death in Wales.' The Parody (by Duncombe) 'An Evening Contemplation in a College' is also contained in this volume.

Gray, Professor Dowden says, probably did not authorize these publications.

XI. STANZAS TO MR BENTLEY.

Richard Bentley was the only son of the famous master of Trinity, Cambridge. Our knowledge of him is mainly derived from the Letters of Horace Walpole, with whom he was constantly staying, as his chief adviser in the architecture and adornment of Strawberry Hill. His Designs for the Six Poems were explained by Walpole for the benefit of the public, in the edition in which they appeared.

Bentley was extravagant and impecunious; he fled to Jersey to escape his creditors and another. Walpole writes to Montagu, 'we don't talk of his abode for the Hecate his wife endeavours to discover it.' (Dec. 6, 1753). In his exile, whilst Walpole was trying to extricate him from his difficulties, he was always plunging his patron into unexpected contracts and bargains. He was a scholar; and had in his possession his father's notes and emendations on the first seven books of Lucan; he undertook to edit Lucan for the Strawberry Hill Press; did so in part, but the task was completed by Richard Cumberland, his nephew.

'Hecate' seems to have died; and Bentley, at Teddington, formed a new alliance of which Walpole did not approve, comparing the parties to Antony and Cleopatra. The versatile Bentley wrote a play, after the manner of the Italian comedy, entitled *The Wishes, or Harlequin's Mouth Opened*. It had a prologue, with an obvious compliment to Gray:

"It represents the god of verse fast asleep by the side of Helicon; the race of modern bards try to wake him, but the more they repeat their works, the louder he snores. At last "Ruin seize thee, ruthless King!" is heard, and the god starts from his trance' (Walpole to Montagu, June 18, 1761).

This prologue however was not spoken; the whole play was, and probably deserved to be, a failure. (Walpole to Montagu, July 28, 1761). Bentley also wrote an Epistle to Lord Melcomb (Bubb Dodington), one of the great patrons of this play. In 1763 he was made a commissioner of the Lottery[1].

Mason attributes these verses to the time when Bentley was still employed upon the Designs; therefore to the year 1752.

2. Gray's Muse is to be silent whilst Bentley leads Painting along. She is pleased with the aid which Painting lends her, yet blushes as conscious of her inferior merit.

3. Mitford compares Pope, Epistle to Jervas, l. 13, 'Smit with the love of *sister-arts* we came,' and Dryden to Kneller, 'Our arts *are sisters*,' and 'Long time the *sister-arts* in iron sleep' etc.

7, 8. Cf. (after Mitford)

"Thence endless streams of fair ideas flow
Strike on the sketch, or in the picture slow."

Ep. to Jervas, l. 42.

and "When life awakes and dawns in every land." *Ib.* l. 4.

16. 'Harmony' may be predicated both of Pope and Dryden, and Gray, it is well known, warmly acknowledged his obligation to Dryden's numbers. Yet it is certainly strange that 'energy' should be given as a distinctive epithet to Pope, in juxtaposition with Dryden. For the *strength* of Dryden is proverbial, and it is his 'energy' which enables him to triumph in the treatment (as in the *Hind and Panther*) of a theme so unsuitable to verse as the controversy of the Churches. Either Gray's devotion to Dryden as his teacher has betrayed him into

[1] He was eccentric and irresponsible, seems to have been at once clever and foppish, but certainly not fastidious. Walpole records that he was always inventing new dishes by compounding heterogeneous ingredients and called it cultivating the 'Materia Edica,' and that he mixed his colours on the same principle and perhaps tasted them too.

an implied antithesis which is not effective, or, what is quite possible, Mason has carelessly transposed the words 'energy' and 'harmony.' Cf. Gray's own note, on *Progress of Poesy*, l. 105.

16. **submit** may be intransitive with 'harmony' for the subject of 'might,' or transitive, the subject of 'might' being 'they.' Cf. *Ode for Music*, ll. 85, 86:

> "And to thy just, thy gentle hand,
> *Submits* the Fasces of her sway."

17—24. Gray implies that a poetry was still possible, measurable by the standard of Dryden and Pope, a poetry in its essence artistic, but lacking the 'diviner inspiration' which belongs to Shakespeare and Milton. The epithet 'benighted' is hard to justify; the age was less 'inspired' just in proportion as it had grown critical. But to Gray the age is 'benighted,' not because it lacks light, but (l. 19) because it lacks fire. Gray, as Mitford says, has in mind Dryden's Epistle to Kneller, an acknowledgment of a portrait of Shakespeare given to the poet by the painter; cf. ll. 73—76:

> "Shakespeare, thy gift, I place before my sight;
> With awe I ask his blessing ere I write;
> With reverence look on his majestic face,
> *Proud to be less, but of his godlike race.*"

Here, as in the ode on the *Progress of Poesy*, Gray notes a diminishing scale of inspiration from Shakespeare and Milton, through Dryden to himself.[1]

20. I have substituted a comma for a full stop after 'heav'n,' as Gray surely means that many special charms, each of which would suffice to make a poet of a secondary order, are by the prodigality of heaven combined in Shakespeare and Milton.

24. Gray here utilizes the last two lines of a translation he made in 1738 from Tasso, *Gerus. Lib.* XIV. 32 sq.

> "The diamond there attracts the wond'ring sight
> Proud of its thousand dies, and luxury of light."

25—30. 'A corner of the only manuscript copy, which Mr Gray left of this fragment, is unfortunately torn; and though I have endeavoured to supply the chasm, I am not quite satisfied with the words which I have inserted in the third line.' Mason supplies 'the chasm' with 'impart' (l. 2) 'flows confest' (l. 3), 'heaves the heart' (l. 4). He seems to have been quite satisfied with 'heaves the heart.' Mitford supplies the *lacunæ* with 'convey,' 'is exprest' and 'dies away'; 'under the shelter,' he says, 'of the supposition that Gray had in his mind

[1] See additional note, p. 293.

Dryden's Epistle to Kneller, from which he partly took his expressions.' I gather that he relies on these *words* and *rhymes* at the end of the Epistle:

"More cannot be by mortal art express'd
But venerable age shall add the rest." l. 154;

and "To future ages shall your fame convey
And give more beauties than he takes away."
ll. 165, 166.

for I can find nothing else in the Epistle, as far as sense goes, which makes for his conjectures more than for Mason's.

XII. THE PROGRESS OF POESY.

The motto from Pindar belongs both to this and to the succeeding Ode. Therefore I have taken it from the place in which it has been set, in all editions of Gray which I have seen, except that of the Two Odes printed by Walpole at Strawberry Hill in 1757. Though it is certain that Gray afterwards permitted it to stand below the title of the first Ode only, perhaps this was but an oversight. The motto includes them both. I could not bring myself to follow Dr Phelps in separating for chronological reasons these companions by interpolating between them the fragment on 'Vicissitude.'

The motto was originally simply

ΦΩΝΑΝΤΑ ΣΥΝΕΤΟΙΣΙ, Pindar, *Olymp.* II.

'The *Critical Review* IV. 167 says, "The author might, with great propriety, have added

ἐς
δὲ τὸ πᾶν ἑρμηνέων
χατίζει."

It is interesting to note that in the edition of 1768 Gray actually adopted this suggestion.' Phelps. On the 7th of Sept. 1757, Gray wrote to Wharton,

Miss Sp. [Speed] seems to understand, and to all such, as do not, she says—φωναντα συνετοισι—in so many words. And this is both my Motto and Comment.'

He refers once more to the motto in a letter to Brown, 17 Feb. 1763, 'The Odes in question, as their motto shows, were meant to be *vocal to the intelligent alone.*'

'I have many shafts in my quiver,' so Pindar is generally understood, 'which have meaning for the intelligent, but for the generality need interpreters.'

Dr Verrall (*Journal of Philology*, vol. IX. p. 129) says, 'In spite of the familiarity of this famous epigram, I am confident that any scholar will upon reflection pronounce the traditional interpretation of it quite indefensible.'

However this may be, Gray undoubtedly followed the traditional interpretation. He knew nothing of the reading ἐς δὲ τοπὰν (which Donaldson gives, recording the MS. reading τὸ πὰν which points to it)—and which Dr Verrall interprets 'for the explanation of words'—i.e. veiled allusions.

It is noteworthy that the fuller motto was given when most of the explanatory notes were added by Gray. The earliest intimation of the *Progress of Poesy* is from Gray to Walpole (in a letter given without date, but probably Dec. 1752), "I don't know but I may send Dodsley very soon (by your hands)...a high Pindaric upon stilts, which one must be a better scholar than he is to understand a line of, and the very best scholars will understand but a little matter here and there. It wants but seventeen lines of having an end."

Mason affirms that he was the innocent cause of Gray's delaying to finish this Ode. '"I told him on reading the part he showed me that though I admired it greatly, and thought it breathed the very spirit of Pindar, yet I suspected it would by no means hit the public taste." Finding afterwards that he did not proceed in finishing it, I often expostulated with him on the subject; but he always replied, "No, you have thrown cold water upon it."' Mason mentions this in illustration of Gray's earlier reluctance to finish *Agrippina* after West's criticisms on it. (See Introductory note there.)

On the 26th of Dec. 1754 Gray sent Wharton the completed Ode, calling it 'Ode in the Greek manner,' and writing: 'If this be as tedious to you, as it is grown to me I shall be sorry that I sent it you....I desire that you would by no means suffer this to be copied; nor even shew it, unless to very few, and especially not to mere scholars, that can scan all the measures in Pindar, and say all the Scholia by heart.'

Though Gray observed the law of Strophe and Antistrophe he did not set much store by it. Writing again to Wharton on March 9, 1755, he says, 'Setting aside the difficulties, methinks it has little or no effect upon the ear, which scarce perceives the regular return of metres at so great a distance from one another. To make it succeed, I am persuaded the Stanzas must not consist of above nine lines each at the most. Pindar has several such odes.'

It will be noted that each strophe and antistrophe consists of 12 lines, each epode of 17; and that every strophe corresponds with every strophe and antistrophe, every epode with every epode, line for line.

Mason (on this letter of Gray) tells us that Gray often made the same remark to him about strophe and antistrophe; and that in consequence the last Ode of Caractacus was formed in shorter stanzas. He sagely remarks, 'Had the regular return of Strophe, Antistrophe and Epode no other merit than that of extreme difficulty, it ought on this very account to be valued; because we well know that "Easy writing is no easy reading."' Perhaps the justification of the true Pindaric Ode lies elsewhere than in this perversion of a common sense maxim, which never meant that we must multiply difficulties before we can be lucid.

'There was nothing,' Mason says, 'which Gray more disliked than that chain of irregular stanzas which Cowley introduced, and falsely called Pindaric; and which, from the extreme facility of execution, produced a number of miserable imitators....It is also to be remarked that Mr Congreve, who first introduced the regular Pindaric form into the English language, made use of the short stanzas which Mr Gray recommends. See his Ode to the Queen.'

'It is sometimes claimed,' says Dr Phelps, 'that Ben Jonson wrote the first Pindaric Ode. In his *Underwoods* there is a Pindaric Ode *To the Immortal Memory and Friendship of that Noble Pair Sir Lucius Cary and Sir H. Morison*. This is divided as Pindar's Odes were divided, into Strophes, Antistrophes and Epodes. Jonson called his Strophe a "Turn," his Antistrophe a Counter-Turn, and his Epode the "Stand"' [?στάσιμον].

Walpole writes to Chute, July 12, 1757: 'On Monday next the Officina Arbuteana [Strawberry Hill Press] opens in form. The Stationers' Company, that is, Mr Dodsley, Mr Tonson, &c. are summoned to meet here on Sunday night. And with what do you think we open? *Cedite Romani Impressores*—with nothing under Graii *Carmina*. I found him in town last week: he had brought his two Odes to be printed. I snatched them out of Dodsley's hands, and they are to be the firstfruits of my press....Now, my dear Sir, can I stir?

Not ev'n thy virtues, tyrant, shall avail.' [*Bard*, l. 6.]

Again, to Sir Horace Mann on the 4th of August he sends 'two copies of a very honourable opening of my press—two amazing Odes of Mr Gray; they are Greek, they are Pindaric, they are sublime!

consequently I fear a little obscure; the second particularly, by the confinement of the measure and the nature of prophetic vision, is mysterious. I could not persuade him to add more notes; he says whatever wants to be explained, don't deserve to be.'

I have a copy of this edition. In it, as in the Irish editions (Cork and Dublin) mentioned on *A Long Story*, *The Progress of Poesy* is headed simply Ode, and the *Bard* simply Ode II. In the Dublin and Cork editions of 1768 mentioned on *Long Story*, they are called Ode I. and Ode II. It will be seen that the drift of the first Ode was mistaken, by some not very bright readers.

To the edition of 1768 Gray has added the following: "*Advertisement.* When the Author first published this and the following Ode, he was advised, even by his Friends, to subjoin some explanatory Notes, but had too much respect for the understanding of his Readers to take that liberty."

With the exception therefore of a brief *advertisement* to the *Bard* and four notes to the same poem, which were given in 1757, Gray's notes belong to 1768.

1. In his manuscript it originally stood:

"**Awake, my lyre: my glory, wake.**" Mason.

"Awake, my glory; awake lute and harp." David's Psalms. Gray. He quotes from the Prayer-Book version, Psalm lvii. 9, which however runs 'Awake *up*' etc. Cf. also Cowley's Supplication (given in Palgrave's *Golden Treasury*):

"Awake, awake, my lyre
And tell thy silent master's humble tale."

Ib. Pindar styles his own poetry, with its musical accompaniments Αἰοληὶς μολπὴ, Αἰολίδες χορδαὶ, Αἰολίδων πνοαὶ αὐλῶν, Æolian song, Æolian strings, the breath of the Æolian flute (*sic*). Gray.

This note was provoked by a writer in the *Critical Review* (IV. 167) who says (as quoted by Phelps) "The first of these odes is addressed to the Æolian lyre, which it emulates in the enchanting softness, ravishing flow, and solemn tones of melody. A severe critic . . . . would censure the sentiment which represents the Loves as dancing to the sound of this lyre. Such an instrument as the Æolian harp, which is altogether uncertain and irregular, must be very ill adapted to the dance, which is one continued regular movement."

The same reviewer, with more truth, suggests that l. 20 ought to mean that the lyre (rather, its magic) was perching on Jove's hand.

Gray, (to Mason, and to Wharton Sept. 7, 1757) attributes this review to Francklin[1], Regius Professor of Greek at Cambridge. The blunder about the Æolian lyre, inexcusable perhaps in a Greek Professor, was not unnatural in less instructed readers. Thomson had in 1748 prepossessed the mind of the reading public with a description of what we commonly call the Æolian harp, in the *Castle of Indolence*:

> "A certain music, never known before,
> Here lulled the pensive, melancholy mind;
> Full easily obtained. Behoves no more,
> But sidelong, to the gently waving wind,
> To lay the well-tuned instrument reclined;
> From which with airy flying fingers light,
> Beyond each mortal touch the most refined,
> The god of winds drew sounds of deep delight,
> Whence, with just cause, the harp of Æolus it hight."
> (Canto I. XL.)

It was necessary however to add a note: 'This is not an invention of the author; there being in fact such an instrument called Æolus' Harp, which when placed against a little rushing or current of air, produces the effect here described.'

In the same year Thomson published an Ode on Æolus' harp, describing it in a note as the invention of Mr Oswald.

2. v. l. MS. **Transport.**

3 sq. The subject and simile, as usual with Pindar, are united. The various sources of poetry, which gives life and lustre to all it touches, are here described; its quiet majestic progress enriching every subject (otherwise dry and barren) with a pomp of diction and luxuriant harmony of numbers; and its more rapid and irresistible course, when swollen and hurried away by the conflict of tumultuous passions. Gray.

The subject, the Progress of Poesy, is not *explicitly* compared to the rush of the streams from Mount Helicon; that would be *simile*, in the ordinary sense. Pindar and Gray may be said to displace simile by

[1] The edition of the two odes of 1757 in my possession has 'Francklin 1757' in MS. on the cover. It was possibly the copy of Gray's sapient critic (vid. *infra*), unless it was that of the *quondam* printer of the *Craftsman*, who strangely enough tenanted a house which became Walpole's, on his little *demesne* of Strawberry Hill. "Can there be," says Walpole, "an odder revolution of things, than that the printer of the *Craftsman* should live in a house of mine, and that the author of the *Craftsman* should write a panegyric on a house of mine?" "Lord Bath," Mr Austin Dobson explains, "if not the actual, was at least the putative writer of most of the *Craftsman's* attacks upon Sir Robert Walpole." He wrote, in part, a praise of Strawberry Hill in verse.

metaphor, which is *implied* simile. The Greek tragedians were apt to pass from the one to the other; thus in the Choephoroe (246 sq.) Æschylus makes Orestes call on Zeus to behold 'the brood bereft of their parent eagle' etc. and then add 'so mayst thou see me and Electra' etc., though he has *identified*, or as Gray would say *united*, the persons and the simile already. The reverse passage from simile to metaphor is seen in the Ajax of Sophocles (167 sq.) where the detractors of Ajax are first explicitly compared to flocks of clamorous birds, and then it is said of them that they dread the mighty vulture and would cower still and dumb if he should appear.

Helicon. Gray does not of course adopt, although he helps us to account for, the common error of the Elizabethans who made Helicon a fountain, instead of a mountain, in Boeotia.

5. **laughing**, a bolder and better translation than 'smiling' of the epithet 'ridens' as applied to flowers, as in Virgil, *Ecl.* IV. 20, Mixtaque *ridenti* colocasia fundet *acantho.*

6. The turn here is very like his favourite Green's:

"And mounting in loose robes the skies
Shed light and fragrance as she flies." *Spleen* l. 79.

which Mitford compares.

8. **Deep, majestic.** Pope (compared by Wakefield) Ode on S. Cecilia's Day l. 11: "The *deep, majestic* solemn organs blow."

Perhaps also, as Mitford suggests, there is some recollection of

"Pour *the full tide* of eloquence *along,*
Serenely pure, and yet divinely *strong.*"—
in Pope's Imitations of Horace, *Ep.* II. ii. ll. 171, 172.

10. Gray must certainly here have had Horace's description of Pindar in mind: *Odes* IV. 2. (5—8).

"*Monte decurrens velut amnis*, imbres
quem super notas aluere ripas,
fervet immensusque ruit profundo
Pindarus ore."

["As when a river, swollen by sudden showers
O'er its known banks from some steep mountain pours,
So in profound, unmeasurable song
The deep-mouth'd Pindar, foaming, pours along." Francis.]

11. **With torrent rapture see it pour** MS.

12. **rebellow**. The equivalent, for Dryden and Pope, of the Latin *reboare.*

13. Power of harmony to calm the turbulent sallies of the soul.

The thoughts are borrowed from the first Pythian of Pindar.' Gray; who adds on l. 20, 'This is a weak imitation of some incomparable lines in the same Ode.'

20. **Perching**. Perhaps Gray had Gilbert West's version of Pindar before him:

"*Perch'd* on the sceptre of th' Olympic King."

A literal translation of the opening lines of the first Pythian, will best enable the reader to measure Gray's obligation to Pindar:

"O golden lyre, joint treasure of Apollo and the dark-tressed Muses, whom the dancers' step ushering in the festive joy obeys, the singers too are guided by thy notes (cf. *infr.* l. 25), whenever, set-a-trill, thou workest the preambles of the choir-leading overtures; moreover thou quenchest the barbèd lightning of ever-flowing fire: and the eagle sleeps on the sceptre of Zeus, drooping on either side the swift pinions,—that prince of birds—whene'er thou sheddest o'er his curvèd head a swart cloud, sweet barrier of his eyelids; and he, slumbering heaves his supple back, subdued by thy vibrations. For e'en headstrong Arês (cf. l. 17 sq.), leaving far away his sharp-pointed spears, melts his heart in trance, and thy shafts soothe the souls of gods, through the skill of Latona's son, and of the deep-zoned Muses."

14. "A soft and *solemn-breathing* sound." Milton, *Comus* 555.

15. **shell**; the equivalent in English poetry to the χέλυς in Greek, and *testudo* in Latin. The name was given to the lyre from the myth of its invention by Hermes out of a tortoise-shell, as described in the Hymn to Hermes (ll. 25 sq.) attributed to Homer.

17. That Thrace was the domain of Ares or Mars is a notion by some traced to the warlike characters of the inhabitants, as old as the *Odyssey* (VIII. 361) and a commonplace of Greek and Latin Poetry. As Phelps remarks, Chaucer, *Knightes Tale* ll. 1114 *sq.*, has splendidly described 'the grete temple of Mars in Trace.'

18. **fury**. Like Jehu the son of Nimshi, Ares drives *furiously*. It is perhaps Jehu that suggests 'fury' to Gray here. Note that as Homer uses ἵπποι (horses) to include the 'car' so Gray conversely uses 'car' to include the horses.

19. Already Collins had represented Valour as subdued through the power of song, by Mercy

"Who oft *with songs*, divine to hear
Winn'st from his fatal grasp the spear,
And hid'st in wreaths of flowers his bloodless sword."

Ode to Mercy ll. 4—7.

Here note also that just before this Gray has said to the shell:

"the sullen Cares
And frantic Passions hear thy soft controul."

as Collins had written of Music (*Passions* ll. 3, 4):

"The passions oft, to hear her shell,
Thronged around her magic cell";

and, lastly, in structure Gray's *Progress of Poesy* bears a marked resemblance to Collins' *Ode to Simplicity*. By *Simplicity* Collins means the voice of nature and genuine emotion expressed in poetry, and like Gray he describes how this genuine poetry fled first from Greece to Rome and then from Rome, with the decline of freedom; unlike Gray, he does not attempt to trace the course of Poetry in England, his theme being more limited; yet like Gray he ends with his own modest aspirations as a poet.

21. Pindar's ἀρχὸς οἰωνῶν, Pythian I. 7. In the *Phœnix and Turtle* (published with Shakespeare's name in 1601) we have

"Every fowl of *tyrant* wing
Save the eagle, *feather'd king*."

22. 'In one of the recesses of the Gallery at Strawberry Hill stood one of the finest surviving pieces of Greek sculpture, the Boccapadugli eagle, found in the precincts of the Baths of Caracalla.' Austin Dobson's *Walpole*, p. 221.

Walpole says "Mr Gray has drawn the 'flagging wing,'" not, I think, meaning that this piece of sculpture suggested the expression, though Gray knew it well, Walpole having bought it in 1745.

23. **dark.** **black** MS.

25 sq. Power of harmony to produce all the graces of motion in the body. Gray.

26. Milton, *Lycidas* 33 '*Tempered* to the oaten flute,' and P. Fletcher, *Purple Island* IX. 111 '*Tempering* their sweetest notes unto thy lay.' Luke.

27. **Idalia's.** Idalia or Idalium a town in Cyprus, where Venus was worshipped.

velvet-green. 'An epithet or metaphor drawn from Nature ennobles Art; an epithet or metaphor drawn from Art degrades Nature.' Johnson.

Mitford quotes:

"At length a fair and spacious *green* he spide
Like calmest waters, plain; like *velvet*, soft."

Fairfax, *Tasso* XIII. 38, [Fairfax has no voucher for the expression in his original].

Also Shakespeare, 'Make boot upon the summer's *velvet* buds.' *Hen. V.* I. 2 [194].

And Young, *Love of Fame* [1725] Sat. v.

"She rears her flowers, and spreads her *velvet-green.*"

Mitford says "Johnson appears by his criticism to have supposed it first introduced by Gray. It was numbered, however, among the absurd expressions of Pope, by the authors of the *Alexandriad* (some of the heroes of the Dunciad)."

30. **antic.** *Macbeth* IV. I. 130:

> "I'll charm the air to give a sound,
> While you perform your *antic* round."

Where Dr Wright remarks that "the word is spelt, as usual, 'antique' in the Folios. Its modern sense of 'grotesque' is probably derived from the remains of ancient sculpture rudely imitated and caricatured by mediæval artists, and from the figures in Masques and Antimasques dressed in ancient costume, particularly satyrs and the like." By *antic* here Gray means quaint, but not ungraceful.

Sport, Sports MS.

31. This line in rhythm is certainly reminiscent of *L'Allegro*. Phelps.

34. **in cadence, the cadence** MS., 'beating' would then be transitive.

35. "Μαρμαρυγὰς θηεῖτο ποδῶν· θαύμαζε δὲ θυμῷ."

Homer *Od.* Θ [8. 265]. Gray.

> "[they *with feet that seemed*
> *To twinkle as they moved,* beat the hard ground.
> Odysseus gazed and marvelled at the sight."
>
> *Earl of Carnarvon.*]

Gray gets the word 'many-twinkling' from Thomson *Spring*, l. 158, [1728]

> "not a breath
> Is heard to quiver through the closing woods,
> Or rustling turn the *many-twinkling leaves*
> Of aspin tall."

But Gray never acknowledged any obligation to *that* source. The word is nevertheless one of the *rough felicities* of Thomson; though Johnson (on Gray) protests against it: 'we may say,' he remarks 'many spotted' but scarcely 'many spotting.' Lyttelton though his beloved Thomson perhaps invented the word, yet seems to have been surprised at it in Gray; and to his objections, Walpole, obviously supposing that Gray got it directly from Homer, writes, "As Greek as the expression is, it struck Mrs Garrick, and she says, on that whole picture, that Mr Gray is the only poet who ever understood dancing," (to Lyttelton, Aug. 25, 1757). Mrs Garrick (Violette) was an authority; she had been a dancer by profession. As the word serves Gray to translate one classic phrase, it serves Keble to translate another:

"When up some woodland dale we catch
The *many-twinkling smile* of ocean."
(*Christian Year*, 2nd Sunday after Trinity),

after the
ποντίων τε κυμάτων
ἀνήριθμον γέλασμα

of Æschylus *P.V.* 89.

36. Compare the following stanza of a poem by Barton Booth, in his *Life*, written in 1718, published 1733

"Now to a *slow and melting* air she moves
So like in air, in shape, in mien,
She passes for the Paphian queen;
The Graces all around her play,
The wond'ring gazers die away.
Whether her *easy body* bend
Or her fair *bosom heave* with sighs;
Whether her *graceful arms extend*,
Or gently fall, or slowly rise;
Or *returning or advancing*,
Swimming round, or sidelong glancing,
Strange force of motion that subdues the soul."
Mitford.

37. "For wheresoe'er she turn'd her face, they bow'd."
Dryden, *Flower and Leaf* l. 191. Mitford.

41. "Λάμπει δ' ἐπὶ πορφυρέῃσι
Παρείῃσι φῶς ἔρωτος."
Phrynichus apud Athenaeum, [XIV. 604 *a*.] Gray.

Given as one line thus in the Tauchnitz text of Athenæus

"Λάμπει δ' ἐπὶ πορφυρέαις παρῇσι φῶς ἔρωτος."

[And on his roseate cheeks there gleams the light of love.]

It was, as we learn from Athenæus (*Ib.* 564 *f.*) a description of the youthful Troïlus. This Phrynichus is the early Tragic poet, in his time the chorus still held the principal place, and the lyric character (as seen in the quotation) preponderated in the drama. Wakefield further compares Virgil, *Æn.* I. 590:

"lumenque juventae
Purpureum, et laetos oculis afflarat honores."

[Venus had breathed on her son the purple light of youth, and the grace of gladsome eyes.] They add that Ovid more than once uses 'purpureus' as an Epithet of 'Amor.'

42 sq. To compensate the real and imaginary ills of life, the Muse was given to Mankind by the same Providence that sends the Day by its chearful presence to dispel the gloom and terrors of the Night. Gray.

52. **MSS. readings.**

> "**Till fierce Hyperion from afar**
> **Pours on their scatter'd rear his etc.**
> **Hurls at their flying rear etc.**
> **Hurls o'er their scatter'd rear etc.**
> shadowy
> **Till o'er from far**
> **Hyperion hurls around his etc.**"

[I give these on the faith of Mitford.]

52. "Or seen the morning's well-appointed star
Come marching up the eastern hills afar." Cowley.

Gray,—who has condensed Cowley's language here, which is (*Brutus, an Ode*, Stanza IV.):

> "One would have thought 't had heard the Morning crow,
> Or seen her well-appointed star
> Come marching up the Eastern Hill afar."

Mitford has noted that in Gray's Journal of his Tour in the Lake District [Letters to Wharton] Gray writes [under Oct. 4, 1769] 'While I was here a little shower fell, red clouds came *marching* up the hills from the east' etc.

Hyperion. The Sun-God. He is the Titan, *father* of Helios (the Sun) according to Hesiod. In Homer the name is an epithet of Helios, but as he gives him also the *patronymic* ὑπεριονίδης he sanctions the same myth. Some ancients derived Hyperion from ὑπὲρ ἰὼν, he that moves above, but the quantity of the ῑ is against this explanation. Liddell and Scott explain the Homeric Hyperion as a shortened form of the patronymic Ὑπεριονίων. The Hyperion of Keats is, after Hesiod, of that older race of Gods, who fell with Cronos (or Saturn) supplanted by Zeus. Gray, though he of course knew better, follows usage in pronouncing Hypérion, not Hyperíon, both here and in *Hymn to Ignorance* l. 12. Shakespeare's 'Hypérion to a satyr' (*Hamlet* I. 2. 140) or 'Hypérion's curls' (*Ib.* III. 4. 56), and his invariable accentuation of the name elsewhere, gave this pronunciation a vogue which it would have been pedantic to contradict. Yet Akenside, Gray's contemporary, pronounced, as Mant observes, with the *i* long, *Hymn to the Naiads* l. 46; but Akenside has been accused of pedantry. Mitford produces two more exceptions to the customary usage of English poets; one from Drummond of Hawthornden (a man of much learning) (1585—1649):

> "That Hyperion far beyond his bed
> Doth see our lions ramp, our roses spread";

the other from Gilbert West's *Pindar* (1749):

> "Then Hyperīon's son, pure fount of day
> Did to his children the strange tale reveal."
> (*Ol.* VIII. 22).

(this is simply a rendering of Ἀπόλλων, but a version from the classics must avoid false quantities).

'lucida tela diei' (Lucretius I. 147; VI. 40) which Munro, after Gray renders '*glittering shafts* of day." Lowell, as Mr Rolfe remarks, has imitated Gray and Lucretius:

> "'Tis from these heights alone your eyes
> The advancing spears of day can see
> Which o'er the eastern hill-tops rise,
> To break your long captivity." *Above and Below.*

Dr Bradshaw notes that Gray twice elsewhere rhymes 'far' with war: *Education and Government*, ll. 46, 47, and the *Translation from Statius* ll. 31, 32, also that the expression 'glittering front of war' had been used in *Agrippina* l. 94.

54—65. Extensive influence of poetic Genius over the remotest and most uncivilized nations: its connection with liberty, and the virtues that naturally attend on it. (See the Erse, Norwegian and Welsh fragments, the Lapland and American songs.) Gray.

Gray here refers to James Macpherson's *Fragments of Ancient Poetry collected in the Highlands of Scotland and translated from the Galic or Erse language*, published at Edinburgh in June, 1760. It is noteworthy that he here accepts these fragments as genuine. Yet in spite of his admiration of them he was from the very first puzzled; and the information which he got from Macpherson himself struck him as 'calculated to deceive, yet not cunning enough to do it cleverly.' The publication of the Epic 'Fingal' in 6 books (Dec. 1761) should have increased his scepticism; but it seems on the contrary to have made his admiration get the better of his doubts. On February 17, 1763 he could write 'Mr Howe would there see that Imagination dwelt many hundred years ago in all her pomp on the cold and barren mountains of

Scotland. The truth (I believe) is that without any respect of climates she reigns in all nascent societies of men, where the necessities of life force everyone to think and act much for himself.'

After this there is a loud silence on this subject in Gray's correspondence, and it is noteworthy that in the very next month (March, 1763) Macpherson published 'Temora,' another Epic in *eight* Books, which was probably too much for Gray. This note of 1768 indicates, I think, that Gray continued to believe that there were some genuine elements in Macpherson's earliest publication, to confirm his thesis expressed both in this place of the *Progress of Poesy*, and in the letter above cited, that the Imagination is vigorous in 'nascent societies of men.' Strangely enough, Gray betrays no suspicion that his own 'Bard' had anything to do with the inspiration of Macpherson. See Introductory note there, and note on l. 20 *ib.*

For the reference Gray makes to 'the Norwegian and Welsh fragments,' see Introductory notes to Norse and Welsh Poems, *infra.*

54. Extra anni solisque vias. Virgil [*Aen.* VI. 797.]

"Tutta lontana dal camin del sole."

Petrarch, Canzon II. Gray.

It is Canzone I. § 3, l. 3 of the *Sonetti sopra vari Argomenti* in the edition before me; the context is nearer Gray than usual :

"Una parte del mondo è che si giace
Mai sempre in ghiaccio ed in gelate nevi
Tutta lontana etc."

"[A clime there is that lies
Ever in ice and hardened snows congealed
All from the solar road remote.]"

Gray's is an improvement on Pope's expression 'walk.'

"His soul proud science never taught to stray
Far as the *solar walk*, or milky way."

(*Essay on Man* I. 102).

Dryden has 'solar walk' in *Threnodia Augustalis* stanza 12, and it was by this time perhaps a commonplace.

55. See *n.* on l. 57 *infr.*

57. **Buried** with **shivering** in the Margin. MS.

Chill with **dull** in Margin. Ib.

'Buried' was perhaps rejected as obscure to all but scholars, for Gray was doubtless thinking of Virgil, *Georg.* III. 376.

"Ipsi in defossis specubus secura sub altâ
Otia agunt terrâ."

[Themselves in caverns deep sunken under earth they fleet their careless leisure. Mackail.] In fact from this place of Virgil the description ll. 54—58 is epitomised. Thus ll. 354, 355,

(Sed jacet aggeribus niveis informis et alto
Terra gelu late, septemque adsurgit in ulnas.)

l. 366 (Stiriaque impexis induruit horrida barbis—) and l. 383 (Gens pecudum fulvis velatur corpora saetis) combine to make up the picture in Gray's line 55.

The substitution of 'dull' for 'chill' is probably motived by 'Chili' in l. 59. 'laid' is in agreement with 'She' (the Muse). Cf. the note on 'reclined,' *Ode on Spring* l. 17.

62. **feather-cinctur'd.** Cf. after Mitford,

"Such of late
Columbus found the American, so girt
With feathered cincture, naked else and wild
Among the trees on isles and woody shores."

Milton, *Par. Lost* IX. 1116.

Also Spenser, *Faerie Queene*, III. 12. 8.

dusky.

"Till the freed Indians in their native groves
Reap their own fruits and woo their sable loves."

Pope, *Windsor Forest* 410.

Gray's epithet, as Dr Warton observes, is the more correct. Cf. *Education and Government* l. 105. Mitford.

64. 'This use of the verb plural after the first substantive is in Pindar's manner,' says Wakefield, quoting *Nem.* X. 91, which is not apposite, and *Pyth.* 4. 318, an instance with plural participle, τὸν μὲν Ἐχίονα, κεχλάδοντας ἥβᾳ, τὸν δ' Ἔρυτον,—Echion, *shouting in their* pride of youth, and Erytus—also Hom. *Il.* V. 774 (a dual) ἦχι ῥοὰς Σιμόεις συμβάλλετον ἠδὲ Σκαμανδρος (lit. where Simois join their two floods and Scamander).

Mitford quotes Dugald Stewart, *Philosophy of the Human Mind* I. 505. "I cannot help remarking the effect of the solemn and uniform flow of verse in this exquisite stanza, in retarding the pronunciation of the reader, so as to arrest his attention to every successive picture, till it has time to produce its proper impression."

64, 65. Shame, used in the sense of αἰδώς, that feeling in the warrior which makes him studious to shun disgrace. Perhaps Gray's association of ideas here is suggested by Milton's

"the unconquerable will,
* * * * * * * *
And courage never to submit or yield."
Par. Lost I. 106—108.

66 sq. Progress of Poetry from Greece to Italy, and from Italy to England. Chaucer was not unacquainted with the writings of Dante or of Petrarch. The Earl of Surrey and Sir Thomas Wyatt had travelled in Italy, and formed their taste there. Spenser imitated the Italian writers; Milton improved on them: but this school expired soon after the Restoration, and a new one arose on the French model, which has subsisted ever since. Gray.

The classic names in this stanza are not inserted at random. The oracle of Apollo at Delphi is mentioned first, as the shrine of the God of Poesy. It was also in a sense the *focus* of a poetry of the severest and most religious type: that of Hesiod for example and Pindar. Thence we pass to the islands of the Ægean to Delos, the mythic birthplace of Apollo where Hymns were yearly sung in his honour, to Lesbos (Sappho and Alcæus), Ceos (Simonides) etc.; the Ilissus, again, represents for us Athens, as the scene in which dramatic poetry reached its perfection (Æschylus, Sophocles, Euripides); the Maeander recalls the poetry of Asia Minor, from the Ionian Coast of which the *Iliad* and *Odyssey*, according to the general belief both of ancient and modern times, first came to Greece proper.

66. **woods** etc. "Dr Chandler flirts at Gray for having clothed 'Delphi's barren steep' with woods." Walpole to Mason, April 8, 1776.

69. **amber.** Gray does not, I think, get this epithet of the Maeander from any classical source. The Maeander is in fact a muddy river, and indeed the sinuosities of its course are attributed by Pliny to its fertilising mud deposits. The original source of this epithet of a river is probably for English poets Virg. *Georg.* III. 520 *Purior electro* campum petit amnis, said of a clear mountain stream; though perhaps Virgil got it from Callimachus, *Cer.* 29:

"—τὸ δ' ὥστ' ἀλέκτρινον ὕδωρ
'Εξ ἀμαρᾶν ἀνέθυε."

Milton, *Paradise Lost* III. 359:

"And where the River of Bliss, through midst of Heav'n
Rolls o'er Elysian flow'rs *her amber stream.*"

Cf. also *Par. Reg.* III. 288, 289:

"There Susa by Choaspes, *amber stream,*
The drink of none but kings."

That Milton follows antiquity in as far as he associates with the word some notion of *pureness* is clear from both these passages, but especially from the second; for he refers to the notion (Pliny, *H. N.* 31, c. 3) that the Parthian kings drank only from this river and another (cf. Tibullus, 4. 1. 140 *regia lympha* Choaspes). Whether he has altogether correctly interpreted antiquity will be questioned by those who follow Servius on Virgil, in explaining 'electrum' of the *metal* of that name. The word is Greek, and there is the same ambiguity in that language as to its meaning. However Milton has a different meaning for 'amber' to Gray's, who has received it from him, but probably uses it of colour, 'yellow,' as 'flavus' was applied to the Tiber, and to the Pactolus. Indeed it might almost seem that he had transferred to the Maeander this epithet of the Pactolus (which flows into the same Ægean), a river so coloured by the sands it carried, that legend affirmed that it ran with gold. Dr Chandler, in his 'Travels' in Greece, 'flirts,' says Walpole, 'at Gray for having converted Maeander's muddy waves into amber, as if amber did not poetically imply the same' (to Mason, April 8, 1776). Not with all poets, as we have seen. Professor Hales (*Folia Litteraria* p. 232) gives the reason why the Maeander is associated with poetry, 'It was a famous haunt of swans, and the swan was a favourite bird with the Greek and Latin writers—one to whose sweet singing they perpetually allude.'

70. **lingering lab'rinths**. Cf. Ovid, *Heroides* IX. 55:

"Maeandros, *toties qui terris errat in isdem*,
Qui *lassas* in se saepe retorquet aquas."

And the description in *Metamorphoses* VIII. 162 sq. rendered by Tasso, *Ger. Lib.* XVI. 8, who again is rendered by Fairfax:

"As through his channel crook'd Meander glides
With turns and twines, and rolls now to and fro,
Whose streams run forth there to the salt sea sides,
Here back return, and to their spring-ward go."

70—71. Milton suggests "by slow Maeander's margent green" as the haunt of the nymph Echo. Phelps.

73. 'In our little journey up to the Grande Chartreuse, I do not remember to have gone ten paces without an exclamation that there was no restraining: not a precipice, not a torrent, not a cliff, *but is pregnant with religion and poetry*.' Gray to West (Nov. 16 N. S. 1739). This thought never left his mind: it finds its first expression in verse in the Latin ode he inscribed in the album of this same Grande Chartreuse on his homeward journey (1741) 'O Tu severi Relligio loci':

"O thou! the Spirit mid these scenes abiding,
Whate'er the name by which thy power be known,
Surely no mean divinity presiding
These native streams, these ancient forests own;
And here on pathless rock or mountain height,
Amid the torrent's ever-echoing roar,
The headlong cliff, the wood's eternal night,
We feel the Godhead's awful presence more
Than if resplendent 'neath the cedar beam,
By Phidias wrought his golden image rose," &c.
(Tr. by R. E. E. Warburton. See *Elegy* ad fin.).

73. Adopted, as Bradshaw notes, by Keble, *Christian Year*, 3rd Sunday in Lent:

"Fly from the 'old poetic' fields
Ye paynim shadows dark!"

76. **Murmur'd a celestial sound.** MS.

80. Cf. *Ode for Music*, l. 6.

green lap. Statius, *Thebais* IV. 786:

"At puer in gremio vernae telluris," &c.

Milton, *Song on May Morning*, l. 4:

"The flowery May, who from her *green lap* throws
The yellow cowslip and the pale primrose." Mitford.

85. **Nature's darling.** Shakespeare. (Gray.) Mitford quotes (for the expression only) Cleveland [1613—1658]:

"Here lies within this stony shade
Nature's darling; whom she made
Her fairest model, her brief story,
In him heaping all her glory."

86, 87. The two lines in Gray, says Mitford, are the same as two in Sandys' Ovid (*Metam.* IV. 515):

"the child
Stretch'd forth its little arms, and on him smil'd."

The expression is the same, but the context is quite different; the babe in Ovid stretches forth its arms to its frenzied father *who dashes it to pieces*. The commonplaces of classic poetry which influenced Gray here are Horace III. 4. 20, (the infant Horace sleeping, covered with bay and myrtle by the doves, in a wild scene, 'non sine dis animosus infans, '*a dauntless child* by the grace of heaven') and 'Incipe, parve puer, risu cognoscere matrem,' Virgil, *Ecl.* IV. 62 (said to the infant son of Pollio of whom heroic things were expected).

89. **pencil.** The pencil is *properly* the painter's brush, and the sense of 'an instrument for writing without ink' is later. Cf. to Bentley, l. 4.

90. "How nature paints her colours." Milton, *Par. Lost* v. 24. Luke.

91. Mitford compares from Young's *Resignation*:

"Nature, which favours to the few
All art beyond, imparts
To him presented at his birth
The key of human hearts."

Milton (*Comus* l. 13 cited by Mitford), has 'golden key' but with a quite different context. Gray writes to Wharton Sep. 7, 1757, 'Dr Akenside criticizes opening a *source* with a *key*.' Where Mitford notes 'But Akenside in his *Ode on Lyric Poetry*, "While I so late *unlock* thy purer *springs*." In *Pleasures of Imagination* Book I., "I *unlock the springs* of ancient wisdom." Akenside's objection is to the 'key.' But even on the *terrain* of the minute criticism of the time he is scarcely right. It is possible both to lock and unlock waters with a key.

93. **Horror. Terror** MS.

94. πηγὰς δακρύων. Soph. *Ant.* 803. Mitford.

97. This alludes to Milton's own picture of himself (*Par. Lost* VII. 12 sq.):

"Up led by thee
Into the Heaven of Heavens I have presumed,
An earthly guest, and drawn empyreal air."

Earlier he had written *Elegy* 5. 15 sq. (anno aetatis 20):

"Iam mihi mens liquidi raptatur in ardua caeli
Perque vagas nubes corpore liber eo;
Perque umbras, perque antra feror, penetralia vatum
Et mihi fana patent inferiora Deum.
Intuiturque [*sic*] animus toto quid agatur Olympo
Nec fugiunt oculos Tartara caeca meos;
Quid tam grande sonat distento spiritus ore?
Quid parit haec rabies, quid sacer iste furor?"
["I mount, and undepressed by cumbrous clay
Through cloudy regions win my easy way;
Rapt through poetic shadowy haunts I fly;
The shrines all open to my dauntless eye;

My spirit searches all the realms of light
And no Tartarean gulfs elude my sight
But this ecstatic trance—this glorious storm
Of inspiration—what will it perform?"

Cowper.] From Mitford.

96. **Flammantia maenia mundi.** Lucret. [I. 74]. So notes Gray, borrowing for the religious Milton the praise of the enemy of religion Epicurus, whom 'neither story of gods nor thunderbolts nor heaven with threatening roar could quell, but only stirred up the more the eager courage of his soul, filling him with desire to be the first to burst the fast bars of nature's portals. Therefore the living force of his soul gained the day; on he passed far beyond *the flaming walls of the world* and traversed throughout in mind and spirit the immeasurable universe; whence he returns a conqueror' &c. (Munro's version of Lucret. *ad loc.*) Munro explains the expression as 'the fiery orb of ether that forms the outer circuit of the world': and refers to Lucr. V. 457—470 for a description of it. He points out also that Milton has imitated Lucretius in his account of 'the etherial quintessence of heaven' (*Par. Lost* III. 716) as flying upward from earth, part turning to stars, while 'the rest in circuit *walls* this Universe' (l. 721).

99. 'For the spirit of the living creature was in the wheels. And above the firmament that was over their heads, was the likeness of a throne, as the appearance of a sapphire stone. This was the appearance of the [likeness of the] glory of the Lord. Ezek. i. 20, 26, 28.' Gray. Cf.

"[That undisturbèd song of pure concent]
Aye sung before the sapphire-coloured throne."

Milton, *At a Solemn Music*, l. 7.

and *Par. Lost* VI. 738;

"Over their heads a crystal firmament,
Whereon a sapphire throne, inlaid with pure
Amber, and colours of the showery arch."

Cf. Ib. 772. Mitford.

100, 101. "Dark with excessive bright thy skirts appear,
Yet dazzle Heaven, that brightest Seraphim
Approach not, but with both wings veil their eyes."

Par. Lost, III. 380 sq.

102. "'Οφθαλμῶν μὲν ἄμερσε· δίδου δ' ἡδεῖαν ἀοιδήν."

Hom. *Od.* [VIII. 64]. Gray.

This is said of Demodocus, the minstrel in the halls of Alcinous:

"Him the Muse
Loved greatly, but to him both good and ill
Had granted: *for of sight she robbed his eyes*
But with sweet song she blessed him."

(Lord Carnarvon.)

There was great variety of choice in classic legend or literature for a comparison with Milton: he associates himself (*Par. Lost* III. 35, 36) with

"Blind Thamyris, and blind Maeonides,
And Tiresias and Phineus, prophets old."

Johnson says "Gray's account of Milton's blindness, if we suppose it caused by study in the formation of his poem, a supposition surely allowable, is poetically true, and happily imagined." Mason, on the other hand, tells us that "this has been condemned as a false thought; and more worthy of an Italian poet than Mr Gray." Count Algarotti, he says, admired it; but Algarotti was an Italian. He would admire it himself, he adds, "had it not the peculiar misfortune to encounter a fact too well known. Milton himself has told us...in his sonnet to Cyriack Skinner, that he lost his eye-sight

'overply'd
In Liberty's Defence, his noble task
Whereof all Europe rings from side to side.'"

He subsequently added a communication from Mr Brand of East Dereham, containing 'a very similar hyperbole' in a commentary on Plato's *Phaedo*, written by Hermias (a Christian philosopher of the 2nd century), and quoted by Bayle—the legend that "Homer keeping some sheep near the tomb of Achilles, obtained, by his offerings and supplications, a sight of that Hero; who appeared to him surrounded by so much glory that Homer could not bear the splendour of it, and was blinded by the sight." Mason rejoices that this disproves the notion that Gray's was a modern *concetto* in the Italian manner, but is convinced that 'he had never seen, or at least attended to this Greek fragment.'

102. "in aeternam clauduntur lumina noctem" (of Orodes).

Verg. *Aen.* X. 746. Wakefield.

"And closed her lids, at last in endless night."

Dryden, as quoted by Mitford[1].

105. **Of etherial race.** The exact expression is Pope's (*Il.* XI. 80),

[1] With no further reference.

as Mitford points out, but Gray's original is, perhaps as Wakefield notes,

"currum, geminosque jugales
Semine ab aetherio, spirantes naribus ignem."

Verg. *Aen.* VII. 280 [a car and two coursers of etherial seed, with nostrils breathing flame].

106. "Hast thou cloathed his neck with thunder?"

Job [xxxix. 19.]

This verse, and the foregoing, are meant to express the stately march and sounding energy of Dryden's Rhymes. Gray.

This answers by anticipation, Johnson's criticism "the *car* of Dryden, with his *two coursers*, has nothing in it peculiar; it is a car in which any other rider may be placed." Gray expresses himself concisely; by rhymes he means rhyming lines, and refers principally to the heroic couplet (hence '*two* coursers') in the management of which Dryden excelled. Johnson himself quotes, as final, the lines of Pope, which Gray had in mind here:

"Waller was smooth; but Dryden taught to join
The varying verse, the *full resounding line*,
The long majestic march, and energy divine."

Ib. **long-resounding**

"Eager, on rapid sleds,
Their vigorous youth in bold contention wheel
The *long-resounding* course."

Thomson, *Winter* 775 [ed. 1742].

And Hymn 77

"to the deep organ join
The *long-resounding* voice." (Mitford.)

107. From Gray's note, *infra*, we may conjecture that he passes here to Dryden in the special character of a lyric poet, after describing him as a master of the heroic couplet.

108. **Bright-eyed. Full-plumed** MS.

110. "Words that weep, and tears that speak." Cowley.

So Gray notes, but Mr Gosse says "the line is the twentieth in 'The Prophet' in *The Mistresse*, 1647, and runs thus:

'Tears which shall understand, and speak.'"

Dugald Stewart, quoted by Mitford, suggests that in Gray's line two different effects of words are indicated: "the effect of *some*, in awakening the powers of conception and imagination; and that of *others* in exciting associated emotions." (*Elem. of the Human Mind*, vol. I. p. 507).

111. Gray notes: "We have had in our language no other odes of the sublime kind, than that of Dryden on St Cecilia's Day; for Cowley, who had his merit, yet wanted judgment, style, and harmony, for such a task. That of Pope is not worthy of so great a man. Mr Mason, indeed, of late days, has touched the true chords, and with a masterly hand, in some of his choruses; above all in the last of Caractacus:

'Hark! heard ye not yon footstep dread,
[That shook the earth with thundering tread?
'Twas Death; in haste
The warrior pass'd:
High tower'd his helmèd head,
I mark'd his mail, I mark'd his shield:
I spy'd the sparkling of his spear,
I saw his giant arm the falchion wield;
Wide wav'd the bick'ring blade and fir'd the angry air[1].'"]

Gray makes no mention of Milton's *Nativity Ode*, as it is commonly called; was it because he did not consider it an ode, or because it did not seem to him sublime? Again, Dryden's Verses on the Death of Anne Killigrew are in the form of an ode,—and the opening stanza, though the rest are a lamentable descent, is perhaps the one piece of Dryden's writing which our own generation would call *sublime*. 'Alexander's Feast,' the *second* Ode on S. Cecilia's Day, to which of course Gray refers, is structurally a fine poem, but if it ever had the power to kindle emotion it has lost it for ever; the words 'burn' no longer.

From the Odes to Obscurity and Oblivion which attacked Gray and Mason, Gray himself has given a quotation (to Wharton, June 1760) which parodies this stanza:

"It tells me, what I never heard before, for (speaking of himself) the Author says, tho' he has

'Nor the Pride, nor Self-opinion
That possess the happy Pair,
Each of Taste the fav'rite Minion,
Prancing thro' the desert Air;
Yet shall he mount, with classick housings grac'd,
By help mechanic of equestrian block;
And all unheedful of the Critick's mock
Spur his light Courser o'er the bounds of Taste.'"

[1] But Mason first wrote:

"Courage was in his van, and Conquest in his rear,"

cf. ll. 61, 64 of *The Bard*.

The writers were Lloyd and Colman, who were soon ashamed of their impertinence. Nevertheless, as Prof. Dowden tells me, in Dublin, 1768, was published an edition of Gray's Poems (probably unauthorized), which contained the *Long Story*, and this burlesque of *The Bard*, the last page representing the rider of Pegasus tumbling from the cliffs and following his wig into mid-air.

112, 113. Probably as true a rhyme to Gray, as it was when the version of 'Veni Creator' was written:

> "Praise to thine Eternal Merit,
> Father, Son, and Holy Spirit."
>
> Book of Common Prayer (Ordination Service).

The pronunciation 'sperrit' still survives, and within living memory was not vulgar.

115. Διὸς πρὸς ὄρνιχα θεῖον. [Pindar] *Olymp.* II. [86—88]. Pindar compares himself to that bird, and his enemies to ravens that croak and clamour in vain below, while it pursues its flight regardless of their noise. Gray.

The words Gray quotes follow close on those he has chosen for the motto of the two Odes. Though Pindar does not name his enemies he indicates that they were *two*; (commonly explained to be Simonides and Bacchylides); Gray who in penning this note, could scarcely have been oblivious of his own *two* assailants, abstains from pointing the allusion. Mitford compares Spenser, *F. Q.* V. 4. 42:

> "Like to an Eagle, in his kingly pride
> Soring through his wide empire of the aire
> To weather his brode sailes."

117. **deep.** With some comparison of the air to a sea; but also some notion of immeasurable height as Euripides, *Medea* 1297 *πτηνὸν ἄραι σῶμ' ἐς αἰθέρος βάθος*, (into the deep of air wing her flight upward), and cf. Shelley 'Skylark' l. 9

> "The blue *deep* thou wingest."

118. Dugald Stewart (*Philosophy of the Human Mind* p. 486) says that "Gray in describing the infant reveries of poetical genius, has fixed with exquisite judgment on that class of our conceptions which are derived from *visible* objects." Mitford.

> **"Yet when they first were opened on the day**
> **Before his visionary eyes would run"** MS.

119. **forms: shapes** MS.

120. **orient,** i.e. brilliant and lustrous, as with the rays of the rising sun; Dr Phelps suggests, less probably I think, "because the

most beautiful jewels came from the east." The word does indeed, as might be expected, occur in connection with jewels, e.g.

"For of o [one] perle, fine orientall,
Her white crowne was imaked all."
Chaucer, *Leg. of Good Women*, Prol.

"Sette with signes called cifers of fine gold, the which were set with great and *oriental perles.*" Hall, *Henry VIII*, an. 12.

"He chose as many as made a faire chaine, which for their... *orientness*, were very faire and rare."
Hakluyt, *Voyages*, vol. III. p. 269.

This third passage (they are all from Richardson) seems to fix the meaning of the other two to 'bright and shining,' even for gems. Cf. Spenser, *Hymne in Honour of Beautie*, l. 79:

"the blossomes of the field
Which are arayd with much more *orient* hew."

It is a favourite word with Milton; e.g.

"Ten thousand banners rise into the air
With *orient colours* waving." *P. L.*, I. 546.

Dr Phelps quotes also,

"His *orient* liquor in a crystal glass." *Comus*, l. 65.

unborrowed, &c. *though* 'orient'. Bradshaw well compares Wordsworth (*Stanzas on the Picture of Peele Castle in a Storm*):

"*The light that never was on sea or land,*
The consecration and *the poet's dream.*"

121 sq. Compare what has been said on the concluding lines of the *Ode on Spring*, *Hymn to Adversity* and *Elegy;* and the Alcaic Ode quoted on the last place.

122. **Yet never can he fear a vulgar fate.** MS.

XIII. THE BARD.

Mason says that the exordium of the *Bard* was finished by March 9, 1755, at which date Gray wrote to Wharton declining to publish the 'Progress of Poesy' *alone*, adding "I have two or three ideas more in my head." Of these it is probable that the fragmentary 'Vicissitude,' which follows, was one. And on the same page of Gray's common place book with the Argument for the *Bard*, given *infra*, Mason found the following:

"All that men of power can do for men of genius is to leave them at their liberty, compared to birds that, when confined to a cage, do but regret the loss of their freedom in melancholy strains, and lose the luscious wildness and happy luxuriance of their notes, which used to make the woods resound." That we have here the *nucleus* of a poem is very likely; and the place in which it is found, makes it possible that this was another of the "two or three ideas" of which Gray speaks, 'the Bard' being the third. We have only Mason's word for the date of the completion of the 'Exordium', but to Gray, on Nov. 26, 1755, he writes of "the fragment of your Welsh Ode, now just warm from your brain."

The Argument above mentioned runs thus:

"The army of Edward I. as they march through a deep valley, are suddenly stopped by the appearance of a venerable figure seated on the summit of an inacessible rock, who, with a voice more than human, reproaches the King with all the misery and desolation which he has brought on his country; foretells the misfortunes of the Norman race, and with prophetic spirit declares, that all his cruelty shall never extinguish the noble ardour of poetic genius in this island; and that men shall never be wanting to celebrate true virtue and valour in immortal strains, to expose vice and infamous pleasure, and boldly censure tyranny and oppression. His song ended, he precipitates himself from the mountain, and is swallowed up by the river that rolls at its foot."

Mason regrets that Gray has departed from this scheme in as far as he has not represented the poets as *exposing Vice and infamous Pleasure* &c.; he suggests that Gray lacked instances in English Poets; Shakespeare made Falstaff amiable, Milton denounced tyranny in *prose*, Dryden was a parasite, Pope, though he detested corruption and bribery, was a Tory, and Addison, though a Whig, was not a great poet!! Mason is scarcely successful in interpreting the workings of Gray's mind. Gray's note is a most rudimentary sketch, it does not include the ghostly chorus of the brother-bards; and it is not the difficulty but the unfitness of the effort that makes him refrain from picturing the poets as satirists of vice and tyranny. It would have been mere *bathos*, and such a threat would have had no meaning for the "ruthless king," though he might be awed by the vaguely foreshadowed horrors that awaited his descendants, and by the strange sense of a spiritual power which his barbarity could not destroy.

On Aug. 6, 1755 Gray writes to Wharton, "What did you think of the *Morceau* I sent you?" this was probably the opening of the *Bard*.

On the 21st he wrote again, "I have sent now to Stonhewer a bit more of the *prophecy* and desire him to show it you immediately; it is very rough and unpolish'd at present."

It is clear from this that the MS. which follows in the Wharton correspondence, [Egerton MSS. Brit. Mus.] comprising the whole of the *Bard* from 'She-Wolf' to the end, was not sent with this letter, and when it was received and inserted in this place of the correspondence I cannot say. It is not that sent to Stonhewer, for it is, *with* the corrections, a complete thing, at least from l. 57; the last 88 lines of the poem almost *verbatim* as we have them now. Moreover on the same 21st of August Gray wrote to Stonhewer, "I annex a piece of the Prophecy which must be true, at least, as it was wrote so many years after the event," and Mason says that this was the second Antistrophe and Epode with a few lines of the third Strophe (i.e. from l. 63 to l. 100 or thereabouts). Ten more lines were added before May, 1757 in which month Gray wrote to Mason, "Mr Parry [the blind Welsh harper] has been here [at Cambridge] and scratched out such ravishing blind harmony, such tunes of a thousand years old, with names enough to choke you, as have set all this learned body a-dancing, and inspired them with due reverence for Odikle [the *Bard*] when ever it shall appear. Mr Parry (you must know) it was that has put Odikle in motion again....You remember the 'Visions of Glory' that descended on the heights of Snowdon, and unrolled their glittering skirts so slowly." And then he adds the third Antistrophe and Epode (i.e. the conclusion of the poem) in a form which varies, as will be noted, from the final text, but almost exactly as does the Wharton MS. in its uncorrected state.

In the textual notes which follow, 'Mason MS.' and 'Wharton MS.' refer to the fragments above described.

The *Bard*, as we have seen, was printed in 1757 with the *Progress of Poesy* at Strawberry Hill, for Dodsley. It was, at this its first appearance, called *Ode II.* It had four notes, to be indicated below by the date (the rest of Gray's notes belonging to 1768), also this preface first appeared in 1757:

"The following Ode is founded on a Tradition current in Wales, that Edward the First, when he compleated the conquest of that country, ordered all the Bards, that fell into his hands, to be put to death."

Dr Phelps thinks that Gray may have found this tradition in the second volume of Carte's *History of England*, which was published in 1750. Carte asserts that Edward ordered all the bards to be hanged, as inciters to sedition, and refers to Sir J. Wynne's *History of the Gwedir Family* written in the 17th century. The edict was perhaps only directed against vagrant minstrels in general, like that of Henry IV. which was a re-enactment of it. See n. on *Long Story* l. 51. The enormous wealth of material in Welsh poetry from the reign of Edward I. to that of Elizabeth is held to prove sufficiently that neither Edward I. nor Henry IV. did much to extirpate the Welsh bards.

The reception of both Odes, but particularly of the *Bard*, was curious. Gray (to Hurd, Aug. 25, 1757) says that a peer believed the last stanza of the *Bard* related to King Charles the First and Oliver Cromwell, and that he has heard of nobody but a player and a doctor of divinity (Garrick and Warburton) that "profess their esteem for them." "O yes," he adds, "a lady of quality, a friend of Mason's, who is a great reader. She knew there was a compliment to Dryden, but never suspected there was anything said about Shakespeare or Milton, until it was explained to her; and wishes there had been titles prefixed to tell what they were about." Gray told Mason about the same time, "Mr Fox, supposing the Bard sang his song but once over, does not wonder if Edward the First did not understand him. This last criticism is somewhat unhappy, for though it had been sung a hundred times under his window, it was absolutely impossible King Edward should understand him; but that is no reason for Mr Fox, who lives almost 500 years after him. It is very well; the next thing I print shall be in Welch,—that's all." It appears from the same letter that Lord Lyttelton and Shenstone admired the poems, but wished them clearer. Walpole's admiration of them was adroitly tempered, according to circumstances. To Lyttelton he deprecates the notion that he is "an enthusiast to Mr Gray"; he even finds the second strophe of the first Ode ('Man's feeble race' &c.) *inexcusable*; he asks, about the *Bard*, "What punishment was it to Edward I. to hear that his grandson would conquer France?" and he thinks the deserted death-bed of Edward III. too common an accident of human life to be a terror worth prophesying. Gray might have retorted that, though Edward might not be scared, that was no reason why Walpole should not be impressed; that the bard's vision has a wider scope than the punishment of the King; that it was surely some Nemesis on the She-wolf of France that her native-land should be desolated by her own son, and that the miserable death of Edward III. is one of the tragic facts of history, just because a common fate of the poor and helpless befell a powerful and victorious king.

On the very same day on which Walpole thus wrote to Lyttelton, he wrote to Montagu, "You are very particular, I can tell you, in liking Gray's Odes—but you must remember that the age likes Akenside, and did like Thomson! can the same people like both?" He knew better; he had just been telling Lyttelton, the friend and admirer of Thomson, that his approbation of Gray was conclusive, and stamped a disgrace on the age which could see no beauty in the 'Odes.'

I have very little doubt that Macpherson had studied the *Bard* to purpose and returned Gray's wares upon his hands in the *Poems of Ossian*. The elaboration of structure in these poems,—impossible to reconcile with the story of their collection,—was probably due to Gray's example, e.g. 'Comala' is a dramatic poem with five persons and a chorus of Bards. And cf. on ll. 20, 28.

Mason has a note recording Gray's suggestions when "Mr Smith, the Musical Composer, and worthy pupil of Mr Handel, had once an idea of setting this Ode." The overture, Gray says, "should be so contrived as to be a proper introduction to the Ode; it might consist of two movements, the first descriptive of the horror and confusion of battle, the last a march grave and majestic, but expressing the exultation and insolent security of conquest. The movement should be composed entirely of wind instruments, except the kettle-drum heard at intervals. The *da capo* of it must be suddenly broken in upon, and put to silence by the clang of the harp in a tumultuous rapid movement, joined with the voice, and not ushered in by any symphony. The harmony may be strengthened by any other stringed instrument; but the harp should every where prevail, and form the continued running accompaniment, submitting itself to nothing but the voice." Compare with this sketch by Gray the beautiful setting of the *Bard* by Professor Villiers Stanford, who worked, as he tells me, not knowing Gray's instructions. He writes to me, "When I began the composition with a march, I thought I was inventing what ought to be there, and lo! I see I only carried out Gray's orders." Again, "The harp *does* enter with the voice without any symphony, and does 'everywhere prevail'."

"The *Bard*," says Johnson, "appears, at the first view, as Algarotti and others have remarked, an imitation of the prophecy of Nereus. Algarotti thinks it superior to its original; and if preference depends only on the imagery and animation of the two poems, his judgment is right. There is in 'the Bard' more force, more thought, and more variety."

Johnson refers to the "Pastor cum traheret" &c. of Horace (*Carm.*

I. 15), wherein Nereus, the sea-god, is represented staying with a calm the voyage of Paris as he is carrying off Helen, whilst he prophesies the war that is to follow and the doom that awaits the seducer. Gray repudiated the notion that he had imitated this, though it was early suggested by a reviewer; he wrote to Wharton (Dec. 2, 1758) "'Pastor cum traheret' was falsely laid to my charge." Johnson knew only Mason's collection, in which this letter did not appear. But Algarotti, whose letter to W. T. How, Dec. 26, 1762, *apud* Mason, Johnson had read, does not say that Gray *imitated* Horace. A comparison between the two poems was nevertheless inevitable.

4. 'Mocking the air with colours idly spread.'

Shakes. *King John* [V. I. 72]. Gray.

5. The hauberk was a texture of steel ringlets, or rings interwoven, forming a coat of mail, that sat close to the body, and adapted itself to every motion. Gray.

'Helm and hauberk,' come together, Mitford says, in *Robert of Gloucester*, Dryden (*Palamon and Arcite* iii. 602); and many times in Fairfax's Tasso.

9. 'The crested adder's pride' Dryden *Indian Queen* [III. I]. Gray.

11. *Snowdon* was a name given by the Saxons to that mountainous tract which the Welch themselves call *Craigian-eryri* [see on l. 38]: it included all the highlands of Caernarvonshire and Merionethshire, as far east as the river Conway. R. Hygden, speaking of the castle of Conway built by King Edward the First, says, 'Ad ortum amnis Conway ad clivum montis Erery'; and Matthew of Westminster (*ad ann.* 1283), 'Apud Aberconway, ad pedem montis Snowdoniae fecit erigi castrum forte.' Gray.

shaggy. Leland says that great woods clothed the different parts of the mountain in his time [1506?—1552]. *Mitford*, who cites Dyer, *Ruins of Rome* (314, 315)

"as Britannia's oaks
On Merlin's mount, or Snowdon's rugged sides,
Stand in the clouds."

If Dyer does not invent, there were, in Gray's time, oaks on the Snowdon range above the cloud-line.

Mitford also compares *Lycidas* 54 "Nor on the shaggy top of Mona high." Cf. l. 23.

13. Gilbert de Clare, surnamed the Red, Earl of Gloucester and Hertford, son-in-law to King Edward. Gray.

14. Edmond de Mortimer, Lord of Wigmore. They both were *Lords-Marchers*, whose lands lay on the borders of Wales, and probably accompanied the King in this expedition. Gray.

17, 18. **With fury pale, and pale with woe,**
Secure of fate, the Poet stood

Gray to Wharton (Aug. 21, 1755), saying, "You may alter *Robed* in the sable &c., almost in your own words thus." He adds "Though *haggard* wch conveys to you the idea of a *Witch*, is indeed only a metaphor taken from an unreclaimed Hawk, which is called a *Haggard*, and looks wild and *farouche*, and jealous of its liberty." See note on *hagged* in *Long Story*, l. 129.

19. The image was taken from a well-known picture of Raphaël, representing the supreme being in the vision of Ezekiel: there are two of these paintings, both believed to be originals, one at Florence, the other at Paris. Gray.

"Moses breaking the tables of the law, by Parmegiano, was a figure which Mr Gray used to say came still nearer to his meaning than the picture of Raphael." Mason.

Keble, who admired Gray, could scarcely have forgotten 'the Bard' when he wrote of Balaam (2nd Sund. after Easter)

"O for a sculptor's hand
That thou might'st take thy stand,
Thy wild hair floating on the eastern breeze,
Thy tranc'd yet open gaze
Fix'd on the desert haze,
As one who deep in heaven some airy pageant sees."

20. [Th' imperial ensign: which full-high advanc'd]
"'Shone, like a meteor, streaming to the wind."
Milton's *Paradise Lost* [I. 537]. Gray.

Gray struggles to his image painfully, by the help of Raphaël and Milton. But, if we believe Macpherson, Ossian's Torcul-torno had long ago outdone 'the Bard': "Thou *kindlest thy hair into meteors*, and sailest along the night." (*Cath-Loda*, Duan I.)

23. Cf. l. 11 n. and, with Mitford, "the woods and desert-caves." *Lycidas* l. 39.

26. **hoarser**, i.e. than their wont.

28 sq. With this enumeration of the bards, and their ghostly presence, cf. the 'Songs of Selma' (Macpherson). [Ossian sings] "I behold my departed friends. Their gathering is on Lora, as in the days of other years. Fingal comes like a watery column of mist! his

heroes are around: and see the bards of song, grey-haired Ullin; stately Ryno! Alpin with the tuneful voice! the soft complaint of Minona! How are ye changed, my friends," &c., &c.

28. Hoel is called high-born, being the son of Owen Gwynedd, prince of North Wales, by Finnog, an Irish damsel. He was one of his father's generals in his wars against the English, Flemings, and Normans in South Wales; and was a famous bard, as his poems that are extant testify. See Evan Evans' *Specimens*, p. 26, 4to.; and Jones, *Relics*, vol. ii. p. 56, where he is called the 'Princely Bard.' Jones says that he wrote eight pieces, five of which are translated by him. The whole are given in Mr Owen's translation in Mr Southey's *Madoc*, vol. ii. p. 162. Mitford.

Hoel, son of Owen, seems to be a later Welsh counterpart of Ossian, the son of Fingal. For other particulars Phelps refers us to Thomas Stephens, *Literature of the Kymry*, 1876, pp. 57 ff.

Llewellyn. "In a Poem to Llewellyn, by Einion the son of Guigan (p. 22), he is called 'a *tender-hearted* prince.' And in another Poem to him, by Llywarch Brydydd y Moch (p. 32), 'Llewellyn, though in battle he killed with fury, though he burnt like an outrageous fire, yet was a *mild prince* when the mead horns were distributed.' Also in an Ode to him by Llygard Gwr (p. 39), he is called 'Llewellyn the *mild* and prosperous governor of Gwynedd [North Wales].' Llewellyn's '*Soft* Lay' is given by Jones in his *Relics*, vol. II. p. 64." Mitford [who surely, however, does not mean us to take 'soft' with 'lay'.]

It is perfectly certain that Gray means his Cadwallo, Urien, and Modred to be contemporaries of his bard, whom he originally named Caradoc. (See ll. 35—42.) Mitford's learned note about these serves only to prove that Gray was but careful to get together in this place names such as Welsh bards had borne and might bear. *His* Urien, for example, cannot be the Urien who died in 560; nor can his Modred be the 'Myrddin ap Morvryn' who "fought under King Arthur in 542."

Ib. **cold.** Cf. the 'fredda lingua' of Gray's quotation from Petrarch on *Elegy* l. 92.

30. 'Uttering such dulcet and harmonious breath,
That the rude sea grew civil at her song.'
Shakesp. *M. N. D.* II. 1. 151. Wakefield.

'Who with his soft song and smooth-dittied song
Well knows to still the wild winds when they roar,
And hush the waving woods.'
Milton, *Comus*, 86, 87. Luke.

Cf. Ib. l. 495. Our English poets derive these hyperboles from the classic legends of the Sirens and Orpheus.

31. **Brave.** Once **Stern**, according to Walpole, who says (to Lyttelton, Aug. 25, 1757) "*brave* is insipid or common-place." I cannot say whether Gray knew when he chose the name that the Urien of bardic history is celebrated, as Mitford notes, in the *Triads*, as one of "the three bulls of war."

33. **Modred.** It is more likely that Gray took this name, simply as euphonious, out of the familiar Arthurian legend, although it there is the name of the traitor, than that he modified it from 'Myrddin ap Morvryn' (see on l. 29) as Mitford suggests.

35. The shores of Caernarvonshire opposite to the isle of Anglesey. Gray.

37, 38. All Nature revolts at the cruel death of the sacred bards; birds of prey, the raven, and the eagle, though famish'd, avoid with instinctive horror the feast which such a crime has offered them. Mitford affirms that this *image* may be found in Lucretius, Ovid, Lucan, and Dryden; on turning to his references, the reader will find that Lucretius and Ovid describe, after Thucydides, one observed fact about corpses that died of *plague*, the reference to Lucan is still more inapposite (the arrival of Erichtho *scares* the birds and wolves from their prey); that from Dryden (*Palamon and Arcite*) describes the birds as shunning 'the bitter blast' near the temple of Mars—of course because it is cold.

38. Camden and others observe, that eagles used annually to build their aerie among the rocks of Snowdon, which from thence (as some think) were named by the Welch *Craigian-eryri*, or the crags of the eagles. At this day (I am told) the highest point of Snowdon is called *the eagle's nest*. That bird is certainly no stranger to this island, as the Scots, and the people of Cumberland, Westmoreland, &c. can testify: it even has built its nest in the Peak of Derbyshire. (See Willoughby's *Ornithol.*, published by Ray.) Gray.

40, 41. 'As dear to me as are the ruddy drops
That visit my sad heart.'

Shakesp. *Jul. Caesar* [Brutus to Portia II. 1. 289, 290]. Gray.

43. The Bard here breaks off his lament, as he discerns his ghostly companions.

Ib. Observe the rhymes here and in *l.* 45; and note that there are rhymes in the middle of the lines in the corresponding places of the two succeeding Epodes. In l. 45 'yet' was probably pronounced 'yit' (cf. 'git' for 'get'). At least the rhyme is Popian:

> "How shall we fill a library with *wit*
> When Merlin's cave is half unfurnished *yet*?"
>
> Ep. to Augustus (354, 355).

47. See the Norwegian Ode, that follows. Gray. Gray refers to 'The Fatal Sisters,' which appeared in the edition of 1768. We may take this note as indicating that when he wrote the *Bard* he had already made some study of Scandinavian poetry. As we have seen, Gray had reached this stage of the *Bard* before Aug. 21, 1755; hence he had probably read the Latin version of Bartholin, from which he translated 'The Fatal Sisters,' before that date. This becomes almost certain when we compare the thrice-repeated refrain of the Sisters

> "Texamus, texamus
> Telam Darradi"

with the similar burden of Gray's Bards. And compare "And weave with bloody hands the tissue of thy line," or "The winding-sheet of Edward's race" with the

> "tela virorum
> quam amicae (the Valkyries) texunt
> rubro subtemine
> Randveri mortis"

of Bartholin's version.

Indeed the resemblance here between the *Bard* and the *Fatal Sisters* led Scott into an error. In the *Antiquary* chap. XXX. he makes Oldbuck say: "'Weave the warp and weave the woof'—you remember the passage in *the Fatal Sisters* which by the way is not so fine as in the original."

It is characteristic that in his correspondence with Mason on the subject of *Caractacus*, Gray suppressed all reference to his own example in *The Bard*. He suggests to Mason, who was inclined to mix alien with Celtic elements too boldly, that we might be "permitted (in that scarcity of Celtic ideas we labour under) to adopt some of these foreign whimsies, dropping however all mention of Woden and his Valkhyrian virgins" &c. [Jan. 13, 1758.]

The conception of spirits weaving the web of destiny, is one which might fitly belong to the poetry of any nation, and Gray had no scruple in adopting it for his Welsh ghosts; but we should have supposed, did not the comparison which he invites tell us otherwise, that he had ingrafted it from the Greek myth of the Fates rather than from a Scandinavian source.

Gray wrote to Mason, early in 1756, "I see, methinks (as I sit on Snowdon) some glimpse of Mona, and her haunted shades, and hope we shall be very good neighbours. Any Druidical anecdotes that I can meet with I will be sure to send you. I am of your opinion, that the ghosts will spoil the picture, unless they are thrown at a huge distance, and extremely kept down." Gray here refers to his own *Bard* and Mason's *Caractacus*, the scene of which is Mona (Anglesey), but his advice about the ghosts concerns *Caractacus*, not *The Bard* as Dr Phelps suggests. By this time Gray's ghosts had been seen "on yonder cliffs" and had asserted themselves very vigorously, having in fact completed their prophecy. But Mason was questioning how far he should employ the spirits from Snowdon in the ode in *Caractacus* beginning 'Mona on Snowdon calls,' l. 49.

49. "They are called upon to 'weave the warp, and weave the woof' perhaps with no great propriety: for it is by crossing the woof with the warp that men weave the *web* or piece." Johnson. Johnson's words leave it more than doubtful whether he himself knew which is the fixed part of the fabric. This is the *warp*, which in the Homeric loom, and the loom of the *Fatal Sisters* (l. 10) was stretched perpendicularly, the weavers crossing it with the woof. Gray's '*weave* the warp' is countenanced by Bartholin, who must by 'tela' mean 'the warp' when he writes

"Jam *hastis applicatur*
cineracea
tela virorum
quam amicae *texunt*" (the *warp* which they weave),

for the 'hastae' or 'lances'

"are the loom
Where the dusky *warp* we strain."

as Gray has it.

By "weave the warp and weave the woof" Gray means 'weave them together'; 'interweave them.'

Ib. The chorus of bards now sings. Their part was indicated in 1757 and in every edition, says Dr Bradshaw, published in Gray's lifetime by double, that of the Bard *solo* by single, inverted commas.

51. Mitford compares Dryden, *Sebastian* Act I. sc. I

"I have a soul that like an *ample* shield
Can take in all, and *verge enough* for more."

52. **Of hell**. "hellish" says Dr Bradshaw "of such a nature as might be expected of evil spirits." Surely not; it is against the drift

of the poem to represent the Bards as 'evil' spirits. They are spirits prophetic of destruction; and 'hell and destruction,' (coupled in Scripture,) are almost cognate ideas. With the same ἦθος Gray writes in the *Fatal Sisters* l. 2,

"Haste! the loom of *hell* prepare";

and though his Bards are Celts, in neither place was he quite uninfluenced by the image of the Hela of Northern Mythology whose palace in Niflheim was Anguish; her table Famine; her bed Care. He wrote to Mason Jan. 13, 1751 "Do not think I am ignorant about either the Gothic Elysium, or the *hell* before, or the *twilight*. I have been there, and have seen it all in Mallet's Introduction to the History of Denmark (it is in French) and *many other places*." See Introduction to *Fatal Sisters*.

55. Edward the Second, cruelly butchered in Berkley Castle. Gray. Mitford compares Drayton, *Barons' Wars*, v. lxvii.

"Berkley, whose fair seat hath been famous long,
Let thy sad echoes shriek a ghastly sound
To the vast air" &c.

56. This line of Gray's is almost in the same words as Hume's description vol. II. p. 359 'The screams with which the agonizing king filled the castle.' Mitford.

Hume may have had Gray's lines in mind; certainly this part of his history was published after the completion of the *Bard*.

57. Isabel of France, Edward the Second's adulterous Queen. Gray.

Ib. Gray took the expression, as Mitford notes, from *Henry VI.* Part III. i. 4. 111, but he uses it more happily:

"She-wolf of France, but worse than wolves of France,
Whose tongue more poisons than the adder's tooth,"

says York to Q. Margaret, 'the faithful Consort' in the *Bard*, l. 89.

58. **the bowels.** With some reference such as poetry and the epithet 'she-wolf' permitted, to the horrible circumstances of the king's death.

59. Triumphs of Edward the Third in France. Gray.

Ib. 'Hangs' is neuter, with 'scourge' as noun after it, says Dr Bradshaw. This may be Gray's meaning, but he has taken little pains to indicate it. We should have expected in the edition of 1757 to find a comma after 'hangs', and 'scourge' printed with a capital. It may be replied however that 'sorrow' and 'solitude' should be so printed there, and yet they are not. Inclining to Dr Bradshaw's view so far, I yet think that Gray's expression comes only indirectly from Scripture, e.g. *Isaiah* x. 26 "The Lord of Hosts shall stir up a scourge for him." Gray would have quoted the title 'the Scourge of God' bestowed on Attila by a Christian monk, and ever after assumed by him.

61. Amazement and Flight are the Δεῖμος ἠδὲ Φόβος of Homer *Il.* IV. 440, present at the clash of the Greek and Trojan hosts; Homer puts them, as does Gray, in sequence, for Δεῖμος is Panic, and Φόβος the ensuing Rout.

For 'Amazement' cf. North's *Plutarch* "Ariovistus...much wondered at Caesar's courage and the more when he saw his own army in *a maze* withall.' Also Shakespeare, *Merry Wives*, IV. 4. 55 'We two in great *amazedness* will fly'; and 'not afraid with any amazement,' A.V. 1 *Pet.* 3. 6 (μηδεμίαν πτόησιν in the Greek).

Solitude. Referring to districts made waste and uninhabited by war.

63. **Conqu'ror,** Wharton MS. with **Victor** superscribed.

64. Death of that king [Edward III.], abandoned by his children, and even robbed in his last moments by his courtiers and his mistress. Gray.

The mistress was Alice Perrers, who is said to have stolen even the ring from the king's finger.

Ib. **the** Wharton MS. with **his** superscribed.

65. **What...what** Wharton MS. With **No...no** superscribed.

67. Edward the Black Prince, dead some time before his father. Gray.

Ib. Mitford quotes Prior, "Hence Edward dreadful with his *sable shield*," but he points out that in Peacham's *Period of Mourning*, 1613, the epithet 'Black' is differently accounted for; Edward is described as

"a goodly prince
Of *swarthy hew*."

69. *Agrippina*, ll. 145, 146,

"The gilded swarm that wantons in the sunshine
Of thy full favour."

Ib. "**The swarm that hover'd in thy noontide ray?**" Wharton MS. erased, with "**in thy noontide ray were born**" superscribed.

70. **day.** Wharton MS. erased, with **morn** at side.

Ib. Compare the saying of Pompey to Sulla, when the Dictator wished to deny Pompey a triumph, 'In vain you oppose me; for men worship the rising rather than the setting sun.'

71. Magnificence of Richard the Second's reign. See Froissard and other contemporary writers. Gray.

71—76. These lines are given on the 4th page of Wharton's MS., but in place of them here are the lines:

> **"Mirrors of Saxon truth and loyalty,**
> **Your helpless old expiring master view,**
> **They hear not. Scarce religion dares supply**
> **Her mutter'd Requiems, and her holy Dew.**
> **Yet thou, proud Boy, from Pomfret's walls shalt send**
> **A sigh, and envy oft thy happy grandsire's end."**

'Mirrors' &c. is of course ironical. For the figure cf. Shakespeare, "the *mirror* of all Christian kings," *Henry V.* II. Chor. 6; "the *mirror* of all courtesy,' *Henry VIII.* II. I. 53; 'the glass of fashion,' *Hamlet* III. I. 161.

Gray says 'Saxon' because so the Welsh bards would call English courtiers, whether of Norman or Saxon descent. 'Religion' scruples to give the king the rites due to the dying or the dead, because of his impenitence as shown by the presence of his mistress in his last hours. 'Requiem' is properly the mass for the dead, so called because of the first words of it, 'Requiem aeternam' &c.; by 'holy Dew' Gray means extreme unction. The 'proud boy' is of course Richard II., in this experiment abruptly introduced, and 'Pomfret' Pontefract Castle, where he died; Edward III. was 'happy' in his end, by comparison with Richard's horrible fate; but the irony here is weak.

Gray had already written Epode 3 when the necessity of a less sudden transition to Richard II. was apparent to him. This could only be achieved by parting with the apostrophe to the courtiers &c. for the laws of the Pindaric Ode, as Gray reminds Mason, are like those of the Medes and Persians, and alter not, and the passage had to be managed within the compass of six lines. As it is, the twice-repeated 'morn,' and the brilliant colours in which it is painted between the two awful sunsets, form one of the most striking effects in the *Bard.* The contrast is feelingly rendered in the music of Professor Stanford.

Coleridge is perhaps right when (*Biographia Literaria*, p. 9) he finds Gray's original here in *The Merchant of Venice* II. 6. 14 sq.,

> "How like a younker, or a prodigal,
> The scarfèd bark puts from her native bay,
> Hugg'd and embracèd by the strumpet wind!
> How like a prodigal doth she return;
> With over-weather'd ribs and ragged sails,
> Lean, rent, and beggar'd by the strumpet wind!"

But when he adds, in censure of Gray, that 'it depended wholly on the compositor's putting or not putting a small capital in this and in many other passages whether the words should be personifications or mere abstracts' it is hard to follow him. Do 'Youth *on the prow*' and 'Pleasure *at the helm*' cease to be personifications if printed without capitals? Is 'Sorrow's *faded form*' any the less a personification because the printer in 1757 gave Sorrow a small 's'? The objection to too much personification was shared by Gray himself in theory; he raised it against Mason in his correspondence with him. That he erred by excess in practice is true; he could not emancipate himself from the fashion of his time, though here, as in other directions, he could point to better things. Coleridge attributes the prevalence of this style of poetry, wholly or in part, to the custom of writing Latin verses. 'Coleridge also observes,' says Dr Bradshaw, 'that the words "realm" and "sway" are rhymes dearly purchased.' See l. 48 of *Education and Government* and note there. Cf. here, with Mitford, Dryden, Vergil, *Georg.* I. 483,

"And rolling onwards with a *sweepy sway*."

Said of the Eridanus (Po) making havoc.

77. Richard the Second (as we are told by Archbishop Scroop and the confederate lords in their manifesto, Thomas of Walsingham, and all the older writers) was starved to death. The story of his assassination by Sir Piers of Exon is of much later date. Gray [1757].

Thomas of Walsingham's *Historia Anglicana* was written within the first quarter of the 15th century, and the historian was a contemporary of Richard II. The charge that Richard II. was starved was made by the Percies before the battle of Shrewsbury: "Thou hast caused our sovereign lord and thine, traitorously within the castle of Pomfret, without the consent or judgment of the lords of the realm, by the space of fifteen days and so many nights, with hunger, thirst and cold to perish." Perhaps Gray had evidence that Scroop, &c. made the same accusation before the later insurrection. Holinshed's *Chronicle*, which was Shakespeare's authority for the death of Richard, first appeared in 1577; the murderer is there called Sir Piers of Exton, and Exton is the name in Shakespeare also. Holinshed himself refers as his authority to a writer (nameless) 'which seemeth,' *i.e.* claims 'to have great knowledge of King Richard's doings,' and this is supposed to have been Creton, who went with Richard to Ireland in 1399. When the body, real or supposed, of Richard II. was exhumed at Westminster, there were no marks of violence on the skull, although "he was felled with a stroke of a pollax which Sir Piers gave him upon his head," according to Holinshed.

Walpole to Lyttelton (*l. c.*) writes, 'Thirst and hunger mocking Richard II. appear to me too hideously like the devils in *The Tempest* that whisk away the banquet from the shipwrecked Duke.' He might as well have instanced Sancho Panza and the physician. He never, we may be sure, treated Gray to this foolish criticism. The true comparison as Dr Berdmore suggests is Virg. *Aen.* VI. 603 (of the punishment of the Lapithae):

"Lucent genialibus altis
Aurea fulcra toris, *epulaeque ante ora paratae*
Regifico luxu: Furiarum maxima juxta
Accubat, et manibus prohibet contingere mensas."

['The high banqueting couches gleam golden-pillared, and the feast is spread in royal luxury before their faces: couched hard by, the eldest of the Furies wards the tables from their touch.' Mackail.]

82. **A smile of horror on** Wharton MS. (uncorrected).

Wakefield compares Milton, *Par. Lost* II. 846:

"Death
Grinned horrible a ghastly smile."

And Mitford the description of Ajax in Hom. *Il.* VII. 212, μειδιόων βλοσυροῖσι προσώπασι, 'smiling with visage grim' as he strides to battle. But we lack a parallel for the bold *oxymoron*, '*scowling* a *smile*.'

83. Ruinous civil wars of York and Lancaster. Gray.

Ib. **bray**. Luke compares *Par. Lost* VI. 209:

"arms on armour clashing brayed
Horrible discord."

Here again Gray is bold. But the '*din brays*' as '*the noise* of battle *hurtles*' in Shakespeare, *J. Cæsar* (II. 2); both 'bray' and 'hurtle' being *distinctive* words; 'bray' being cognate (vid. Skeat) with 'break' and implying *suddenness* as well as loudness.

84. "Harry to Harry shall, hot horse to horse,
Meet," &c. Shakespeare, *Henry IV*. Pt. I. IV. I. 122.

Also Massinger, *Maid of Honour*:

"Man to man, and horse to horse." Rogers.

86. So Lucan, at the beginning of the *Pharsalia* 'cognatas acies,' 'kindred squadrons.' The whole passage is very like Gray:

"infestis obvia signis
Signa, pares aquilas, et pila minantia pilis."

[Standards encountering standards, eagles matched against eagles, *pila* menacing *pila*.] But there is a special force in Lucan; for these all distinguish a Roman army from the rest of the world, and the fratricidal nature of the struggle is marked in every word.

87. **Ye. Grim** struck through, with **Ye** superscribed. Wharton MS.

87 sq. Henry the Sixth, George Duke of Clarence, Edward the Fifth Richard Duke of York, &c. believed to be murdered secretly in the Tower of London. The oldest part of that structure is vulgarly attributed to Julius Caesar. Gray.

It is certainly of line 87 that Gray writes to Walpole (July 11, 1757), 'If you will be vulgar, and pronounce it *Lunnun*, instead of London, I can't help it.' This shows a fashionable vulgarism in pronunciation shared by Walpole at this date. He probably objected to the sequence in the line of so many liquid sounds, which the proper pronunciation of *London* breaks with a *d*. Gray, as far as I can discover, has the poets with him: e.g. Wither (1588—1667) in his *Christmas*,

> "Good farmers in the country nurse
> The poor that else were *undone*,
> Some landlords spend their money worse
> On lust and pride in *London*";

and Gay in his *Polly* (1729):

> "The more in debt run in debt the more
> Careless who is *undone:*
> Morals and honesty leave to the poor
> As they do at *London*."

For Gray's fondness for liquids see note on l. 134 *infra*.

88. We are told in the same stanza how 'towers' are 'fed.' Johnson. To this criticism there is no answer, except that Gray sometimes emulates the boldness of Æschylus or Shakespeare.

Scott heads the 28th chapter of *The Fortunes of Nigel* with ll. 87, 88 of the *Bard*, and remarks that Bandello, long before Gray, 'has said something like it.' This I have no opportunity to verify.

89. **Consort's**. Margaret of Anjou, a woman of heroic spirit, who struggled hard to save her husband and her crown. Gray.

Ib. **Father's**. Henry the Fifth. Gray.

90. **holy. hallow'd** Wharton MS. uncorrected.

Ib. Henry the Sixth very near being canonized. The line of Lancaster had no right of inheritance to the Crown. Gray. Cf. *Eton Ode*, l. 4 and note.

91. **Above, below**; i.e. on the loom.

Ib. The white and red roses, devices of York and Lancaster. Gray.

92. In *twined*, Dr Bradshaw thinks there is a reference to the union of the two houses, by the marriage of Henry VII. with Elizabeth of York; but the sequence is awkward; under the thorny shade of the intertwined rose-trees *Richard the Third* wallows in infant gore. If there is here a reference to marriage (as I incline to think) rather than the grapple of foes, it is probably to the marriage of Edward IV. with the Lancastrian Elizabeth Woodville, Lady Grey, of which union the murdered princes were the issue. Cf. *Ode for Music*, l. 43, where, on the same principle, Elizabeth is called the *paler* rose, having *become* so by her marriage with Edward of York. Shakespeare (?) it is to be noted, is mistaken when he makes Elizabeth's first husband to have been a Yorkist (3 *Henry VI.* III. 2, 6, 7)[1]. Sir John Gray was a Lancastrian, and his lands were seized on by Edward IV. after the battle of Towton.

93. The silver boar was the badge of Richard the Third; whence he was usually known in his own time by the name of *the Boar*. Gray.

Ib. **infant-gore.** Gray *hyphenates* when the substantive is used adjectivally, cf. evening-prey (l. 76), lion-port, virgin-grace, ll. 117, 118; velvet-green, *Progress of Poesy* (l. 27). The reference is of course to the murder of the two young princes 'Edward the Fifth and Richard Duke of York,' whom Gray has mentioned on l. 87.

96. They return, at the conclusion of their chant, to the chief object of their vengeance.

98. Gray here shows that he knows well enough the difference between 'woof' and 'warp.' See on l. 49.

99. **Half of thy heart.** Cf. 'animae dimidium meae' ['half of my soul' or 'life'] Hor. *Od.* I. 3. 8. Bradshaw.

Eleanor of Castile died a few years after the conquest of Wales. The heroic proof she gave of her affection for her lord is well known. The monuments of his regret for her are still to be seen in several parts of England. Gray [1757]. In n. of 1768 he writes 'Northampton, Geddington, Waltham and other places.' These are places between Grantham and Westminster, on the road by which Eleanor's funeral passed. The heroism of Eleanor had been celebrated in the *Edward and Eleanora* of Thomson in 1739; it is better, but more briefly commemorated in Tennyson's *Dream of Fair Women*.

101. The ghosts now vanish; and the Bard speaks alone.

Ib. **thus** superscribed on **here** struck through, Wharton MS.

102. **your despairing Caradoc** Wharton MS. with **me unbless'd. Unpitied here** superscribed.

'The mountain in Shropshire is called Caer Carădoc: but Mr Gray

[1] The error is corrected in *Richard III.* I. 3.

asserts that the middle syllable is long, or he could have used it in his poem of the *Bard*.' Cradock. So Gray wrote to Walpole, July 11, 1757, but he also said (ib.) 'Caradoc I have private reasons against'; we may suspect that he did not like any possible confusion between his *Bard* and Mason's *Caractacus*. He pronounces Carădoc in the Welsh Fragment so named (l. 4). Walpole to Lyttelton (*l. c.*) counts the change in the *Bard* a correction for the worse. Gray chose the name just as he chose those in ll. 29—33; see note there.

103. **clouds.** Wharton MS. struck through; **track** superscribed.

104. **sink.** Wharton MS. with **melt** superscribed.

solemn
105. **Ah! what** ^ **scenes ~~of Heaven~~.** Wharton MS.

106. **golden** Wharton MS. with **glitt'ring** superscribed.

Ib. **skirts.** The word in this connection is Miltonic, as

"Dark with excessive bright thy *skirts* appear."
Par. Lost, III. 380.

And (Adam speaks) Ib. XI. 332

"I now
Gladly behold though but his utmost *skirts*
Of glory."

where Newton refers us to Exodus xxxiii. 22, 23. In fact, though the word is Milton's, the idea is Scriptural, in reference to 'a vision of glory'; cf. Isaiah vi. 1 'His *train* filled the temple.'

109. **From Cambria's thousand hills a thousand strains**
Triumphant tell aloud, another Arthur reigns.

Wharton MS. with our text written along the side.

Ib. It was the common belief of the Welsh nation that King Arthur was still alive in Fairy-land, and should return again to reign over Britain. Gray.

In 'Some Remarks on the Poems of Lydgate' Gray mentions the notion that Arthur was so 'translated' and should come again to restore the Round Table:

"This errour abideth yet among Britons
Which founded is upon the prophesie
Of old Merlin, like their opinion;
He as a King is crowned in faërie,
With scepter and sworde, and with his regalie
Shall resort as lord and soveraine
Out of faërie, and reigne in Britaine" &c.
[*Fall of Princes*] B. VIII. c. 24.

He notes on this passage that 'Peter of Blois' who lived in 1170, says ironically in his *Epistles*, 57

"Quibus si credideris
Expectare poteris
Arturum cum Britonibus."

Lydgate attests the belief in the 15th century; and Dr Phelps remarks that Gray might have noted the same thing in the *Polychronicon* of Higden, ad ann. 1177, a work which he quotes on l. 11, *supr.*

110. **All hail.** Accession of the House of Tudor. Gray [1757].

Ib. Both Merlin and Taliessin had prophesied that the Welsh should regain their sovereignty over this island; which seemed to be accomplished in the House of Tudor. Gray.

The prophecies of Merlin (Merddin) and Taliessin, here referred to, have been proved by Thomas Stephens not to be earlier than the 12th century, and hence to have nothing to do with those bards, whose date is in the 6th century. See his *Literature of the Kymry*, 2nd ed. ch. ii. sect. 4, pp. 198 ff. Phelps.

Girt with many a
111. ~~**Youthful knights and**~~ **Barons** Wharton MS.
Haughty Knights &c. To Mason, May, 1757.

Ib. Cf. Sir Richard Baker on the "state" of Queen Elizabeth (*Chronicle of the Kings of England*, ed. of 1684, p. 400) "Never Prince kept greater State with less stateliness: Her Pensioners and Guard were always the tallest and goodliest Gentlemen and Yeomen of the Kingdom: her Maids of Honour and other Women about her, the fairest and most beautiful Ladies of the Realm; and yet her self a *Diana* among the Nymphs." Phelps. But his note should have come later. See next note.

112. **With dazzling helm and horrent spear.** Wharton MS. and to Mason, *l. c.*; struck through in Wharton MS. and text superscribed.

By the change he makes ll. 111, 112 more distinctly refer to the Tudor sovereigns *before* Elizabeth; the two following lines obviously describe her court. Cf. preceding note and *Long Story*, l. 13.

Milton, *Ode on the Passion*, l. 18

"He, *sovran* Priest...
His *starry front* low-roofed beneath the skies."

The expression is classical; and as descriptive of the face is commonest in *later* Latin poetry; e.g. Valerius Flaccus, *Argonautica*, 4. 330

"ire cruores
Siderea de *fronte* vident."

And Claudian, *ad Serenam*, l. 58

"*sidereo* laeta *supercilio*."

Mitford, cp. Petrarch, *Son*. CXLVIII. (167), l. 9

"Gli occhi sereni e *le stellanti ciglia*."

In most examples the sense is simply 'radiant,' but in Milton and Gray there is perhaps the further notion of the diadem.

114. **In. Of** to Mason, *l.c.* To the same, June, 1757, "In bearded majesty," was altered to "Of" only because the next line begins with "In the midst" &c.

115. Elizabeth is described in the style of the courtly poets of her time; the Welsh Bard sees the Tudors in their brightest colours.

116. **Her eye.** Micheli, the Venetian, described Elizabeth in 1557 (the year before her accession) as having fine eyes; a testimony more trustworthy than the praise of her courtiers. This eye Gray makes characteristic of the Tudors; cf. *Installation Ode*, l. 70

"Pleased in thy lineaments we trace
A Tudor's *fire* &c."

And his *Bard* refers it to their Celtic origin.

Ib. **of...line. Born of Arthur's line.** Gray to Mason, May, 1757.

117. **A...an.** Wharton MS. struck through, **Her...her** superscribed.

lyon-port. Speed, relating an audience given by Queen Elizabeth to Paul Dzialinski, Ambassador of Poland, says, "And then she, lion-like rising, daunted the malapert Orator, no less with her stately port and majestical deporture, than with the tartnesse of her princelie checkes." Gray.

Gray's expression may have excited comment, which led to this note. He writes to Mason, May, 1759, "Mr Hurd himself allows that 'lion-port' is not too bold for Queen Elizabeth." And as, between 1753 and 1759 (see *Gray and His Friends*, p. 191), he was reading exactly that sort of literature, he might have found before he wrote 'lion-port' the anecdote told by Puttenham in his *Art of Poesie*, of the Queen forgiving a knight who had behaved insolently to her before she came to the throne. "Do you not know," she is reported to have said, "that we are descended of the *lion*, whose nature is not to harm or prey upon the mouse?" &c.

119, 120. Great efflorescence of poetry in the reign of Elizabeth; it centres round her court, and she is often the object of its homage, hence 'round her.' And it is, fittingly, the sound of lyric poetry, the music of the harp, that the Bard's ear first catches, to tell him that his art, spite of the tyrant's barbarity, will not be lost. This is faintly indicated in '*strings* symphonious'; and it is certainly not till after 'The verse adorn *again*' that allusion is made to the *greater* poems of Spenser and Shakespeare. In this stanza they figure, if at all, as the Shakespeare of 'the Sonnets,' the Spenser of the 'Hymnes,' or the goodly company of Sidney and the numerous bards of 'England's Helicon.'

121. Taliessin, Chief of the Bards, flourished in the 6th century. His works are still preserved, and his memory held in high veneration among his countrymen. Gray [1757].

Cf. n. on l. 110 supr. Gray, as Phelps points out, says in a note to his *Observations on the Pseudo-Rhythms* (written after 1761), "If the remains of Taliessin be not fictitious."

122. **breath** is Gray's spelling in Wharton MS.

123. **Rapture.** What Walpole means when he writes to Lyttelton (*l. c.*) "I can even allow that image of Rapture hovering *like an ancient grotesque*, though it strictly has little meaning" it would be hard to say. The image, as every one else has seen, is from the skylark, which Shelley says, is "like an unbodied joy." Mitford says Gray drew from Congreve, *Ode to Lord Godolphin*, st. VI.

"And soars with rapture while she sings."

He scarcely needed to draw from any one here; but we may also *compare* Waller,

"*Singing she mounts;* her airy wings are stretched
Towards Heaven, as if from Heaven her note she fetched."
(*Of and to the Queen*, ll. 7, 8);

and, with Bradshaw, Shelley, 'To a Skylark,' l. 10

"And singing still dost soar and soaring ever singest."

Gray's implied simile well expresses the spontaneous, exuberant character of Elizabethan song; the epithet 'many-coloured' its variety.

Ib. **calls. wakes.** To Mason, 1757.

125—144. The conclusion of the *Bard* was much criticized, even by Gray's admirers. Walpole (*l. c.*) says, "The last stanza has no beauties for me. I even think its obscurity fortunate, for the allusions to Spenser, Shakespeare, Milton, are not only weak, but the two last returning again, after appearing so gloriously in the first Ode, and with so much fainter colours, enervate the whole conclusion."

We must bear in mind the difficulty of Gray's plan at this point. It would have been absurd and incongruous to attribute to prophecy and the Welsh Bard the distinctness which belongs to a poetic retrospect. The 'fainter colours' are absolutely necessary; and as it is there is too much of *criticism* underlying 'pleasing pain,' "Truth severe by fairy Fiction drest," and too much learning in 'buskined measures.'

Gray himself thought the last part of the poem 'weakly,' and adds to Mason, "and you think so too," but he hoped that the "ten last lines would have escaped untouched." Mr Bonfoy and Mr Neville, he says, "like the first Ode (that has no *tout-ensemble*) the best of the two and both somehow dislike the conclusion of the *Bard*, and mutter something about antithesis and conceit in 'to triumph, to die,' which I do not comprehend, and am sure it is altered for the better. It was before

'Lo! to be free to die, are (*sic*) mine.'

If you like it better so, so let it be. It is more abrupt, and perhaps may mark the action better: or it may be,

'Lo! liberty and death are mine.'"

[to Mason, June, 1757].

"Let it be observed," says Johnson, "that the ode might have been concluded with an action of better example; but suicide is always to be had without expense of thought." This shows that Johnson was in the first instance a moralist and only in the second a critic; but it also shows that an autocratic position, such as his, in literature, may make a man's utterances quite fatuous.

125. "I understand what you mean about 'The verse adorn again.' You may read

'Fierce War, and faithful Love
Resume their &c.'

But I do not think it signifies much, for there is no mistaking the sense, when one attends to it." Gray to Mason, June, 1757. The suggested change is imperfectly indicated, but does not seem to be an improvement.

126. "Fierce wars and faithful loves shall moralize my song."

Spenser's *Proeme to the Fairy Queen* [l. 9]. Gray.

127. This line tersely describes Spenser's design in the *Faerie Queene*, of which he himself says, in the letter to Sir Walter Raleigh which serves as his preface, "To some, I know, this Methode will seeme displeasaunt, which had rather have good discipline delivered plainly in way of precepts, or sermoned at large, as they use, then [than] thus clowdily enwrapped in Allegoricall devises." Cf. also Milton in his *Areopagitica*, § 23, "Our sage and serious poet Spenser whom I dare be known to think a better teacher than Scotus or Aquinas"; and note that Una, whose fortunes, with those of the Red

Cross Knight, form the subject of the first Book of the *Faerie Queene* is in Spenser another name for Truth.

128. **buskin'd.** Shakespear. (Gray.)

Cf. Milton, *Il Penseroso*, 101, 102:

> "Or what (though rare) of later age
> Ennobled hath the buskin'd stage."

The buskin is the cothurnus (*κόθορνος*) which was worn by tragic actors, and hence became the emblem of Tragedy, as the *soccus* of Comedy. Masson is probably right in supposing that Milton's lines refer mainly to Shakespeare. It is the counterpart in *Il Penseroso* to the reference to Comedy in *L'Allegro*:

> "If Jonson's learned *sock* be on,
> Or sweetest Shakespeare, Fancy's child
> Warble his native wood-notes wild."

Var. Lect. **mystic**, to Mason, May, 1757, which surely was better; but perhaps changed to avoid alliteration.

129. **pleasing Pain.** "Sweet pleasing payne," Spenser, *Faerie Queene*, IX. X. 3 [of the passion of love]. Luke. But the origin of Gray's *idea* is Aristotle, *Poetics*, XXVII. τὴν ἀπὸ ἐλέου και φόβου διὰ μιμήσεως δεῖ ἡδονὴν παρασκευάζειν τὸν ποιητὴν, the [tragic] poet must provide that *pleasure* which arises from *pity and fear*.

130. **With Horror wild that chills the throbbing breast.**

[to Mason, May, 1757.]

To the same, June,—"'That chills the throbbing," &c. I dislike as much as you can do. What if we read

"**With Horror, tyrant of the throbbing breast**'."

Accordingly, *teste* Mitford, 'tyrant of the' is superscribed, *l. c.* in Mason's writing.

131. Milton. Gray. With special reference, as the next line shows, to *Paradise Lost*.

133. The succession of Poets after Milton's time. Gray.

134. 'Why you would alter "lost in long futurity" I do not see unless, because you think "lost" and "expire" are tautologies, or because it looks as if the end of the prophecy were disappointed by it, and that people may think that poetry in Britain was, some time or other, really to expire, whereas the meaning only is that it was lost to his ear from the immense distance. I cannot give up "lost," for it begins with an *l*.' Gray to Mason, June, 1757.

135—138. There is a remarkable resemblance, though it is probably only coincidence, between these lines and the passage quoted by Mitford from **Vida** (an Italian Latinist of the Renaissance, born *circ.* 1490), *Hymnus D. Andreae Apostolo*, l. 99 sq.:

"Impie, quid furis? . . . . .
Tene putas posse illustres abscondere caeli
Auricomi flammas, ipsumque extinguere solem?
. . . .
Forsitan humentem nebulam proflare, brevemque
Obsessis poteris radiis obtendere nubem.
Erumpet lux: erumpet rutilantibus auris
Lampas; et aurifera face nubila differet omnia."

[Impious Man! Why dost thou rage? Thinkest thou that thou canst hide the splendid flames of the golden-tressed heaven, and quench the sun himself? Thou wilt, mayhap, avail to raise by thy breath a dark mist, and curtain with a momentary cloud his encumbered rays. Yet his light shall burst forth; forth with reddening gleam his torch shall burst, and scatter all the rack with a flood of golden fire."]

The idea, apart from its treatment, is a commonplace of poetry. When Dekker, quoted by Mitford, *If it be not good, the Divel is in it*, wrote in 1612

"Think'st thou, base lord,
Because the glorious sun behind black clouds
Has awhile hid his beams, he's darken'd for ever,
Eclips'd never more to shine?"

he had been preceded by Shakespeare, *Rich. II.* III. 3. 63 *sq.*

"See, see, King Richard doth himself appear
As doth the blushing discontented sun
From out the fiery portal of the east
When he perceives the envious clouds are bent
To dim his glory and to stain the track
Of his bright passage to the occident."

And comp. also *Henry IV.* Pt. I. I. 2. 219 sq.

"...the sun
Who doth permit the base contagious clouds" &c.

137. Milton, *Lycidas*, 168, 169

"So sinks the day-star in the ocean bed,
And yet anon *repairs* his drooping head."

Mitford.

No doubt the context (q.v.) has also influenced Gray.

A thoroughly Latin use of the word; the older meaning of *reparare* is to get once more, to recover; the sense of 'mend' is later. Cf. (with Mitford) Lucretius, v. 734,

atque alia illius *reparari* in parte locoque

["and another [moon] be produced in its room and stead." Munro.]

Nearer to the later sense is Horace, *Carm.* IV. 7. 13,

Damna tamen celeres *reparant* coelestia lunae,

["The seasons' difference rolling moons *repair*." Merivale.]

but Hor. preserves the older in *Carm.* III. 3. 60 (avitae Tecta velint *reparare* Trojae).

XIV. ODE ON THE PLEASURE ARISING FROM VICISSITUDE.

This is in a handwriting said to be Stonhewer's in the 3rd vol. of Pembroke MS. It is there called 'Fragment of an Ode found among Mr Gray's papers after his decease and here transcribed from the corrected Copy.' On the other side of the page he gives the variations in the first copy which are recorded below. The title of the Fragment is probably Mason's.

In the same vol. the same hand, I think, gives the following among 'Extracts from Mr Gray's Pocket Books':

"P.B. of 1754:

Contrast between the Winter Past and coming Spring. Joy owing to that Vicissitude. many that never feel that delight. Sloth envy Ambition. how much happier the rustic that feels it tho he knows not how.

"Then follow a few lines of the Ode 'Now the golden Morn' etc. so that the above note appears to be a kind of Argument to that Fragment. Four lines also as follow are among the others:

Rise my soul [etc. ll. 17—20]."

"On another page

Gratitude

The Joy that trembles in her eye
She bows her meek and humble head
in silent praise
beyond the power of sound."

Perhaps these hints on 'Gratitude' were also intended for this Poem, as expressing the feelings of a convalescent, or possibly the mute thanksgiving of the rustic (*vide supra*).

This attempt may have been inspired by the spring of 1754; Dr Phelps is probably right, chronologically, in placing it between *Progress of Poesy* and *the Bard*, for the date of commencement; but their common motto links those two poems inseparably.

Mason writes, "I have heard Mr Gray say that M. Gresset's *Épître à ma Sœur* gave him the first idea of this Ode." He finds resemblance chiefly in the 7th Stanza; see n. there. Gray mentions and quotes Gresset for the first time in a letter to Wharton of June 5, 1748, in which he speaks of this *Épître* to the sister. He was Gray's contemporary and survived him, dying in 1777. His *Ver-Vert* (the Story of a Parrot) is still popular; Gray thought his *Le Méchant* the best comedy he had ever read. Green (see on *Eton* Ode), another contemporary (d. 1737) like Gresset, fascinated Gray by a tone of gentle meditation, expressed sometimes by Gresset, always by Green, with an almost colloquial ease which our poet made no attempt to imitate[1].

Gresset's style is so discursive, and his tone so varied in the course of his long poem, that it is mainly towards the end of it that Gray's obligation to him appears. Gresset's poem was on his own recovery from sickness (*Sur ma Convalescence*). His description of his sufferings is in the most conventional style of the French poetry of his day, with abundance of heathen mythology; but he becomes more natural as he proceeds:

> "Tout nous appelle aux champs, *le Printemps va renaître*
> *Et j'y vais renaître avec lui.* (cf. *infra* ll. 17—20.)

In this correspondence between the *renaissance* of Nature and Man is the common ground of Gray and Gresset; but from l. 21 to l. 44 of Gray's poem has no counterpart in Gresset; and is in a strain quite beyond his reach. Indeed he is as inferior to Gray in reflection as Gray is to him in lightness of touch on more trivial themes. He served Gray only as *stimulus* and starting-point, as when he says, 'Tout s'émousse dans l'habitude,' but he illustrates this, in conclusion, with a prosaic contrast between two men of pleasure, *Cléon*, who has not been ill and is therefore *blasé*, and *Lisis* (*sic*) who has, and in consequence finds Society charming.

[1] The history of their lives offers another curious resemblance between Green and Gresset. They both deserted their spiritual instructors, Green the Quakers, and Gresset the Jesuits, with sentiments of respect; Gresset's tone on this subject anticipating that of Renan in his *Souvenirs*.

Commentators find in ll. 49—62 an anticipation of Wordsworth; they would probably have found much that was far more Wordsworthian if Gray had described the "happiness of the rustic" more fully. He begins to do this in ll. 53—56 in a manner *not* Wordsworthian; but in the words (*vide supra*) 'that feels *it though he knows not how*' we have a hint to which the 'silent praise' and 'beyond the power of sound' recorded above, may conceivably belong; out of these something might have been made as near to the mind of Wordsworth as Gray's epoch was capable of attaining. How far Mason could get in this direction by the help of Gray's sign-post he lets us know in his bold attempt to complete the poem:

> "He, unconscious whence the bliss,
> Feels, and owns in carols rude,
> That all the circling joys are his
> Of dear Vicissitude." etc.

His filling-up of what in our text is the last fragment of the poem should always be preserved as an 'object-lesson':

> "To these if Hebe's self should bring
> The purest cup from Pleasure's spring
> Say, can they taste the *flavour high*
> *Of sober, simple, genuine Joy?*"

Mitford quotes from a letter of Langhorne's to Hannah More, "I have heard something that Mason has done in finishing a half-written Ode of Gray. I fear he will never get the better of that glare of colouring, 'that dazzling blaze of song,' an expression of his own, and ridiculous enough, which disfigures half his writings."

3. **vermeil-cheek.** See *Bard*, l. 93 n. Luke cites Milton, *Comus*, 752:

> "What needs a vermeil-tinctured lip for that," etc.

8. Gray writes to Wharton, Aug. 26, 1766, describing the road to Canterbury, 'it was indeed owing to the bad weather, that the whole scene was dress'd in that *tender emerald-green* which one usually sees only for a fortnight in the opening of spring.'

9. Mitford quotes *Lucretius*, I. 260:

> "nova proles
> *artubus infirmis* teneras lasciva per herbas
> ludit, [lacte mero mentes perculsa novellas]"

(a new brood *with weakly limbs* frisks and gambols over the soft grass. Munro).

And T. Warton *On the First of April*:

"O'er the broad downs, *a novel race*
Frisk the lambs with *faultering pace*,"

published in 1777[1].

10. **V.L. Quaintly ply.**

11. **Rous'd from their long and wintry trance.**

13—17. These four lines on the skylark will stand comparison with Wordsworth's and Shelley's poems on the same subject. Phelps.

15. **lessening,** v.l. **towering.** Luke.

16. Lucretius v. 28. *liquidi fons luminis.* Milton, *Par. Lost*, VII. 362 'drink the *liquid light*.'

17—20. The place of these four lines, as will be seen from the Introductory Note, is conjectural; but Mason is probably right in setting them here. The four more lines wanting to the stanza Mason supplied, in very common-place fashion.

22. **snowy,** v.l. **scowling** *or* **snow in.**

29—32. Shakespeare is Gray's teacher here, not only in *Hamlet*, IV. 4. 36, 37:

"He that made us of such large discourse,
Looking before and after,"

but in the distinction drawn between man and the brute creation, in that man's impressions are modified by reflection. Cf. for instance *Merchant of Venice*, V. 1. 69—71:

'*Jes.* I am never merry when I hear sweet music.
Lor. The reason is, your spirits are attentive:
For do but note a wild and wanton herd," etc.

33. **past,** v.l. **black.**

49 sq. Gresset says of his own feelings on recovery:

"Tout m'interesse, tout m'enflamme,
Pour moi l'univers est nouveau.
Sans doute que le Dieu qui nous rend l'existence,
À l'heureuse Convalescence
Pour de nouveaux plaisirs donne de nouveaux sens:
* * * * * * *

[1] Warton's *Ode* bears a great resemblance to Gray's. He seems here to have sought variety by 'faultering pace' and by fetching 'novel,' from Lucretius;—thus justifying Johnson's sarcastic lines about him,

"Wheresoe'er I turn my view
All is strange, yet nothing new."

"He puts," said Johnson, "a very common thing in a strange dress, till he does not know it himself, and thinks other people do not know it either."

Les plus simples objets, le chant d'une fauvette,
Le matin d'un beau jour, la verdure des bois,
La fraîcheur d'une violette,
Mille spectacles, qu'autrefois
On voyait avec nonchalance,
Transportent aujourd'hui" etc.

Commentators have found something like Wordsworth in these four lines of Gray. But Wordsworth claims for himself a sympathy with Nature more profound and limitless than Gray could ever have conceived. The lines often quoted here as a parallel are really a contrast. Gray describes the feeling of every convalescent. But when Wordsworth says:

"To me the meanest flower that blows can give
Thoughts that do often lie too deep for tears,"

he expresses in robust health a sentiment so little shared by the average man, that even Dr Arnold, who writes of 'the deep delight with which he looks at wood anemones or wood sorrel' finds in these lines something morbid; 'life,' he said, 'is not long enough to take such intense interest in objects themselves so little.' Again, Wordsworth reproaches Peter Bell because

"A primrose by the river's brim
A yellow primrose was to him
And it was nothing more."

But Lowell confesses to moods in which he asks himself, 'Why it should be anything more?' There is no real analogy between a delight possible for all men (this is what Gray describes), and thoughts only given to rarer spirits.

55. Crystálline is the pronunciation in Milton, as Mason notes:

"On the crystálline sky, in sapphire thron'd."

Par. Lost, VI. 772.

57. Mason's restitution here does not even pretend to complete what Gray has left incomplete, but boldly alters and dislocates it:

"*While* far below the *madding* Crowd
Rush headlong to the dangerous flood,
Where broad and turbulent it *sweeps*
And perish in the bourdless *deeps*."

Gray certainly did not mean to put any epithet to 'crowd,' still less to repeat the epithet in the *Elegy*; and to make the last two lines Mason by compressing and suppressing has put together what Gray may have meant to keep quite distinct.

Gray's real sources are not always those which he more directly indicated. Here he was trying to give a somewhat different expression to Gresset, not in the *Épître à ma Sœur*, but in his *Ode sur la Médiocrité* (Gray's *Humble Quiet*) :—

"Aux bords d'une mer furieuse
Où la fortune impérieuse
Porte et brise à son gré de superbes vaisseaux,
* * * * * * * *
Dans un temple simple et rustique
De la nature ouvrage antique,
Ce climat voit régner la Médiocrité.
Là, conduite par la sagesse
Tu te fixas, humble Déesse,
* * * * * *
Tu rassembles, loin du tumulte
Le vrai, les plaisirs purs, les sincères vertus.
Séduits par d'aveugles idoles,
* * * * *
Le vulgaire et les grands ne te suivirent pas," etc.

XV. TOPHET.

This is a kind of phonetic anagram of Etough[1]. These verses were written by Gray under an etching of the Rev. Henry Etough made by Mr Tyson of Bene't (Corpus Christi) College, Cambridge, and presented by him to the poet. The sketch was a small full length, possibly like that figured in Mitford's edition of Gray's *Works* (vol. I. p. 159) and in Bell's Aldine edition by Bradshaw (p. 272).

Etough was originally a Jew, and is said to have renounced his religion for the sake of a valuable living. The second line of *Tophet* refers to the fact that he "kept the conscience" of Sir Robert Walpole, and advised him about preferments. He was rector of Therfield, Herts, and Colmnorth, Bedfordshire. His epitaph in the church at Therfield states that, "With a robust constitution, through a singular habit of body, he lived many years without the use of animal food, or of any

[1] Tophet was a place close to Jerusalem, infamous for sacrifices to Moloch, and consequently regarded as a place of abomination, the very gate or pit of Hell. Isaiah xxx. 33.

fermented liquid, and died suddenly, Aug. 10, 1757, in the 70th year of his age."

The lines were first printed in the *Gentleman's Magazine*, May, 1785, according to Dr Bradshaw, with the exception of ll. 3 and 4. They are said to be in Stonhewer's handwriting in Pembroke MS. with the heading "Inscription on a Portrait."

I cannot fix the exact date of *Tophet*. We may suppose that the sketch was made in Etough's lifetime, but even this is uncertain.

1, 2. V.L. in Pembroke MS.

"**Such Tophet was, so looked the grinning Fiend**
Whom many a frighted Prelate called his friend."

A note indicates that lines 3 and 4 are "additions in the first copy.' Bradshaw.

XVI. EPITAPH ON MRS JANE CLARKE.

This epitaph is on a mural tablet of slate and marble in the Church at Beckenham, Kent. The inscription is:

JANE CLARKE

Died March 27, 1757. Aged 31. (Bradshaw.)

Dr John Clarke was a physician at Epsom, and one of the oldest of Gray's college friends. Gray writes to Wharton from Florence, Mar. 12, 1740, "If my old friends Thompson, *or Clark* fall in your way [at Cambridge] say I am extremely theirs." And to Clarke himself 20 years later (Aug. 12, 1760) he writes about the Erse fragments and gives a grotesque account of the death of Chapman, the Master of Magdalene, the publication of which by Mason greatly offended Chapman's friends.

6. Mitford quotes

["If Science raised her head]
And *soft Humanity* that from rebellion fled."
Dryden, *Threnodia Augustalis*, st. XII.

"Bred to the rules of *soft humanity*."
Dryden, *All for Love*, II. I.

Pope, *Epitaph on General Withers*.

"[O born to arms! O worth in youth approved!]
O *soft humanity*, in age beloved!"

But perhaps in the first example the expression refers to the liberal arts, literature, 'the humanities' as the Scotch say; whilst in the others, as in Gray, it stands for the gentle courtesies of life.

6. V.L. after l. 6 in place of the four next:

> "**To hide her cares her only art,**
> **Her pleasure, pleasures to impart,**
> **In ling'ring pain, in death resign'd,**
> **Her latest agony of mind**
> **Was felt for him, who could not save**
> **His All from an untimely grave.**" Mason.

In the wife's solicitude about the husband's pain, as Gray expresses it in the text,

> "In agony, in death resign'd
> *She felt the wound she left behind*,"

there is such an allusiveness as the difference of circumstances permitted to the words of Arria to Pætus, when she hands him the sword, in Martial (I. 14)

> "Si qua fides, *volnus*, quod feci *non dolet*, *inquit*,
> Sed quod tu facies, hoc mihi Paete dolet."
> ["'Tis not the wound that I have made, said she,
> But that which thou wilt make, that paineth me."]

9, 10. Dr Bradshaw says here that Mrs Clarke died in childbirth. I can find no evidence for this, except the statement of Mr Gosse. It is certainly no proper inference from these two lines, and that Gray should have made no use of a fact which lent itself so easily to pathos[1], is almost inconceivable. But it is clear from the preceding note that in the first draft of the verses he had forgotten the existence of the child altogether; and if the circumstances were as Mr Gosse represents them, this should have the distinction of being quite the worst epitaph ever written by a poet of name. As it is, the sentiment of the last two lines, whatever we may think of it, is not Christian; and of even pagan poets not all would affirm that time, when it puts an end to life, puts an end to memory and to love.

[1] Cf. the following epitaph on a lady who *did* die in child-birth, the child surviving her:

> "I, quære, lector, an non sit lucrum mori,
> Quum moriens mater vitam dat et accipit
> Mortalem nato, aeternam sibi."

XVII. EPITAPH ON A CHILD.

In 1758 Dr Wharton lost his eldest and at that time his only son, a child of tender years. And on the 9th of April in that year Gray wrote him a letter of condolence, far more valuable than this epitaph, but too long to quote. The letter is indorsed by Wharton 'On Robin's Death.' The epitaph was written after June 18, 1758, on which day Gray wrote to Wharton, "You flatter me by thinking that any thing that I can do, could at all alleviate the just concern your late loss has given you: but I can not flatter myself so far & know how little qualified I am at present to give any satisfaction to myself on this head, and in this way, much less to you. I by no means pretend to inspiration, but yet I affirm, that the faculty in question is by no means voluntary. it is the result (I suppose) of a certain disposition of mind, w[ch] does not depend on oneself, and w[ch] I have not felt this long time. you that are a witness, how seldom this spirit has moved me in my life, may easily give credit to what I say."

Johnson says of Gray, "He had a notion not very peculiar, that he could not write but at certain times or at happy moments; a fantastic foppery, to which my kindness for a man of learning and virtue wishes him to have been superior." There could be no more conclusive evidence that Gray's was no affectation than this epitaph, written, as we have seen, *invitâ Minervâ*, to oblige a friend. It is quite the feeblest poem in the present collection. I have not found it recorded that Wharton ever made use of it; perhaps he never even received it, for Gray may very properly have concluded that it was not worth sending him.

Mr Gosse has printed it as here reproduced 'from a copy in the handwriting of Alexander Dyce, found slipped into a book at South Kensington, and made by him when the original MS. was sold in 1854.' Dr Bradshaw reports that there are two copies by Mitford in the British Museum, one of which was made from Gray's MS., the other from a MS. not by Gray. These are here designed Mitford MS. (1), Mitford MS. (2).

1. **freed.** **free** Mitford MS. (2).

6. **Here** Mitford MSS. (1 and 2)...**his, the** Mitford MS. (2).

XVIII. THE FATAL SISTERS.

The *Fatal Sisters*, according to a note to the original MS. at Pembroke College, was written in 1761. (Gosse.) [Before May 5, *vide infra.*] It was first published as the seventh in the Poems of 1768. In a letter to Beattie, 1st February, 1768, Gray states that the "sole reason" for publishing this and the following odes is "to make up for the omission of the *Long Story*," which he did not include in his poems in 1768. (Bradshaw.)

To the edition of 1768 Gray prefixed the following:

'Advertisement. The Author once had thoughts (in concert with a friend) of giving *the History of English Poetry*. In the Introduction to it he meant to have produced some specimens of the Style that reigned in ancient times among the neighbouring nations, or those who had subdued the greater part of this Island, and were our Progenitors; the following three Imitations made a part of them. He has long since dropped his design, especially after he heard, that it was already in the hands of a Person well qualified to do it justice, both by his taste, and his researches into antiquity.'

The 'friend' was Mason, as appears from a letter of Walpole to George Montagu, May 5, 1761: 'Gray has translated two noble incantations from the Lord knows who, a Danish Gray, who lived the Lord knows when. They are to be enchased in a history of English bards, which Mason and he are writing; but of which the former has not written a word yet, and of which the latter, if he rides Pegasus at his usual foot-pace, will finish the first page two years hence.' The 'Person' in whose favour Gray resigned the task was Thomas Warton. He was probably encouraged by the intimation that Gray had abandoned his own History, and by the compliment to himself in this Advertisement, to apply to Gray through Hurd for 'any fragments or sketches' of Gray's design. But it was not until April 15, 1770, when he was told that Warton's first volume was in the press, that Gray replied by sending him the sketch to be found in the letter to Warton of that date. As a matter of fact Warton's first volume only appeared in 1774, after our poet's death.

Gray followed the Advertisement in 1768 by a *Preface* which runs thus:

'In the eleventh century, Sigurd, Earl of the Orkney-islands, went with a fleet of ships and a considerable body of troops into Scotland, to the assistance of *Sictrygg with the silken beard*, who was then making war on his father-in-law *Brian*, King of Dublin; the Earl and all his forces were cut to pieces, and Sictrygg was in danger of a total defeat; but the enemy had a greater loss by the death of *Brian* their king, who fell in the action. On Christmas Day (the day of the battle) a native of *Caithness* in Scotland saw at a distance a number of persons on horseback riding at full speed towards a hill, and seeming to enter into it. Curiosity led him to follow them, till looking through an opening in the rocks, he saw twelve gigantic figures resembling women: they were all employed about a loom: and as they wove, they sung the following dreadful song; which when they had finished, they tore the web into twelve pieces, and (each taking her portion) galloped six to the North, and as many to the South.'

Professor Kittredge points out that "Christmas day" is a slip; Torfaeus puts the battle on Good Friday. It was the Battle of Clontarf, April 23, 1014. He (or Dr Phelps) notes also that Brian was king of Ireland, and Sigtrygg king of Dublin, that Brian was Sigtrygg's step-father, and that both fell in the battle.

It is to be noted however that Gray's Preface accords with the Ode, whether in the Latin version, or his own, in ignoring the death of the younger king; and he could scarcely have had Torfaeus before him for the day of the battle, for the Latin of Torfaeus as cited in Phelps, Appendix, p. xliv., though curiously worded, is explicit for Good Friday. On p. 162 of Phelps' *Gray* it is stated that 'the accompanying prose of the original (in the Nialssaga) furnishes an introduction and a conclusion which are put together by Gray in his Preface.' As it is stated in the same volume that Gray in his Preface followed Torfaeus, I suppose Torfaeus followed the Nialssaga, with which his account certainly tallies.

Mitford gives Gray's Preface and Preliminary Note (*infra*) combined, with certain additions; after 'a native of Caithness in Scotland' come the words 'of the name of Darrud' (an error which Gray himself corrects on the Latin version); and at the end of the note the following:

'Their numbers are not agreed upon, some authors representing them as *six*, some as *four*. See Magni Beronii diss. de Eddis Islandicis, p. 145, in *Ælrichs. Dan. et Sued. lit. opuscula*, vol. I.'

Whether these statements are Gray's I do not know.

Mason gives on the Argument a MS. note of Gray, in explanation of the date *Christmas Day*.

"The people of the Orkney islands were Christians, yet did not become so till after A.D. 966, probably it happened in 995; but though they, and the other Gothic nations, no longer worshipped their old divinities, yet they never doubted of their existence, or forgot their ancient mythology, as appears from the history of Olaus Tryggueson." Mason then refers us to Bartholinus, t. i. p. 615.

It has been questioned whether Gray translated these Norse Odes from the originals or from the Latin versions. Mason's statement is capable of being construed either way: he speaks of 'the Latin versions of the originals from whence they were taken.' In his observations on the *Pseudo-Rhythmus*, which were written after 1761, Gray has a note in which he quotes from the *Ransom of Eigil* (*sic*) to show that it is in rhyme, and though this can be recognized without any knowledge either of the grammar or the meaning, and is besides no evidence of the state of his acquirements when the two Norse Odes were written, it is more likely that he had in some measure understood the original of the *Ransom* before 1761 (see what is said on his note to the Latin version of the *Fatal Sisters*, *infra*). Gray's notes on *the Descent of Odin* will be discussed in their place; from them (in Phelps' *Gray*) Professor Kittredge, who has dealt carefully with the question, infers that Gray had gained out of the books to which he had access that sort of knowledge of the language which was inevitable to such sagacity as his, but probably nothing like mastery. There is only one point which Professor Kittredge and Dr Phelps leave untouched. They have passed over the above-mentioned note by Gray on the Latin version of the *Fatal Sisters*. Gray there corrects Torfaeus, from whom he extracted the Latin, but Torfaeus only repeats Bartholin, and Bartholin owns his obligation to the learned Arni Magnússon with respect to the Latin versions. (Phelps' *Gray*, Appendix, xliii. n. 4.) From this it would seem that Gray not only consulted the originals, but had an opinion of his own as to their meaning and claimed the right to differ from a recognized authority on the subject. (Professor Kittredge however has convinced me that I am here in error.)

Torfaeus (Torfason) 'b. 1636, d. 1719, was a learned Icelander and one of the founders of the science of Northern Antiquities. His most important works (chiefly historical) were written while he was the King of Denmark's historiographer royal for Norway. His *Historia Orcadum* is the work to which Gray refers.' Professor Kittredge. The other authority is *Antiquitatum Danicarum de Causis contemptae Mortis a Danis adhuc Gentilibus Libri Tres*. [Three books of Danish Antiquities concerning the causes of the contempt of Death by the Danes while they were still Heathens.] Copenhagen, 1689. 'The author was

Thomas Bartholin the younger (1659—1690), Professor at Copenhagen.' *Id.*

'The Old Norse words quoted by Gray form a part of the opening sentence of the song:

> "Vítt er orpit fyr val-falli
> rifs reiði-ský."

'The pendent cloud of loom is stretched out wide before the slaughter' (Phelps and Kittredge). Scott in *The Pirate* [chap. XV. and note D] tells how when Gray's *Fatal Sisters* reached one of the Orkneys, a clergyman there read it to some of the old inhabitants, who after hearing a few lines of it, told him that they knew the song well in the Norse language, and had often sung it to him when he asked them for an old song. They called it the Magicians or the Enchantresses. This was probably in Gray's lifetime.

I give, after Mason, the Latin, as Gray found it in Torfaeus; and beside it a version for English readers:

	Late diffunditur	Wide is spread
	Ante stragem futuram	Before the coming havoc
	Sagittarum nubes:	The cloud of arrows:
	Depluit sanguis:	Down raineth the blood:
5	Iam hastis applicatur	Now to lances is fastened
	Cineracea	The ashen-hued
	Tela virorum	Warp of Warriors
	Quam amicae texunt	Which the Sisters weave
	Rubro subtegmine[1]	With the red woof
10	Randveri mortis.	Of Randver's death.
	Texitur haec Tela	This web we are weaving
	Intestinis humanis,	Of human entrails:
	Staminique strictè alligantur	And to the warp are straitly tied
	Capita humana,	Human heads;
15	Sunt sanguine roratae	There be blood-besprinkled
	Hastae pro Insilibus	Lances for treddles:
	Textoria Instrumenta ferrea	Iron is our weaving-gear
	Ac Sagittae pro Radiis:	And Arrows for Shuttles:
	Densabimus Gladiis	With Swords will we close-pleach
20	Hanc Victoriae Telam.	This Web of Victory.
	Prodeunt ad texendum Hilda	Forth come to the weaving Hilda
	Et Hiorthrimula,	And Hiorthrimula,

[1] i. q. subtemine.

	Sangrida et Swipula	Sangrida and Swipula
	Cum strictis Gladiis;	With drawn Swords;
25	Hastile frangetur,	The Spear shall be broken,
	Scutum diffindetur,	Cloven the Target,
	Ensisque	And Sword
	Clypeo illidetur.	Be dashed against Shield.
	Texamus, texamus	Weave we, weave we
30	Telam Darradar[1]!	The Web of Darradar!
	Hunc (Gladium) Rex Juvenis	This [Sword] the Young King
	Prius possidebat.	Erst wont to wear.
	Prodeamus,	Forth let us go
	Et Cohortes entremus	And join the Squadrons
35	Ubi nostri Amici	Where our Friends
	Armis dimicant!	Contend in battle!
	Texamus, texamus	Weave we, weave we
	Telam Darradi[2];	The Web of Darrad;
	Et Regi deinde[3]	And to the King, [then,]
40	Deinde adhaereamus!	Then, let us cleave
	Ibi videbant	*There* were seen
	Sanguine rorata scuta	Blood-sprent shields
	Gunna et Gondula	By Gunna and Gondula
	Quæ Regem tutabantur.	Guarding the King.

[1] *sic, ap.* Mason.

[2] "So Thormodus interprets it, as though Darradar were the name of the Person who saw this vision, but in reality it signifies a *Range of Spears* from *Daur*, Hasta, and *Radir*, Ordo." Gray.

I am enabled by the Rev. W. C. Green, translator of the *Egilssaga* (Stock, 1893) to state that the expression *vefr darradar* 'web of spear' occurs in Egil's *Head-ransom*, in a passage which Mr Green (p. 132) has rendered:

> "*Lances, a woven fence*
> Well-ordered, bristle dense."

As we have seen, Gray knew Egil's *Ransom*, and perhaps through this very passage in it (?as interpreted by Wormius) he is enabled to correct Bartholinus or Torfaeus here. Mr Green says, "Gray's acceptation of *darradar* as a compound word is doubtful: there is no trace of such a compound in Vigfússon's Lexicon. And yet it is quite possible that some one has taken the word as Gray explains it. For *darr* is 'a dart, plural *dörr*, which might often in old books be printed *daur*. And *rada* is a word 'to arrange.' But *ar* is the common genitive singular termination of several Icelandic declensions, and *darradar* is 'of a dart.'"

The name of the song is *Darradar Liod*, and Vigfússon and Powell point out that it is called in the lay itself (l. 42 of their text) *geir-hliod*, which can only mean 'lay of darts.' The mistake about 'Darrad' dates from the *Nialssaga*.

[3] *sic, ap.* Mason.

45	Texamus, texamus	Weave we, weave we
	Telam Darradi!	The Web of Darrad!
	Ubi Arma concrepant	Where rattle the Arms
	Bellacium Virorum	Of warlike Heroes
	Non sinamus eum	We must not suffer *him*
50	Vitâ privari:	Of Life to be reft:
	Habent Valkyriae	The Valkyries have
	Cædis potestatem.	Control of Slaughter.
	Illi Populi terras regent[1]	Lands shall those Tribes rule
	Qui deserta Promontoria	Who on desert Headlands
55	Antea incolebant.	Hitherto wont to dwell.
	Dico potenti Regi	O'er the mighty King I say
	Mortem imminere	Death impendeth
	Jam Sagittis occubuit Comes:	Already neath Arrows hath fallen the Earl.
	Et Hibernis	And the Hibernians
60	Dolor accidet,	Grief shall befall
	Qui nunquam	Which never from mind
	Apud Viros delebitur.	Of Men shall be blotted.
	Jam Tela texta est.	Now the Web is woven:
	Campus vero (Sanguine) roratus:	Blood-bedabbled the Plain:
65	Terras percurret	O'er the lands shall sweep
	Conflictus Militum.	Strife of armèd Men.
	Nunc horrendum est	Now dreadful is it
	Circumspicere	To cast the eyes round
	Cum Sanguinea Nubes	For a Cloud of Blood
70	Per Aera volitet:	Through Air is racking:
	Tingetur Aer	The Air shall be dyed
	Sanguine Virorum,	With Blood of Warriors
	Antequam Vaticinia nostra	Ere our Weird-Words
	Omnia corruent.	All fall to the ground.
75	Bene canimus	Well sing we
	De Rege juvene,	Of the Youthful King
	Victoriae carmina multa:	Many Songs of Victory:
	Bene sit nobis canentibus!	Good be our guerdon!
	Discat autem ille	But let that man learn
80	Qui auscultat	Who is hearkening,

[1] Two lines *ap.* Phelps

	Bellica Carmina multa	Many a warlike Song
	Et Viris referat.	And tell it among Men.
	Equitemus in Equis	Let us ride upon Horses:
	Quoniam efferimus gladios strictos	Since drawn swords from forth
85	Ex hoc loco.	This place we carry.

There is a copy of the *Fatal Sisters* in the Pembroke MSS., and another, a transcript by Wharton, in the Egerton MSS. in the British Museum. The Wharton MS. is headed (doubtless *from* Gray), 'The Song of the weird Sisters translated from the Norwegian written about 1029.' The date thus fixed by Gray, whencesoever derived, tallies with the statement of the American editors, that "the poem must be nearly contemporary with the event which it celebrates."

Scott was no doubt thinking of this version in passage quoted, *Bard*, l. 47, *ad fin.*

Note. "The Valkyriur were female Divinities, servants of *Odin* (or *Woden*) in the Gothic mythology. Their name signifies *Chusers of the slain*. They were mounted on swift horses, with drawn swords in their hands; and in the throng of battle selected such as were destined to slaughter, and conducted them to *Valhalla*, the hall of *Odin*, or paradise of the Brave: where they attended the banquet, and served the departed Heroes with horns of mead and ale." Gray.

This account, say the American editors, is derived from Bartholin, Bk. II. chaps. 11 and 12, and "accurately represents the belief that obtained among the vikings at the time when the poem was composed, but must be regarded as a special Scandinavian development, forming itself gradually among the warrior class in what is known as the 'viking age' (A.D. 750—1050 roughly) and not as a general Germanic creed (Gray's Gothic in this connection doubtless = Germanic, Teutonic), nor even as a creed ever accepted by the common people in Scandinavia."

2. **Hast** Wharton MS. For the pronunciation to which this points, cf. Dryden, *Threnodia Augustalis*, st. 4:

"Friends to congratulate their friends made *haste*,
And long inveterate foes saluted as they *pass'd*."

And the same rhyme, *infra* XXIII. ll. 8, 10.

3. "How quick they wheel'd, and flying, behind them shot
Sharp sleet of arrowy shower[s][1]."
Milton's *Par. Reg.* [III. 323, 324]. Gray.

[1] *shower* in original edition of *Par. Reg.* but noted there as an *erratum*.

16—2

"it toto turbida coelo
Tempestas telorum et ferreus ingruit imber."
[Through all the air goes a thick storm of weapons and faster falls the iron hail. Mackail.] Virg. *Aen.* XII. 284. Mitford.

4. "The noise of battle hurtled in the air."
Shakesp. *Jul. Caesar* [II. 2. 22]. Gray.

8. "Gray here follows Bartholin's Latin, which misrepresents the original. The Icelandic has 'the friends of the slayer of Randvérr,' i.e. 'the friends of Odin,' i.e. 'the valkyrjur,' a typical skaldic phrase." (Phelps and Kittredge.) For 'Orkney's woe' Gray has no original. It is clear indeed that the statements which he has embodied in his Preface are not a proper Argument to the original poem, though they have affected his interpretation of it. The song is altogether one of triumph, and no disasters to the side protected by the Sisters are recorded in it. The 'Comes,' therefore, in l. 59 of the Latin version is not the Earl of the Orkneys, though Gray so took it, unless Sigurd fought on Brian's side; whoever he was, his fall is among the calamities of *Erin*.

15. **Sword.** **Blade** Wharton MS.

It will be noticed that Gray has transferred to this place the reference to the Monarch's sword which comes later in the Latin (l. 31). Nor does he make it the young King's sword. The passage in the original speaks of 'the Young King' but is obscure.

17 sq. "**Sangrida, terrific Maid**
Mista black, and Hilda see" Wharton MS.

The four names Latinized *ap.* Torfaeus (ll. 21—23) are rendered in Vigfússon and Powell "War and Sword-clasher, Sangrid and Swipple." Gray rejects the awkward *Hiorthrimol*, and substitutes Mista. This and Geira (l. 31) he found, say the American editors, 'in Bartholin's translation (p. 554) of a stanza in another poem of the *Poetic Edda* (the Grimnismál), where they occur in a long list of names of *valkyrjur*.' [Vigfússon and Powell, I. 75].

22. **Blade.** **Sword** Wharton MS.

24. **Hauberk.** See Gray's note on l. 5 of the *Bard*.

25. With the weaving here and in the *Bard* compare the paraphrase of the gipsy's song in *Guy Mannering* [c. IV.]:

'Twist ye, twine ye! even so
Mingle shades of joy and woe,
Hope and fear, and peace and strife
In the thread of human life.
* * * * * *

Now they wax and now they dwindle
Whirling with the whirling spindle' &c. Bradshaw.

27. Cf. *Bard*, l. 142.

29, 30. Notice the semi-classical and conventional character of these two lines. The eighteenth century poet found it hard to keep this out of his verses however romantic or primitive the theme. Johnson was accustomed to laugh at the attempts made in his day to imitate the vigorous simplicity of old romantic poetry; he could, he said, do it better himself; and to prove it extemporized four lines of translation, the third of which runs:

"Where *confused in mutual slaughter*" [!]

Gray also fails here occasionally, though he has chosen a measure very suitable to a sort of incantation; it is that of the witches in *Macbeth*; and Dr Phelps remarks that

"Keep the tissue close and strong,"

reminds us by the rhythm of

"Make the gruel thick and slab."
(*Macb.* IV. I. 32.)

We may add that l. 21

"Ere the ruddy sun be set,"

has in the opening Witch-scene of *Macbeth* (I. I. 4, 5),

"When the battle's lost and won,
That will be ere the set of sun,"

a counterpart which Gray did not find in his original, and I cannot doubt that he had *Macbeth* lurking in his mind.

31. **Gunna and Gondula** Wharton and Pembroke MSS. (The readings in Pemb. MS. are given on the faith of Mr Gosse.)

No doubt Gray came to the conclusion that it should be *Gondŭla*, not *Gondūla*. Cf. his rejection of Caradoc in the *Bard*, l. 102. I think he changed *Gunna* to *Geira* (see on l. 17) for greater variety in the sound after *Gondula*.

Notice the imperfect tenses in the Latin ll. 42, 45, from which Gray here departs. The original as translated *ap.* Vigfússon and Powell is "Battle and Gondol that guard the king shall bear bloody shields."

32. **Youthful King**. Sigtrygg, cf. l. 50 of the Latin.

33. **slaughter. havock** Pembroke MS.

37. **They** &c. The Northmen, hitherto confined to the seabord of Erin.

41. **Earl.** Brian's son (Vigfússon and Powell), see on l. 8. But *Gray* probably means *Sigurd.*

44. **Shall.** **Must** Wharton MS.

45. **His.** **Her** Pembroke MS.

48. Cf. for the diction on l. 29.

50. **Blot.** **Veil** Wharton MS.

57. **Mortal.** The original has, in this context, as translated *ap.* Vigfússon and Powell:

"We have spoken words of might round the young King, we have sung him many a joyous Lay of Victory, many a Lay of Spears. Now let him that hath heard them learn them and sing them among men."

This seems to be only an injunction to those that heard the songs in praise of Sigtrygg to transmit them; much as David enjoined that his 'Song of the Bow' (the dirge over Saul and Jonathan) should be taught; but the writer in the *Nialssaga*, building his story in part out of the song, and misinterpreting its title, invents the listener Darrad &c.[1]

59, 60. **Scotland.** There is nothing corresponding to this in the original. It is in fact an excrescence upon an excrescence. See prec. note.

winding. **ecchoing** Wharton MS.

61—65. "**Sisters, hence! 'tis time to ride:**
Now your thundering falchion wield:
Now your sable steed bestride:
Hurry, hurry to the field."
Wharton and Pembroke MSS.

[1] This legendary setting of the song assumes a guise almost historic in Scott's Diary, *ap.* Lockhart (*Life of Scott*, c. XXIX) "On Duncansby head appear some remarkable rocks, like towers, called the Stacks of Duncansby. Near this shore runs the remarkable breaking tide called the *Merry Men of Mey*, whence Mackenzie takes the scenery of a poem—

'Where the dancing men of Mey
Speed the current to the land.'

[Lockhart here refers us to Henry Mackenzie's Introduction to the "Fatal Sisters." *Works*, 1808, vol. viii. p. 63.] "Here according to his locality, the Caithness man witnessed the vision, in which was introduced the song translated by Gray."

XIX. THE DESCENT OF ODIN.

For date of writing and publication of the *Descent* &c. see preceding Ode.

'The Icelandic line should read "Upp reis Óðinn aldinn gautr," Uprose Odin, the old Creator.' P. and K.

In the Wharton MS. it is headed 'The Vegtams Kwitha [*sic*] from Bartholinus, L. 3, c. 2, p. 562.' 'Vegtamskviða (i.e. *The Song of Vegtamr*, name assumed by Odin). Known also as *Baldrs Draumar* (Baldr's Dream[1]).' P. and K. See note on l. 37 *infra*.

The Persons of the Dialogue are not indicated in Wharton's transcript in Brit. Mus. There is probably a Pembroke MS., but I have not seen it, and find no record of its readings in books accessible to me. Mason is said to have extracted the notes on these Odes which he signs G [Gray] from the Pembroke MSS.

Bartholin omits the first stanza of this Ode, and inserts ten lines which are spurious. In these respects Gray follows him. (P. and K.)

Vigfússon and Powell say that the original is evidently by the author of *Thrymskviða*, a humorous story describing how Thor recovered his hammer from the giant Thrym. If I am not mistaken, they would assign both poems to the last years of the 10th century. (*Corpus Poetarum Boreale*, v. 1. p. lxvi.)

The legend of the death of Balder son of Odin says that he had dreams of danger to his life. He told them to the gods. Then Frigga, his mother, took an oath from all things that they would not hurt Balder. But she omitted, as too weak a thing, the mistletoe "that grows on the eastern side of Valhalla." So Balder, like Achilles, was invulnerable except that there was one unlikely thing that could hurt him, as Achilles had one unlikely place in which he could be hurt. The gods were wont to amuse themselves by throwing darts and stones at Balder. But the evil Loki found out that the mistletoe had not taken the pledge; and he put it in the hands of Hoder, who being blind was not joining in the sport, and directed his arm, and so Balder was slain. Ere this however Odin had gone disguised to Hela, to discover the doom of Balder, as described in the Poem that follows. The first stanza, perhaps omitted

[1] But Vigfússon and Powell say the original *title* is lost. They head it *Balder's Doom*.

by Bartholin because it seems to be a fragment, is of four lines, thus rendered in Vigfússon and Powell: "...At once the Anses [Æsir] all went into council, and all the goddesses to a parley. The mighty gods took counsel together that they might find out why dreams of evil haunted Balder."

Bartholin's Latin Text (*ap.* Mason).

	Surgebat Odinus,	Uprose Odin
	Virorum summus	Chief of Men
	Et Sleipnerum	On Sleipner
	Ephippio stravit.	Laid he the saddle;
5	Equitabat deorsum	Downwards he rode
	Niflhelam versus.	Toward Niflhel:
	Obviam habuit Catellum	He met the Whelp coming
	Ab Helae habitaculis venientem.	From Hela's abodes.
	Huic sanguine aspersa erant	Bedabbled in blood
10	Pectus anterius,	Were the brute's gorge,
	Rictus, mordendi avidus,	Muzzle, eager to bite,
	Et maxillarum infima:	And under jaw:
	Allatrabat ille,	He barked
	Et Rictum diduxit	Wide-grinning
15	Magiae Patri,	At the Father of Spells,
	Et diu latrabat.	Long did he bark.
	Equitavit Odinus	Odin rode on
	(Terra subtus tremuit)	(Earth trembled beneath him)
	Donec ad altum veniret	Till he came to the lofty
20	Helae Habitaculum.	Dwelling of Hela.
	Tum equitavit Odinus	Then rode Odin
	Ad orientale ostii Latus	To the East side of the Portal
	Ubi Fatidicae	Where he knew was
	Tumulum esse novit.	The Barrow of the Prophetess.
25	Sapienti Carmina	To the Wise One Charms
	Mortuos excitantia cecinit,	He sang waking the Dead,
	Boream inspexit,	He looked to the North Wind,
	Literas [Tumulo] imposuit,	Placed runes [on the Barrow],
	Sermones proferre cœpit	Spells to speak he began:
30	Responsa poposcit,	For answers he called,
	Donec invita surgeret,	Till she rising unwilling

	Et mortuorum sermonem proferret.	Spake speech of the dead.
	Fatidica. Quisnam hominum	*Prophetess.* Who of men
	Mihi ignotorum	To me unknown
35	Mihi facere praesumit	Takes on him to make
	Tristem Animum?	Sad my Soul?
	Nive eram, et	Upon me snow
	Nimbo aspersa,	Was shed, and cloud;
	Pluviâque rorata	With rain was I washed;
40	Mortua diu jacui.	Long dead have I lain.
	O. Viator nominor,	*Odin.* My name is 'Traveller,'
	Bellatoris Filius sum;	'Warrior's' son:
	Enarra mihi quæ apud Helam geruntur.	Tell me what passeth in Hela:
	Ego tibi quae in mundo:	I thee what passeth in the world:
45	Cuinam sedes Auro stratae sunt	For whom are the seats strewn with gold
	Lecti pulchri,	The fair couches,
	Auro ornati?	With gold adorned?
	F. Hic Baldero Medo	*Pr.* Here for Balder Mead
	Paratus extat,	Is set forth ready,
50	Purus Potus,	Pure Drink,
	Scuto superinjecto:	A shield covers the goblet:
	Divina verò soboles	The sons of the gods
	Dolore afficietur.	Grief shall visit.
	Invita haec dixi,	Unwilling have I said this
55	Jamque silebo.	And now will be silent.
	O. Noli, Fatidica, tacere.	*Od.* Prophetess, be not silent.
	Te interrogare volo,	Fain would I question thee
	Donec omnia novero.	Till all I know.
	Adhuc scire volo,	Yet would I learn
60	Quisnam Baldero	Who on Balder
	Necem inferet,	Death shall inflict,
	Et Odini Filium	And the Son of Odin
	Vitâ privabit?	Of Life shall deprive?
	F. Hoderus excelsum fert	*P.* 'Tis Hoder brings thither
65	Honoratum Fratrem illuc.	His high, honoured Brother.
	Is Baldero	'Tis he who on Balder
	Necem inferet,	Death shall inflict,

	Et Odini Filium	And the Son of Odin
	Vitâ privabit.	Of Life shall deprive.
70	Invita haec dixi	Unwilling have I said this
	Jamque tacebo.	And now will be silent.
	O. Noli tacere, Fatidica,	*O.* Prophetess, be not silent,
	Adhuc te interrogare volo	Yet would I question thee
	Donec omnia novero.	Till all I know.
75	Adhuc scire volo,	Yet would I learn
	Quisnam Hodo [*sic*]	Who to Hoder
	Odium rependet,	Hate shall repay
	Aut Balderi Interfectorem	And Balder's slayer slaying
	Occidendo rogo adaptet?	Make meet for the pyre?
80	*F.* Rinda Filium pariet	*Pr.* Rinda shall bear a Son
	In Habitaculis occidentalibus:	In the dwellings of the West
	Hic Odini Filius	He, Odin's Son,
	Unam noctem natus, armis utetur;	But one night old, shall wield weapons;
	Manum non lavabit,	He shall not wash hand
85	Nec Caput pectet,	Nor comb head,
	Antequam Rogo imponet	Ere he shall set on the pyre
	Balderi inimicum.	Balder's Foe.
	Invita haec dixi,	Unwilling have I said this,
	Jamque tacebo.	And now will be silent.
90	*O.* Noli tacere, Fatidica,	*O.* Prophetess, be not silent,
	Adhuc te interrogare volo,	Yet would I question thee
	Quaenam sunt Virgines,	Who are the Virgins
	Quae prae Cogitationibus lachrymantur	Who for [sad] thoughts weep
	Et in Caelum jactant	And towards Heaven cast
95	Cervicum pepla?	Their Neck-veils?
	Hoc solum mihi dicas,	This one thing tell me,
	Nam prius non dormies.	For till then sleep thou shalt not.
	F. Non tu Viator es,	*Pr.* Thou art not Traveller,
	Ut antea credidi;	As ere this I deemed;
100	Sed potius Odinus	But Odin rather
	Virorum summus.	Chief of Men.
	O. Tu non es Fatidica,	*O.* No Prophetess thou,
	Nec sapiens Fœmina,	Nor Wise-Woman,
	Sed potius trium	But the Dam rather

105	Gigantum Mater.	Of the Giants Three.
	F. Equita domum Odine,	*Pr.* Ride home, Odin:
	At in his gloriare:	But boast thee herein:
	Nemo tali modo veniet,	None in such sort shall come
	Ad sciscitandum	Question to ask
110	Usque dum Lokus	Till the day that Loki
	Vinculis solvatur,	Be released from his bonds,
	Et Deorum Crepusculum	And of the Gods' Twilight
	Dissolventes aderint [*sic*].	Come the Destroyers.

It will be noticed that Gray's Poem is upon the whole nearer to the Latin text than is the case with *The Sisters.* I have translated Bartholin's Latin (which here and there seems wrong grammatically) according to his *intended* meaning.

1. **King of Men.** Gray follows Bartholin. Vigfússon and Powell 'the ancient Sire.'

2. **steed.** *Sleipner*, who however in the *Prose Edda* (as given in Mallet's *Northern Antiquities*, § 42, p. 432, ed. Bohn) is described at his birth as 'a *grey* foal, with eight legs.' Though Odin is not an infernal deity, Gray is no doubt so far affected by the Latin mythology that in describing this *visit* to Hell, he gives him one of Pluto's *coal-black steeds.*

4. Hela, in the Edda, is described with a dreadful countenance, and her body half flesh-colour and half blue. Gray.

Ib. Niflheimr, the hell of the Gothic nations, consisted of nine worlds [hence 'portals nine,' l. 16] to which were devoted all such as died of sickness, old age, or by any other means than in battle. Over it presided Hela, the Goddess of Death. Gray.

The form in the original, *Niflhel* (cf. Bartholin, l. 6) is translated Mist-Hell, *ap.* Vigfússon and Powell.

"This comes from Bartholin, pp. 387, 585, and is based on a passage of the *Prose Edda.* It represents, like the Valhalla creed, a late stage of Viking belief. The Old Norse form of the goddess's name is Hel. Hell in this note should be understood as *Hades*, not as a place of torment." (P. and K.)

5. 'Called *Managarmar* in the *Edda.*' Mason. *Garm* in the *Volo-Spa.* He fed, says Mason, on the lives of men.

7 sq. In this description Bartholin and Gray must have rendered some spurious lines. The original, as translated *ap.* Vigfússon and Powell, has only: "there was blood on its breast, as it ran by the way; barking at the Father of Spells."

11. **fruitless.** **ceaseless** Wharton MS.

14. **shakes.** **quakes** Wharton MS.

16. **nine,** added by Gray, see on l. 4.

17. A line from *L'Allegro*, l. 59—as Mitford points out; but in a very different setting:

> "Right against the eastern gate,
> Where the great Sun begins his state."

17—26. There is scarcely anything to separate these lines in the diction and rhythmic expression from Scott. Short as they are these two Norse Odes, but particularly *The Descent of Odin*, permanently influenced him, and perhaps directly or indirectly helped to determine the choice of the measure in which the narrative part of his best known 'Lays' is in the main set. We constantly hear from him the echoes[1] of such lines as

> "Where long of yore to sleep was laid
> The dust of the prophetic Maid,"

or

> "The thrilling verse that wakes the dead[2]."

When he had shown his translation of Burger's *Lenore* to his friend's sister, Miss Cranstoun, she wrote, "Upon my word Walter Scott is going to turn out a poet,—something of a cross I think between Burns and Gray." No doubt she had these Norse Odes in mind in naming Gray; and in naming Burns too, probably she thought of Tam O'Shanter. In the young Harold of the *Lay of the Last Minstrel* (Canto VI. st. 22), Scott described the sources of his own inspiration: for instance, the Saga that told

> "Of those dread Maids, whose hideous yell
> Maddens the battle's bloody swell,"

(he refers us in a note to Gray's *Fatal Sisters*); adding however, how

> "...by sweet glen and greenwood tree
> He learn'd a milder minstrelsy,
> Yet something of the Northern spell
> Mix'd with the softer numbers well."

Compare with *The Fatal Sisters* the *Song of Harold Harfager* in *The Pirate*, Chap. XV.

21. For this line there seems to be no warrant in the original *ap.* Vigfússon and Powell. Whoever interpolated the text which Bartholin translated perhaps forgot that Odin had *reached* Hela, and that the

[1] The resemblance is noted, I find, by the Earl of Carlisle.

[2] In 1792 Scott had transcribed the *Vegtams Kvitha*, the Norse Original, the Latin of Bartholin and the English of Gray, with an account appended of the death of Balder from the *Edda* and other sources.

reason for turning to the north, viz. that Hela lay northwards, was, in the instance of his spell, wanting.

Clime, Grk. κλίμα (κλίνω) is the supposed *slope* of the earth from the equator to the pole, and hence means *region*, any notion of *temperature* is secondary. Gray uses it with some idea of *regio*, used, in the language of Roman augury, for the line marking segments of earth or sky in divination.

22. **thrice**. A touch *added* by Gray (cf. the Latin l. 28) from Greek, Roman, and perhaps almost every superstition.

"*Thrice* the brinded cat hath mewed." *Macbeth*, IV. 1. 17.

Notice that Gray omits the 'tumulo' which Bartholin has inserted to explain the Norse; but in fact the whole line is an interpolation of which, say the American editors, the text is quite as vague as Gray's 'traced.' Probably 'graved' was meant. Mitford says, "In a little poem called the *Magic of Odin*, see Bartholinus (p. 641), Odin says, 'If I see a man dead, and hanging aloft on a tree, I engrave Runic characters so wonderful, that the man immediately descends and converses with me.'" The fragment of a Spell Song *ap*. Vigfússon and Powell, which tells of the origin of Runes, begins "The Sage read them, *graved* them." Egil (Green's Egilssaga, c. 75) recovers a sick woman by graving spell-words in runes.

'Runic is a term applied to alphabets used by the Scandinavians and other Germanic races before the adoption of the Roman letters.' P. and K.

23. **accents. Murmurs** Wharton MS.

24. The original word is Vallgaldr, from *Valr*, mortuus, and *Galdr*, incantio. Gray (as quoted by Mason). P. and K. say the note is from Bartholin, p. 640.

26. "Mine ear but heard *the sullen sound*
Which like an earthquake shook the *ground*,"
Scott, *Lady of the Lake*, Canto VI. 19,

27. **call. voice** Wharton MS.

27, 28. The seeress' unwillingness to be disturbed recalls the words of Samuel when evoked by the Witch of Endor, "Why hast thou disquieted me to bring me up?" 1 Sam. xxviii. 15. The idea is familiar to all nations. Phelps.

my troubled. a weary Wharton MS.

31—33. "the bones of men
....
...bleached by drifting wind and rain."
Scott, *Lady of the Lake*, III. 5.

35. **he. this**, Wharton MS.

37. **A Traveller.** *Viator ap.* Bartholin, *Vegtamr* in the original, rendered *ap.* Vigfússon and Powell 'Way-wise'; the word Gray renders 'Warriour' is there 'Warwise.' These Odin passes on the Prophetess as proper-names, as Bartholin shows, "Viator *nominor*" (l. 41). Gray, perhaps designedly, neglects this touch of primitive simplicity, which may be compared with the disguise of Ulysses as *Outis* (Noman) (*Od.* IX.) which deceived the Cyclops.

41, 42. Bartholin and Gray seem to mistake the original here, though the text is apparently doubtful: Vigfússon and Powell render "For whom are the benches strewed with 'mail-coats' and the hall so fairly decked with painted shields?"

44. Mead, made from honey. Gray's periphrasis is his own; even the epithet 'pure' seems to come from a mistake or interpolation in Bartholin's Norse text.

45. Gray certainly departs from Bartholin here, for I can give no meaning to 'scuto superin*jecto*' but that in my rendering l. 51. He is much nearer to Vigfússon and Powell's "*the walls decked with shields.*" See what is said on Gray's note on version of Torfaeus in *Fatal Sisters.*

47. Wharton having written **giv'n** corrects to **given.**

48. So Bartholin (ll. 53, 54); the original, according to Vigfússon and Powell is much less effective, "While the sons of the Anses are in merry mood."

Ib. **heaven**, Wharton MS.

51. Mason here extracts from Gray's MS.:

"Women were looked upon by the Gothic nations as having a peculiar insight into futurity: and some there were that made profession of magic arts and divination. These travelled round the country, and were received in every house with great respect and honour. Such a woman bore the name of Volva Seidkona or Spakona. The dress of Thorbiorga, one of these prophetesses, is described at large in Eirick's Rauda Sogu (*ap.* Bartholin, l. I. cap. IV. p. 688). She had on a blue vest spangled all over with stones, a necklace of glass beads, and a cap made of the skin of a black lamb lined with white cat-skin. She leaned on a staff adorned with brass, with a round head set with stones; and was girt with an Hunlandish belt, at which hung her pouch full of magical instruments. Her buskins were of rough calf-skin, bound on with thongs studded with knobs of brass, and her gloves of white cat-skin, the fur turned inwards.

"They were also called *Fiolkyngi*, or *Fiol-kunnug* (*sic*); i.e.

Multi-scia: and *Visindakona*; i.e. Oraculorum Mulier, *Nornir*; i.e. Parcae."

This note, say the American editors, is almost wholly from Bartholin. They correct some inaccuracies in the Icelandic; e.g. what Gray writes as *Fiolkyngi* is, they say, a noun, and means *the prophetic art*. The Nornir or Norns are really the Norse *Fates*. They are, however, confounded with ordinary seeresses in a story quoted by Bartholin, p. 685 (cf. p. 612). See on l. 75.

Scott, from Mason's *Gray*, or from the sources there quoted (cf. on ll. 17—26 *supra*), has borrowed the description of 'Norna of the Fitful-Head' in *The Pirate*, c. 5; and he says, "The name assigned *her*, which signifies one of those fatal sisters who weave the web of human fate, had been conferred in honour of her supernatural powers." For the same reason, perhaps, it was once given commonly to 'spae-wives.'

51, 52. **Prophetess, my call obey,**
Once again arise, and say Wharton MS.

55. **In Hoder's** *hand*. Here again Gray seems to have some inkling of the meaning of the original: "Lo, Hod is *bearing* a tall branch of fate." Vigfússon and Powell. The reference must be to the fatal mistletoe (cf. the *Volo-Spa*, 101—103, V. and P. vol. I.), p. 197, but Bartholin's version has no trace of this (ll. 64, 65 *supra*).

59, 60. **Once again my call obey,**
Prophetess, arise and say Wharton MS.

61, 62. **"By whom shall Hoder's blood be spilt**
Who the avenger of his guilt?" Wharton MS.

64. **wond'rous.** **Giant** Wharton MS.

66. "King Harold made (according to the singular custom of his time) a solemn vow never to *clip or comb his hair* till he should have extended his sway over the whole country. Herbert, Iceland. Transl. p. 39." Mitford. Analogous among Hebrew customs is the Nazaritic vow, in which the hair was unshorn until the vow had been fulfilled, or in the best-known instances (Samson, Samuel, St John the Baptist) for all the lifetime. But cf. next note.

68. This line obscurely renders the original and Bartholin. The wond'rous Child (named Wali) was one night old when he slew Hoder (Lat. vers. l. 83). One might question the reference to a *vow* in l. 66 under the circumstances, if we looked for coherence in these legends; and perhaps there too the words point to the infant's prompt action. Matthew Arnold in *Balder Dead* makes Hoder slay himself.

69. **corse.** Spelt **coarse** in Wharton's MS.

74. **awake.** **arise** Wharton MS.

75. "Probably the Nornir; their names were Urda, Verdandi, and Skulda; they were the dispensers of good destinies. As their names signify Time past, present, and future, it is probable they were always invisible to mortals: therefore when Odin asks this question on seeing them, he betrays himself to be a god." Mason.

77. **flaxen.** **flowing** Wharton MS.

83. **The mightiest of the mighty line**, Wharton MS.

An amplification by Gray.

86. "In the Latin 'Mater trium Gigantum.' He means, therefore, probably Angerbode, who, from her name, seems to be 'no Prophetess of good,' and who bore to Loki, as the Edda says, three children, the Wolf Fenris, the great Serpent of Midgard, and Hela, all of them called Giants in that mythology." Mason.

But P. and K. say (doubtfully), "Odin recognizes the seeress as the goddess Hel herself." In that case perhaps 'Mother of *three* Monsters' (V. and P.) has no specific reference; but is an imputation extemporized by Odin to relieve his feelings, with a detail to give it more sting.

87. **Hie thee, Odin, boast** Wharton MS.

89. **iron-sleep.** Cf. *Bard*, l. 93 n.

χάλκεον ὕπνον, Hom. *Il.* XI. 241; and "ferreus somnus," Virg., *Aen.* XII. 309. Mitford.

90. **has.** **have** Wharton MS.

"*Lok* is the evil Being who continues in chains till *the Twilight of the Gods* approaches, when he shall break his bonds; the human race, the stars, and sun shall disappear; the earth sink in the seas, and fire consume the skies: even Odin himself and his kindred-deities shall perish. For a farther explanation of this mythology see Mallet's Introduction to the *History of Denmark*, 1755, Quarto." Gray.

"Gray had himself no doubt used Bartholin, pp. 567 ff., where a part of the Voluspa (the Sibyl's soothsaying) is quoted and translated." P. and K.

According to the Prose Edda, Loki after compassing the death of Balder and preventing his return from Hela, was caught and imprisoned in a cavern, bound with *three*-fold bonds of iron; and a serpent was suspended over him dropping venom, which his wife Siguna receives in a cup, which she empties as often as it is filled; but while she empties it, the venom drops on Loki's face, and he writhes; which is the cause of earthquakes. "There will Loki lie until Ragnarök" says the Edda. Ragnarök Gray with all the older interpreters took to mean "the

Twilight of the Gods." P. and K. say it merely means "the Fates of the Gods." So for the two last lines of Bartholin's version here Vigfússon and Powell give, "And the Destroyers come at the *Doom* of the Powers." Bartholin must have supposed that the 'Twilight' preceded the final catastrophe.

91—94. This is an expansion of the simple original; inspired in part by the *Volo-Spa.* In *substantial* Night, Gray's meaning is much the same as Milton's (*Par. Lost,* II. 150), 'uncreated' or 'unoriginal' (*Ib.* X. 477) Night. But Milton speaks also of *unessential* Night (II. 439), the very reverse of Gray's *substantial*, for it means having *no* substance, *οὐσία*, essence, and this strictly speaking is the right epithet, Darkness being only *absence* of light and colour. But Gray means that Darkness *was*, before the creation of anything, and will *survive* the destruction of all things.

92. **Has reassum'd. Reassumes her** Wharton MS.

XX. EPITAPH ON SIR WILLIAM WILLIAMS.

On the 23rd of October, 1760, Gray wrote to his friend Brown, 'In my way to town I met with the first news of the expedition from Sir William Williams, who makes a part of it, and perhaps may lay his fine Vandyck head in the dust.'

And on May 5, 1761, Walpole writes to George Montagu, 'We have lost a young genius, Sir William Williams; an express from Belleisle, arrived this morning, brings nothing but his death. He was shot very unnecessarily, riding too near a battery; in sum, he is a sacrifice to his own rashness, and to ours. For what are we taking Belleisle?'

The same to Mann, May 14. 'Sir William Williams, a young man much talked of, for his exceeding ambition, enterprising spirit, and some parts, in Parliament, is already fallen there [at Belleisle]; and even he was too great a price for such a trumpery island—we have dozens as good in the north of Scotland, and of as much consequence.'

Belle-Île is off the coast of Morbihan, almost direct south of Quiberon, and west of the mouth of the Loire.

Sir W. Williams, according to Walpole (to George Montagu, May 14, 1761), 'made Fred. Montagu heir to all his debts.'

His full name was William *Peere* Williams. He was a baronet, member for Shoreham, captain in Burgoyne's dragoons, a regiment raised in 1759, now the 16th Lancers. It was his executor, Frederick Montagu, who, perhaps at Mason's instigation, prevailed on Gray to write this epitaph 'for a monument which he means to erect at Belleisle.' (Gray to Mason, Aug. 1761.)

The affairs of Sir W. Williams seem to have been embarrassed, this may account for a statement quoted by Mitford, that '*in the recklessness of a desponding mind* he approached too near the enemy's sentinels, and was shot through the body.'

His younger brother, George James Williams, known as 'Gilly Williams,' was the bosom friend of the witty George Selwyn; and one of the three (the other two being Selwyn and 'Dick' Edgcumbe) in that 'Conversation' piece by Sir Joshua Reynolds, which now, I believe, is at the top of the staircase in the National Gallery.

The text of the epitaph printed by Mason differs from that given by Mitford in *Letters of Gray and Mason* (Aug. 1761), and in Mitford MSS. in the British Museum, doubtless transcribed from that letter. Gray (*ib.* Aug. 1761) says he does not like the epitaph, and does not expect Montagu will; he asks for Mason's 'real opinion'; perhaps this may have encouraged Mason 'to wreak his wicked will.' So Dr Bradshaw thinks.

5. **uncall'd his maiden** Gray to Mason, *l.c.* **his voluntary** Mason. Mitford points out that Scott has imitated Mason's text:

"Since riding side by side our hand
First *drew the voluntary* brand."

Marmion, Introd. to Canto IV. ll. 9, 10.

'Sir William Williams, in the expedition to Aix, was [a volunteer] on board the *Magnanime* with Lord Howe; and was deputed to receive the capitulation.' Mason.

The capture (Sept. 28) of the fortified island of Aix, at the mouth of the Charente, was an incident in the unsuccessful expedition against the arsenal of Rochefort, in 1757. Howe, then a captain, anchored his ship within 50 yards of the fort, and after an hour silenced the batteries. General Conway (Horace Walpole's cousin) took possession of the citadel. See also Chesterfield to his Son, Oct. 10, 1757.

But that it omits the fact that Williams saw service at Aix for the first time, Mason's text is an improvement on the original draft here.

6. **glory** Gray to Mason, *l. c.* **honour** Mason.

9. **intrepid** G. to M. **undaunted** Mason.

It may be questioned whether Gray would have made the change to 'undaunted.' He studied variety; and having given the village Hampden a 'dauntless breast' in a line of the *Elegy* by this time familiar, he would choose another word here.

10. **Victor &c.** Ignorance is bliss for annotators of this epitaph; in the light of actual fact it seems artificial and unreal. Le Palais, the citadel of Belle-Île, capitulated on the 7th of June, 1761, more than a month after the death of Sir W. Williams.

XXI. SKETCH OF HIS OWN CHARACTER.

This was published by Mason in 1775, in a note to Gray's Letter to Stonhewer, Aug. 18, 1758. This is, I think, our only authority for the text.

1. Mitford quotes Swift to Gay [Jan. 8, 1722—3], but the passage is mutilated by him to make it square. There is one point of superficial resemblance. Swift says that poets are 'too *poor to bribe* porters, and *too proud* to cringe to second-hand favourites in a great family.'

4. Pope, *Prologue to the Satires* (Ep. to Arbuthnot), ll. 267, 268,

> "I was not born for courts or great affairs:
> I pay my debts, believe, and say my pray'rs."

Gray wrote to Wharton, Aug. 5, 1763, 'Mrs Jonathan told me, you begun your evening prayer as soon as I was gone and that it had a great effect upon the congregation: *I hope you have not grown weary of it, nor lay it aside when company comes.* poor Mrs Bonfoy (*who taught me to pray*) is dead.'

Gray's religious opinions were never much defined by him; there was nothing distinctively Christian about them from the point of view of doctrine. That he was religiously minded is beyond question; the Deism which was in his day general among men of letters was not in his case the cover for atheism or materialism. [See on *Alliance of Education and Government*.]

Berkeley in his *Alciphron* (1732) gives us, in Alciphron, the picture of a disciple of Shaftesbury, and in Lysicles (the counterpart of Thrasymachus in Plato's *Republic*), an unbeliever of a rougher type, who flouts Alciphron for conceding 'the belief of a God, virtue, a future state, and such fine notions.' (*Dial.* v. § 29.) In the letter to

Stonhewer above mentioned Gray contemptuously accounts for the 'vogue' Shaftesbury once enjoyed, but says 'an interval of above forty years has pretty well destroyed the charm. The mode of free-thinking is like that of Ruffs and Farthingales, and has given place to the mode of not thinking at all: once it was considered graceful half to discover and half conceal the mind, but now we have been long accustomed to see it quite naked.' In fact Lysicles had elbowed Alciphron aside.

In Bolingbroke's *Works*[1] Gray found a censure of Wollaston[2], for expressing regrets like those in the *Elegy*, "For who to dumb forgetfulness" &c. and also a theory, which has been revived in our own time in the cause of orthodoxy, that we can know nothing of the moral attributes of the Deity. On both these topics Gray made a commentary, which Mason has preserved as an appendix to the letter to Stonhewer above cited. It is a valuable relic, not only as a piece of reasoning, but as evidence of a *real* belief in God, in a man who had been taught to pray. Let us remember also Gray's aversion to Voltaire, and his entreaty to Norton Nicholls not to visit him; and his opinion of Hume as expressed in a letter to Beattie, July 2, 1770.

A post or a pension. In 1757, when the Laureateship was vacant, Gray wrote to Mason (Dec. 19), 'Though I well know the bland emollient saponaceous qualities both of sack and silver, yet if any great man would say to me "I make you rat-catcher to his Majesty, with a salary of £300 a year and two butts of the best Malaga, and though it has been usual to catch a mouse or two, for form's sake, in public once a year, yet to you, sir, we shall not stand upon these things," I cannot say I should jump at it' &c.

The only post in the gift of the crown which he was anxious to obtain was the Professorship of History at Cambridge, for which he made unsuccessful endeavours in 1762 (see *Gray and His Friends*, pp. 184, 185), and which was bestowed on him in 1768.

Charles Townshend. A meteoric statesman (in some respects the Randolph Churchill of his time), who died (in his 42nd or 43rd year) in 1767. In 1761 he was Secretary at War, he was subsequently Paymaster of the Forces, and at the time of his death, Chancellor of the Exchequer.

[1] That blunderbuss, as Johnson called it, against religion and morality, which he had not resolution to fire off himself, but left half-a-crown to a beggarly Scotchman (Mallet) to draw the trigger after his decease.

[2] Norton Nicholls says, 'I believe Gray liked Wollaston's *Religion of Nature*.'

"Our comet Charles Townshend is dead...that eccentric genius, whom no system could contain, is whirled out of existence" (Walpole to Mann, Sept. 27, 1767). Walpole's judgment of his character was unfavourable; Gray seems to have shared it.

Burke in 1774 paid a kindly tribute to Townshend's memory, in his Speech on American Taxation, though he describes him as 'officially the reproducer of that fatal scheme.' He refers to the skill with which he brought a comparatively small stock of knowledge to bear; says, he 'hit the House just between wind and water,' and 'seemed to guide, because he was always sure to follow it'—speaks of 'the *ferment* he was able to excite in everything by the violent ebullition of his mixed virtues and failings'; 'his ardent passion for fame'; and adds, 'to please universally was the object of his life,' but 'to *tax* and please is not given to men, though *he* attempted it.'

The sketch which Smollett gives of Charles Townshend, in *Humphry Clinker*, confirms the picture of him which friendly and unfriendly critics combine to make. He was brilliant and fascinating; but you could not trust him. His famous "Champagne" Speech was delivered in the last year of his life; when Chatham's seclusion left his motley government without guidance. In the course of it Townshend, gibing at himself and everybody, said 'Government had become what he himself had often been called, a Weathercock.'

Squire. It is noteworthy that in this very year (1761) Squire became Bishop of S. David's. He was *quondam* Fellow of S. John's, Cambridge,—one of the Royal Chaplains (Gray to Mason, 1757) and Dean of Bristol. Warburton said of him that he made *religion his trade*, as another dean *made trade his religion*. He obtained his bishopric before May 9, 1761[1]. These verses may have been written earlier than those on Sir W. Williams. The notion that Goldsmith took hints from them for 'Retaliation' must be rejected. 'Retaliation' (whenever written) was printed in 1774, after Goldsmith's death; these verses first appeared in Mason's *Life and Works of Gray* in 1775.

[1] Gray to Wharton of that date: Squire's Chaplain was the infamous Dr Dodd, by Squire introduced to Lord Chesterfield, who made him tutor to his son.—Dodd forged the son's name and was hanged for it.

XXII. AMATORY LINES.

A rather absurd title, retained for the sake of convenience. According to Bradshaw it was bestowed by Mitford in 1814. That the lines are Gray's we know from the statement of the Rev. Mr Leman, who received them with the following poem from the Countess de Viry (Miss Speed), while on a visit to her at her castle in Savoy, in 1780. Of these lines the anonymous editor of Sharpe's *Poems of Gray* (1826) says that they were "produced on a request that Miss Speed made to the poet one day, *when he was in company with Mr Walpole*, that she might possess something from his pen on the subject of love." If this is exact, this is the earlier of the two poems, for *Thyrsis* is certainly on that subject.

Mr Leman gave these lines to Joseph Warton, I believe, soon after he received them, and they appeared, according to Mitford, in Warton's edition of Pope, vol. I. p. 285.

Dr Glynn, Gray's friend and physician at Cambridge, sent this and the following poem to a friend, G. S. Calcott, at Bristol, July 1, 1791. From his letter I find that it was headed 'A song without a tune,' and the 'Thyrsis &c.' was called 'The Inconstant.'

XXIII. SONG.

Walpole wrote to the Countess of Ailesbury, Nov. 28, 1761, "You will like...to see some words which Mr Gray has writ at Miss Speed's request to an air of Geminiani: the thought is from the French."

On the same day, writing to Montagu, Walpole announces that Miss Speed is going to marry the 'Baron de Perrier.' [Gray's letter, cited in the *Long Story*, to the effect that she *is* married is misdated (by himself) Jan. 1761; should be 1762.]

Gray was in London at this interesting epoch in Miss Speed's life; he had witnessed the coronation in September, and in October and November seems to have been very busy 'choosing papers' &c. for his friend Wharton. One letter to Wharton, of Nov. 13, is mutilated; we have nowhere any extant evidence that Gray was other than heart-whole while the Baron was paying his court. In Walpole's brief and incomplete *Memoir of Gray* he assigns these verses to Oct. 1761. My text is that of Mr Gosse, which, he says, is printed "from a copy by Stonehewer at Pembroke College." Dr Bradshaw affirms that this statement is incorrect. How far this is the case I have no means of judging.—The lines, as printed in Walpole's Letter to the Countess of Ailesbury (ed. Cunningham), are before me; Mitford notes variations in Park's edition (1808), and I quote also, after Bradshaw, the variations in Stephen Jones's edition, 1799 (though I do not know whether these have any authority), and in Mitford MSS. in Brit. Mus.

What was Gray's *French* original no one seems to have discovered. One thinks of Horace's 'Quid fles, Asterie' (*Carm.* III. 71):

"Why thus, Asterie, weep thy lord?
Him with rich eastern cargo stored
Spring's earliest breeze across the main
Will to thy fond arms waft again
His faith unstained." (Wrangham.)

But the application of "one swallow does not make a spring" to the consolation of the lover, is I suppose, what Walpole calls "the thought." Otherwise this of Mlle. Deshoulières is a specimen of the sort of thing Gray imitates here:

Air.

"Pourquoi revenez-vous, printemps? Qui vous rappelle?
Le chant des rossignols et leurs tendres amours
Redoublent ma douleur mortelle.
Que le cruel hiver ne durait-il toujours?
Tircis, hélas! Tircis est infidèle:
Hé! qu'ai-je à faire de beaux jours?"

which again has a superficial resemblance to the Sonnet on the Death of West.

1. **We parted. he left me** Jones and Park.

2. **Ere. In** Park.

3. **yon violet. the opening** Jones and Park.

4. **buds...deck. bud...decks** Walpole, and apparently all texts, except Pembroke MS. (*vide supra*).

5, 6. Transposed in Jones and Park.

7. **green**, i.e. verdure, foliage. Often used (sometimes in plural) in a way which our present taste rejects as common: e.g. by Addison in 1728:

"The barren wilderness shall smile
With sudden *greens* and herbage crown'd."
(*Version of Ps.* 23.)

For 'green' Mitford MS. has **Bloom** for which there is no corresponding rhyme.

8. **this.** **Such** Jones and Park.

haste. For the rhyme, see *Fatal Sisters*, l. 2, n.

9. **Western.** **Gentle** Jones. **Warmer** Mitford MS.

skies. **sky** Jones and Park.

10. **Cannot prove that winter's past.** Mitford MS. **Prove not always winter past.** Jones and Park.

11. **Cease.** Addressed to 'notes' and 'green.'

12. "Originally," says Cunningham on the text in Walpole's *Letters* (l. c.), "**Dare not to reproach my love.**" And so Mitford MS. This makes one question the independent value of the text thus annotated.

XXIV. TRIUMPHS OF OWEN.

Published by Gray with the *Norse Odes* in 1768, in place of the *Long Story*.

In the title, perhaps reprinted according to ed. 1768, *Evan's* should be *Evans'* or *Evans's*. The name was Evan Evans, but Gray gives the gentleman's possessive case just in the same way elsewhere. (See *Gray and His Friends*, p. 190.) But in 1760 (June), he writes to Wharton, after speaking of Macpherson's *Fragments*, "the Welch Poets are also coming to light: I have seen a Discourse in MS. about them (by one Mr Evans, a Clergyman) with specimens of their writings. This is in Latin, and tho' it don't approach the other, there are fine scraps among it."

In Johnson's Notes of a Journey into North Wales in 1774 (in Birkbeck Hill's *Boswell's L. of Johnson*, vol. V. p. 443), under Aug. 5 we have, "Poor Evan Evans was mentioned as incorrigibly addicted to strong drink." He was Curate of Llanvair Talyhaern in Denbighshire (*ib.* VI. 71), and the title of his work was *Some Specimens of the Poetry of Antient Welsh Bards translated into English, with Explanatory Notes on the Historical Passages, and a short account of Men and Places mentioned in the Bards, in order to give the Curious some Idea of the Tastes and Sentiments of our Ancestors, and their Manner of Writing*. London, R. and J. Dodsley, 1764.

This volume included, I believe, the Latin 'Dissertatio de Bardis' of which Gray speaks in his letter to Wharton. (See on following *Versions*.)

Gray prefixed to his rendering the following:

"Advertisement. Owen succeeded his Father Griffin in the Principality of North-Wales, A.D. 1120. This battle was fought near forty years afterwards." [The father's name is now said to be Gruffydd ab Cynan, and the date of Owain's succession, 1137.]

Mason says, "Mr Gray entitles this Ode a Fragment, but from the prose version of Mr Evans it will appear that nothing is omitted except a single hyperbole at the end, which I print in italics:

Panegyric upon Owain Gwynedd, Prince of North-Wales, by Gwalchmai, the son of Melir, in the year 1157[1].

1. I will extol the generous Hero, descended from the race of Roderic, the bulwark of his country; a prince eminent for his good qualities, the glory of Britain, Owen the brave and expert in arms, a Prince that neither hoardeth nor coveteth riches.

2. Three fleets arrived, vessels of the main; three powerful fleets of the first rate, furiously to attack him on the sudden; one from Jwerddon[2], the other full of well-armed Lochlynians[3], making a grand appearance on the floods, the third from the transmarine Normans, which was attended with an immense, though successless toil.

3. The Dragon of Mona's Sons was so brave in action, that there was a great tumult on their furious attack; and before the Prince himself there was vast confusion, havoc, conflict, honourable death, bloody battle, horrible consternation, and upon Tal Malvre a thousand banners; there was an outrageous carnage, and the rage of spears, and hasty signs of violent indignation. Blood raised the tide of Menai, and the crimson of human gore stained the brine. There were glittering cuirasses, and the agony of gashing wounds, and the mangled warriors prostrate before the chief, distinguished by his crimson lance. Lloegria was put into confusion; the contest and confusion was great; *and the glory of our Prince's wide-wasting sword shall be celebrated in an hundred languages to give him his merited praise.*"

"The battle of Tal y Moelvre, which this poem celebrates, is thought to be identical with 'the defeat of the fleet entrusted by Henry II. to Madoc ab Meredydd in 1159.' See Thomas Stephens, *Literature of the Kymry*, 2nd ed. p. 17." Phelps.

Whilst Gray refers to Evans's *published* work as his authority, it is

[1] See Evans's *Specimens of Welch Poetry*, p. 25, and for the original Welch, p. 127. [Mason.]

[2] Ireland. [Mason.]

[3] Danes and Normans. [Mason.]

quite possible that this and the following versions were made between 1760 and 1764, from the MSS. which Gray had seen, and perhaps made excerpts from.

3. **Roderic's stem.** "Owain Gwynedd...was descended in a direct line from Roderic the Great (Rhodri Mawr), prince of all Wales (in the tenth century), who (according to tradition) divided his principality amongst his three sons." Evans's note (ap. Phelps).

4. **Gwyneth.** North-Wales. Gray.

"i.e. Gwynedd (Venedotia). Owain took the surname Gwynedd on succeeding to this principality." Phelps.

6. I do not know that Gray had any original for this line; and it has rather a modern savour.

8. Scott, *Marmion*, Canto I. x. 10:

"Welcome to Norham, Marmion!
Stout heart, and open hand!"

Cf. on *Fatal Sisters*, ll. 17—26.

11. **Eirin.** Ireland, cf. *Fatal Sisters*, l. 45.

13. **shadow.** "Canning, in his celebrated simile, speaks of 'those tremendous masses now reposing on their shadows in perfect stillness'." Candy.

Dr Bradshaw and Dr Phelps agree to refer "long and gay" to "Lochlin" in the next line; and Dr Phelps interprets "The Danish fleet (Lochlin) in a long and gay line, sails on its own shadow." I cannot think that Gray, to express this, would have been contented to say "long and gay Lochlin" at all; still less that he would have divided "Lochlin" from its epithets in this awkward fashion. The epithets undoubtedly belong to "shadow," though a "gay shadow" is very like nonsense. He surely wrote

"Upon her shadow long and *gray*" &c.

He has sufficiently expressed "making a grand appearance upon the floods" in Evans's version by "proudly riding," v. 12, and it will be noted that he enlarges freely, here and elsewhere, upon his thin and prosaic original.

14. **Lochlin.** Denmark. Gray. Cf. *Lay of the Last Minstrel*, Canto VI. l. 325:

"For thither [to the Orkneys] came, in times afar,
Stern Lochlin's sons of roving war."

and also Norna in "the Pirate" *passim*; also Macpherson's *Ossian*, *passim*.

20. "The red Dragon is the device of Cadwallader, which all his

descendants bore on their banners." Gray. "The Dragon-Son of Mona" is Owen.

Mona, Anglesey. When Mason was writing his *Caractacus*, and Gray his *Bard*, Gray wrote "I see, methinks, as I sit on Snowdon, some glimpse of Mona [the scene of *Caractacus*] and her haunted shades, and hope we shall be very good neighbours." It is pretty certain that Mason was puzzled at this, mistaking the locality of his own Mona, and wondering how he and Gray could be 'neighbours.' For Gray says (July 25, 1756), "I can only tell you not to go and take the Mona for the Isle of Man [also called Mona]; it is Anglesey, a tract of plain country, very fertile, but picturesque only from the view it has of Caernarvonshire, from which it is separated by the Menai, a narrow arm of the sea. Forgive me for supposing in you such a want of erudition." Mason, by combining these two passages of Gray's in *one* letter, has smothered up the fact that he really fell into this blunder, and his own letter, which would have betrayed it, has disappeared. Nevertheless, the descriptive colouring of *Caractacus* conforms not to Anglesey but to the Isle of Man.

25. **Talymalfra.** Moelfre, a small bay on the north-east coast of Anglesea. (Bradshaw.)

27—30. Gray did not print these four lines though they have their counterpart in Evans' version (*q.v.*) *supra*. Perhaps because ll. 27, 28 are an exaggeration of an exaggeration. Mason printed them in 1775, as an "addition from the Author's MS."

31 sq. Gray has changed the order from that of the original in this paraphrase. I cannot find in it the 'genius' which Mitford attributes to it; nor is it easy to construe. Dr Bradshaw says 'Marking' (in l. 35) agrees with 'he' (l. 33). If this is so, surely we must transpose ll. 33 and 34,

> "Hasty, hasty Rout is there
> Where he points his purple spear
> Marking &c."

By the awkward 'Fear to stop, and shame to fly' we must understand, not two sets of warriors, but one, those namely who would fain run away, if they were not restrained by shame (pudor, *αἰδώς*), if we take 'indignant' in its ordinary sense.

XXV. THE DEATH OF HOEL.

This and the following short studies were probably made at the same time as the *Triumphs of Owen*, but were first published by Mason in 1775, in whose text this follows the *Triumphs*. Gray's heading in Pembroke' MSS. is 'From Aneurin, Monarch of the Bards, extracted from the Gododin.' The two following fragments Mason printed in his notes to *The Death of Hoel*. Mason says that Aneurin "flourished about the time of Taliessin, A.D. 570." Aneurin with the flowing Muse is said to have been brother to the historian Gildas.

Dr Phelps says: "The *Gododin*, from which these three pieces are extracts, is one of the few genuine relics of ancient (sixth century) Welsh poetry....The occasion of the original poem is disputed, but the most general opinion seems to be that it celebrates a battle between the Strathclyde Britons and Northumbrian Saxons (see D. W. Nash, *Taliesin*, 1868, p. 65; but cf. Thos. Stephens, *Lit. of the Kymry*, 2nd ed. p. 3)."

The Latin version, upon which it seems agreed that Gray depended, is as follows in Evans, pp. 71, 73 (acc. to Phelps):

"'Si mihi liceret sententiam de Deirorum populo ferre
Æque ac diluvium omnes una strage prostrarem [*sic*];
3 Amicum enim amisi incautus,
Qui in resistendo firmus erat.
Non petiit magnanimus dotem a socero,
Filius CIANI ex strenuo GWYNGWN ortus.

Viri ibant ad CATTRAETH, et fuere insignes,
Vinum et mulsum ex aureis poculis erat eorum potus.
....
Trecenti et sexaginta tres aureis torquibus insigniti erant;
10 Ex iis autem qui nimio potu madidi ad bellum properabant
Non evasere nisi tres, qui sibi gladiis viam muniebant
Sc. bellator de *Aeron* [Mason *Acron*] et CONANUS DAEARAWD [Mason *Dacarawd*]
Et egomet ipse (sc. Bardus Aneurinus) sanguine rubens,
Aliter ad hoc carmen compingendum non superstes fuissem.'

In the first line Mason gives '*vindictam in Deirorum populum ferre*,' I know not on what authority. I suppose 'sententiam ferre' is meant to bear the sense which I give it in the following English version.

'Were it permitted me to give my doom upon the Deirans:
Like a flood I would lay them all low in one ruin:
3 For by my heedlessness I have lost my friend
Who was stout in resisting.
High-souled, he asked not dower from his father-in-law
He, the son of Cian, and sprung from stalwart Gwyngwn.
Warriors went to Cattraeth, and bravely-decked were they:
Wine and mead were their drink, from golden goblets.

* * * * * * * *

Three hundred and sixty-three there were adorned with golden torques;
Howbeit, of them, who soaked in excess of wine, hurried to battle
There escaped but three who with swords fenced themselves a passage
The warrior of Aeron, and Conan Daearawd,
And I myself (the bard Aneurin) red with blood;
Else had I not survived to compose this song.'"

3. **Deïra**, three syllables: remember the famous pun of Gregory about the Saxon slave-boys from Deïra (Northumbria), "They must be delivered *de irâ*, from the wrath (of God)."

5. Gray departs from Evans here (cf. l. 3 and Eng. vers.).

9. This line refers to the 'maid.' Gray's arrangement of words is often very careless: cf. l. 35 of *Triumphs of Owen*, if the text there is right; and several other instances already noted.

Nectar, &c. For a similar periphrasis for 'mead' cf. *Descent of Odin*, l. 44. Mitford comp. Eur. *Bacchae*, l. 143 ῥεῖ δὲ μελισσᾶν νέκταρι, honey.

11. **Cattraeth.** In Yorkshire near Richmond. Stephens supposes it to be the Roman town Cataracton, now Catterick. Phelps.

19. "How well has he turned the idea of the line 'Ex iis qui nimio potu madidi' [l. 10 in Evans, see English vers.] and the conclusion 'Aliter ad hoc Carmen compingendum,' &c. The former of which is ridiculous; the latter insipid." Mason.

Whether it is 'well done' to efface a trait of primitive simplicity may be questioned. Gray's *inevitable* defect as a traveller into new regions of poetry was, that he did not always report what he found but gave readers what he thought they would prefer instead of it. The poets of our own time would have brought into distinct relief these wine-soaked warriors; note how Tennyson in the *Voyage of Maeldune* and Aubrey de Vere in *Bard Ethell* enhance peculiarities of race which may be interesting poetically, just because they are what Mason calls 'ridiculous.'

23, 24. Here Mason's praise is much better bestowed. There is no poetry whatever in the crude words of the original, if Evans has here interpreted them correctly; they are worthy of that burlesque of the genuine *Erse* fragments which Scott gives in the 30th Chapter of the *Antiquary*. Gray has made them worthy of Scott's *Last Minstrel*.

XXVI. CARADOC.

Also from the *Gododin*. Evans's Latin (p. 73) as given by Mason is

"Quando ad Bellum properabat Caradocus
Filius apri silvestris qui truncando mutilavit Hostes,
Taurus aciei in pugnae conflictu, (*sic*)
Is lignum (i.e. hastam) ex manu contorsit."

When Caradoc hurried to battle
(Like) the son of the forest boar who rends and shears his foes
Like a bull, in the clash of the fight of the spear-point [?]
So did he hurl the wood (his javelin) from his hand.

2. '*sullen* roar' applied to the 'curfew' in Milton's *Il Penseroso*, l. 76.

4. **Carădoc.** See on *Bard*, l. 102.

XXVII. CONAN.

From the same. Evans (p. 75).

"Debitus est tibi cantus qui honorem assecutus es maximum,
Qui eras instar ignis, tonitrui (*sic*) et tempestatis,
Viribus eximie, eques bellicose, Rhudd Fedel, bellum meditaris."

To thee, who hast attained greatest honour, song is due:
Thou, who wast like fire, thunder and storm,
O splendid in strength, knight of prowess, Rhudd Fedel, meditatest war.

These are but hints for Gray's verses.

2. **Build.** Cf. Milton's *Lycidas* 10, 11

'he knew
Himself to sing, and build the lofty rhyme,'

which "has its original acc. to Newton, either in Horace's 'seu condis amabile carmen' (*Epist.* I. iii. 24) or, as Hurd pointed out, in the still bolder phrase of Euripides ἀοιδὰς ἐπύργωσε (*Supplices* 998)." (Masson.)

XXVIII.

These lines were prefixed to a letter from Gray to Mason dated July 16, 1765, and were followed by the words "Tell me if you do not like this, and I will send you a worse." And Mason replied (July 22 from his living at Aston) "As bad as your verses were they are yours, and therefore when I get back to York I will paste them carefully in the first page of my Shakespeare to enhance its value, for I intend it to be put in my marriage settlement as a provision for my younger daughters." There is a copy of this in Mitford MSS. in British Museum which however differs in some particulars from that which he printed in *Correspondence of Gray and Mason.* Of this Dr Bradshaw has taken notes. Variations are noted *infra.* It will be observed that Gray tries here and there to imitate the Shakespearian manner.

Mistris, Mitford (in *G. and M.*), after the Elizabethan spelling. One is reminded of "fair Mistress Anne" in the *Merry Wives.*

stint. stop.

"And, pretty fool it *stinted* [left off crying] and said 'Ay.'"
Romeo and Juliet I. iii. 48.

St Charitie. "By Gis [Jesus] and by Saint Charity" is in one of poor Ophelia's songs, *Hamlet* IV. 5.

3. **Willey**, Mitford (in *G. and M*).

right. adverb. "I am *right* loath to go," *Merchant of Venice* ii. 5. 16.

proper. fine, handsome. "As proper a man as ever went on two legs," (*Tempest* II. ii. 63).

5. **canker'd. crabbed** in Mitford MSS.

canker'd means 'venomous,' 'malignant,' cf. *King John* II. 193, 194.

"a wicked will!
A woman's will's a *canker'd* grandam's will!"

A typical example of the 'canker'd critic' is Thomas Rymer the historiographer, more creditably known for his *Foedera*, who in 1693 published 'A Short View of Tragedy: its original excellency and corruption. With some Reflections on Shakespeare and other Practitioners for the Stage.' Rymer says of *Othello*, "There is in this play some burlesque, some humour and ramble of comical wit and some mimicry to divert the spectators; but the tragical part is plainly none other than a bloody farce, without salt or savour."

6. **fumbling**, bungling, incompetent. The reference is to Sir Thomas Hanmer, who in 1743 edited the Shakespeare published at Oxford. He had been Speaker of the House of Commons in the reign of Queen Anne. He is described by the editors of the *Cambridge Shakespeare* as "a country gentleman of great ingenuity and lively fancy, but with no knowledge of older literature, no taste for research, and no ear for the rhythm of earlier English verse, who amused his leisure hours by scribbling down his own and his friends' guesses in Pope's Shakespeare, and with this *apparatus criticus*, if we may believe Warburton 'when that illustrious body, the University of Oxford, in their public capacity, undertook an edition of Shakespeare by subscription, thrust himself into the employment.'"

Poor Collins at Oxford Dec. 3, 1743, in his Epistle to Sir Thomas Hanmer, represents the Baronet's edition as *final*:

"Those sibyl leaves, the sport of every wind,
(For poets ever were a careless kind),
By thee disposed, *no farther toil demand*,
But, just to nature, own thy forming hand."

poets small. Rowe (1709) and Theobald (1733) were 'small' poets, and Shakespeare editors at the dates named; I fear that Gray had in mind Theobald, whose merits were never fully recognized until the publication of the *Cambridge Shakespeare*; I am not so sure that he was thinking of Rowe. Nor is it very likely that he thought of Johnson, whose Shakespeare did not appear until October of this year, although his *Observations on Macbeth* were published in 1745.

7. Dr Aldis Wright kindly explains this for me, comparing Pope, *Dunciad* IV. 568, who speaks of the children of Dulness:

"of more distinguish'd sort
Who study Shakespeare at the inns of Court."

Gray was no doubt thinking of Thomas Edwards, the author of the *Canons of Criticism*, which contains a severe attack on Warburton. The book first appeared in 1747 under the title of 'A supplement to Mr Warburton's edition of Shakespeare....By the other Gentleman of Lincoln's Inn.' In the third edition (1748) it was called 'Canons of Criticism.' Leslie Stephen in the *Dictionary of Biography* says that the *first* 'Gentleman of Lincoln's Inn' was Philip Carteret Webb, who published a pamphlet under that name in 1742. Edwards' book went through seven editions between 1747 and 1765. The last has his name. Another 'pert barrister' might be John Holt, 'a Gentleman, formerly of Gray's Inn,', who attempted to rescue Shakespeare from the errors 'falsely charged on him by his several Editors.'

"Among the parsons might perhaps be reckoned Zachary Grey and John Upton. The latter in 1746 wrote 'Critical Observations on Shakespeare'; and Grey in 1752 'Critical and Explanatory Notes on S.'" Dr Aldis Wright.

Warburton may be included in the list, though that very pretentious person would have been much enraged at being so described. His edition, based on that of Pope, appeared in 1747; he was, at that date, Preacher at Lincoln's Inn.

I believe *Gray's* Mason never published anything on Shakespeare.

8. **worst of all.** **Worse than all** Mitford MSS.

12. **residence.** Gray to Wharton Jan., 1762 [wrongly dated, by himself, '61]. "The best piece of news I have to send you is, that Mason is Residentiary of York, wch is worth near 200£ a year:...the Precentorship (worth so much more) being vacant at the same time, L^d^ H[oldernesse] has obtain'd that too for him." But, Oct. 10, 1763, (to Robinson) he describes the ever-discontented Mason as "repining at his four-and-twenty weeks residence at York, unable to visit his bowers, the work of his own hands, at Aston [his living], except in the depth of winter; and longing for the flesh-pots and coffee-houses of Cambridge."

marriage. Mason's marriage was in contemplation. His 'gentle Argentile' as he called her, in reference to his play of *Argentile and Curan*, was Mary, daughter of William Sherman, of Kingston-upon-Hull. He married her on the 25th of September, 1765, and she died March 27, 1767, aged 28. See on XXX. *infra*.

sore eyes. There are several references to Mason's infirmity in his correspondence with Gray, who cautions him against reading at night.

The Mitford MS. has **mince pies** instead of 'sore eyes.' The 'variation' may have some meaning known to Gray and Mason and perhaps the Cloisters at York. Gray writes to Mason at York 29 December, 1768, "Come away to Cambridge when your Christmas duties and *mince-pies* are over."

13. **wicked will.** cf. on l. 5.

14. **at the hour,** &c. Mrs Anne is to wait until Mason goes out to the service in the Minster, and when the sound of the organ, audible in

the cloister-houses, tells her that the procession is entering the choir, or that worship has begun, she may safely proceed to business.

17—20. In Mitford MS. this verse is the third. Bradshaw.

21. Clouet was cook to the Duke of Newcastle. He was the Ude or Brillat-Savarin or Soyer of his day, though I do not know that he *wrote*. But he *inspired* Verral's *Book of Cookery* (1759), a copy of which, once Mitford's, is now in the British Museum. It is annotated by Gray (who was great on the subject) with much minuteness and system. Verral calls his Master in the Art 'Monsieur *de St* Clouet.'

22. **works. work** Mitford MS.

24. **To glorious cheesecakes** Mitford MS.

XXIX. IMPROMPTU.

In June, 1766, Gray was on a visit to his friend the Rev. William Robinson, at Denton in Kent, "eight miles east of Canterbury on the skirts of Barhamdown" as he himself describes the locality (to Wharton Aug. 26, 1766). Mitford tells us that when he left, these lines were found in the drawer of the dressing-table of the room which he occupied. They seem to have got into circulation and even into print, before Gray's decease. This might be inferred from what Walpole writes to Mason Dec. 1, 1773. "I think you determined not to *reprint* the lines on Lord H. I hope it is now a resolution. He is in so deplorable a state, that it would aggravate the misery of his last hours." It was still more distinctly affirmed by the same to Lady Ossory Aug. 19, 1784. They were of course, if this is so, printed anonymously; and perhaps the *authorship* of them is the secret to which Gray refers when he writes to Mason on the 29th of December, 1768, "Oh, wicked Scroddles! There have you gone and told my *arcanum arcanorum* to that leaky mortal Palgrave....Hitherto luckily nobody has taken any notice of it, nor I hope ever will." The reference seems to me somewhat doubtful: it should be remembered, however, that Gray had just been appointed Professor of History at Cambridge, when his secret, evidently of a political character, was told by Mason; at such a time he would be extremely anxious not to be known as the writer of a bitter lampoon[1].

[1] But for positive statements, I should prefer, if this reference is rightly interpreted, to think that these verses were written when Gray visited Robinson in the summer of 1768, and got into circulation before his appointment in August.

A fragment of Gray's, a History of Hell, contained political views of his. See Walpole's Letters v. p. 447, ed. Cunningham.

"The first four stanzas appeared in the supplement to the *Gentleman's Magazine* for 1777....In February, 1778, the two last stanzas were supplied, but incorrectly, by another correspondent; and in January, 1782, in a third letter to the *Gentleman's Magazine* the errors in the previous one were pointed out. The first edition of Gray's Poems in which the verses appeared was Stephen Jones' [1799]." Bradshaw.

They were published in Nichols' *Select Poems*, vol. VII. p. 350, from which Mitford records various readings. There is a copy in Wharton's handwriting in the British Museum. In this the title is

"On L^d H——d's Seat near W——e. K^t."

Perhaps 'W——e' stands for 'Westgate.' The heading commonly given is, I think, from the Magazines. Lord Holland *was* 'a deceased nobleman' when the verses there appeared; *not* when Gray wrote them.

"Dallaway in his *Anecdotes of the Arts*, p. 385, says that this house was built by Lord Holland as a correct imitation of Cicero's Formian villa, at Baiae, under the superintendence of Sir Thomas Wynne, Bart., afterwards Lord Newborough." (Mitford.) The ruins were *imitation* ruins, such as may be seen at Virginia Water. Put up to mimic collapse, this freak did actually give way, to the enhancement of its picturesque effect, and that probably before Gray saw it. Cowper writing to Unwin in July, 1779, describes what he recollected having seen on a visit to Margate, I think in 1763. "One sight however (in the Isle of Thanet) I remember engaged my curiosity, and I went to see it—a fine piece of ruins, built by the late Lord Holland at a great expense, which the day after I saw it, tumbled down for nothing. Perhaps therefore it is still a ruin; and, if it is, I would advise you by all means to visit it, as it must have been much improved by this fortunate incident. It is hardly possible to put stones together with that air of wild and magnificent disorder which they are sure to acquire by falling of their own accord."

These mimic ruins, if Cowper saw them in '63, were in all likelihood made *before* Fox became a peer (the first Lord Holland). Horace Walpole's deprecation and regrets about the publication of Gray's verses will be understood when we remember that Fox served his political apprenticeship under Horace's father, Sir Robert. Fox became Lord Holland after the retirement of Lord Bute in 1763. He had accumulated great wealth, for his preference was for lucrative offices. As Bute's colleague and adviser he practised all the intimidation and corruption which had disgraced the government of Walpole; and the naturally sweet temper which he transmitted to his more famous son was soured by the unpopularity into which his measures brought him, especially with the citizens of London.

The names in the earlier printed copies are slightly disguised after the fashion of the time.

2. **form'd.** **took** Wharton MS. 3. **a.** **some** Wharton MS.

6. **Goodwin.** **Godwin** Wharton MS.

8. **shipwreckt** Wharton MS. **dread.** **fear**, Nichols.

10. **No tree.** Churchill had written in 'the Scot's Pastoral'

"No bee was heard to hum, no dove to coo."

(See the whole passage in Chambers' *Cyclopaedia of Eng. Lit.* under *Churchill.*)

11. **could not.** **cannot** Wharton MS.

12. **horrors.** **terrors** Nichols.

13. **Here.** **Now** Wharton MS. We should conclude from the description in this stanza, that the 'Formian Villa' was the 'seat' not 'the ruins.'

14. **Arches and turrets** Wharton MS.

15. **monast'ries.** **palaces** Wharton MS.

our. **his** Wharton MS.

17. **Bute.** "In all these acts of harshness Fox to the surprise of his friends was more eager and forward than any of his colleagues. 'Fox has grossly deceived me,' said his Royal Highness of Cumberland to Lord Waldegrave. 'I thought him good-natured, and yet in all these transactions he has shown the bitterest revenge and inhumanity.'" Lord Mahon's *History of England* (vol. v. c. XLI. pp. 23, 24). Bute in 1762 had preferred Brockett, tutor to Sir John Lowther, to Gray for the Professorship of History at Cambridge.

18. I do not know to what original the names in the text generally printed are to be traced. Mitford, printing 'M—'s, R—'s, B—'s,' no doubt after the text he follows, says that these are to be interpreted 'Mungo's, Rigby's, Bradshaw's,' and refers us to Mason's *Heroic Epistle* l. 95: "The Rigby's, Calcrafts, Dysons, Bradshaws there."
But this attack on the 'minor plunderers of the age' published in 1773 whilst it may account for the appearance of these names in late and unauthoritative editions of Gray's lines, are no evidence of what he really wrote. Richard Rigby, according to the talk of the time, was at once the creature and controller of the Duke of Bedford. Gray tells Wharton (Jan. 23, 1760), that in the disturbances in Dublin, the people, at the same time that "they pulled Sir Thomas Prendergast by the nose (naturally large) until it was the size of a cauliflower, would have hanged Rigby if he had not got out of a window." Of the same

transactions Walpole writes to Montagu (Dec. 23, 1759) "There wanted nothing but a Massaniello to overthrow the government, and luckily for the government and for *Rigby*, he, *who was made for Massaniello*, happened to be first minister there." He was "Master of the Rolls in Ireland, afterwards Paymaster of the Forces; a statesman of the second class, and a *bon vivant* of the first" (Croker). "He died (1788) involved in debt with his accounts as Paymaster of the Forces hopelessly unsettled," says Cunningham. Enough and to spare will be found about Rigby in the Letters of Junius, which however only began in '69. It was no doubt from this man that Disraeli took the name Rigby which he bestowed in Coningsby on John Wilson Croker. The Bedford faction, led by Rigby, had brought their reluctant chief to the support of the Bute administration.

Mungo was Jeremiah Dyson, more creditably known as the friend and patron of the poet Akenside. He was like Rigby of those who called themselves 'the king's friends,' and he supported Bute.[1]

Bradshaw, according to Junius, was at first "a contractor for forage and afterwards exalted to a petty post in the War Office." After being, with Stonhewer, secretary to the Duke of Grafton, he received, according to the same authority, a pension of £1500 a year. Walpole to Mason Nov. 11, 1774, relates that "he shot himself yesterday se'nnight. He has been a very active minister of the second or third class. Instead of making a great fortune he has spent one, and could not go on a week longer."

But two of the three names in this line in the received text were probably substituted in later editions of the poem, and possibly not by Gray. It is questionable whether either Dyson or Bradshaw were important enough in 1766 to be mentioned even in satire as the friends of Lord Holland as early as 1763; whilst at a later date Gray would have scrupled to stigmatize the colleague of his friend Stonhewer. Accordingly I have printed the readings of the Wharton transcript; except that he writes **Calcroft's**.

Lord Shelburne in 1763 was only twenty-six years old; but in this year, after Bute's retirement from the premiership, he became Chief of the Board of Trade. He had negotiated for Fox's peerage, but confessed that he had exaggerated, in letting Bute suppose that Fox would resign the Paymastership. "These misrepresentations Lord Bute called 'a pious fraud.' 'I can see the fraud plain enough,' cried Fox, 'but where is the piety?'" Ld. Mahon, vol. V. c. 41. Shelburne's supposed duplicity earned him the name of Malagrida after a famous Jesuit of that name.

[1] See additional note, p. 293.

About this time also Calcraft was talked of for an Irish peerage. He was particularly attached to Fox; but the complaint in the text, in connection with *his* name, may be illustrated by Walpole to Conway May 1, 1763, "They found among Wilkes's papers an unpublished 'North Briton' designed for last Saturday. There was a dialogue in it too between Fox and Calcraft; the former says to the latter 'I did not think you would have served me so, 'Jemmy Twitcher.'"

The reference is to Gay's *Beggar's Opera*; and no doubt this discovery of this satire of Wilkes' in April was talked about and made the public more quick to apply the same nickname to *Lord Sandwich* in November. Lord Sandwich at the opening of the Session Nov. 15, 1763, denounced Wilkes, his own boon-companion, as the author of an infamous poem, with which Sandwich had been long familiar; in fact it was *addressed* to him. A few days afterwards at Covent Garden Theatre the *Beggar's Opera* was acting. When Macheath (the highwayman hero) came to the words 'That Jemmy Twitcher should peach I own surprises me'—"the whole audience," says Lord Mahon, "with one unanimous shout of applause marked the application." In 1764 when Sandwich was a candidate for the Lord High Stewardship at Cambridge Gray wrote a bitter lampoon, 'Jemmy Twitcher, or the Cambridge Courtship,' which we do not reprint.

Nor C—s, nor B—d's promises been vain Nichols. It is possible this may have been Gray's, but not quite in this form. 'C—s' is I suppose '*Calcraft's*'; what Gray wrote therefore was

Nor Calcraft's, Bedford's, promises &c.

He could scarcely have pronounced *C* as a letter, and *Bedford* in full.

19. **better.** **other** Wharton MS.

blest. **bless'd** Wharton MS. **grac'd** Nichols.

20. **beauties which.** **ruins that** Wharton MS. **horrors which** Nichols.

21. **purified.** **beautifyed** Wharton MS.

23. **would.** **might** Wharton MS. **should** Nichols.

St Peter's choir. The choir of Westminster Abbey.

choir. **Quire** Wharton MS.

XXX. CONCLUDING LINES OF EPITAPH ON MRS MASON.

"The last four lines of Mason's epitaph on his wife were written by Gray: *I saw them in his handwriting, interlined in the MS. which he shewed me*, and the words of Mrs Mason, when she had given up all hope of life." Norton Nicholls' "Reminiscences of Gray" in Mitford, vol. v. pp. 39, 40.

Gray expressly claims the line 'Heaven lifts' &c. to Mason, May 23, 1767, whilst mentioning that Hurd found fault with it. This letter Mason did not publish. Mitford, *ad loc.*, assigns the last *three* lines to Gray. Of the lines for which these were a substitute Nicholls says, he only remembers "that they were weak, with a languid repetition of some preceding expressions. Mr Gray said, 'That will never do for an ending, I have altered them thus.'"

Gray wrote to Mason, March 28, 1767, "if the last struggle be over, if the poor object of your long anxieties be no longer sensible to your kindness, or to her own sufferings, allow me (at least in idea, for what could I do, were I present, more than this?) to sit by you in silence, and pity from my heart, not her, who is at rest, but you who lose her." "This," Mason says, "which I received at the Hot Wells, at Bristol, then breathed, and still seems to breathe the very voice of Friendship in its tenderest and most pathetic tones." He replied to Gray from Bath on April 1st, "The dear testimonial of your friendship reached Bristol about the time when the last offices were done to my lost angel at the Cathedral, and was brought to me hither just now."

The inscription on a tablet in Bristol Cathedral runs thus:

"Take, holy earth! all that my soul holds dear:
  Take that best gift which Heaven so lately gave:
To Bristol's fount I bore with trembling care
  Her faded form: she bowed to taste the wave,
And died. Does Youth, does Beauty read the lines?
  Does sympathetic fear their breasts alarm?
Speak, dead Maria! breathe a strain divine:
  E'en from the grave thou shalt have power to charm.
Bid them be chaste, be innocent like thee;
  Bid them in Duty's sphere as meekly move;
And if as fair, from vanity as free,
  As firm in friendship, and as fond in love,
Tell them," &c.

The context seems to show that the first of the four lines was at least in part Mason's.

XXXI. COUPLET ABOUT BIRDS.

"I will set down...two verses made by Mr Gray as we were walking in the spring in the neighbourhood of Cambridge," says Nicholls (*Reminiscences* in Mitford, vol. v. p. 34), quoting these lines. The date of them it is impossible to determine, but Nicholls' acquaintance with Gray belongs to the latter part of the poet's life.

Canon Ainger pointed out that Rogers followed this couplet in *Human Life*: ——"What time the wood-lark there
Scatters his loose notes on the sultry air."

XXXII. ODE FOR MUSIC.

The full title of this Ode is 'Ode | Performed in the | Senate-House at Cambridge | July 1, 1769, | at the Installation of his Grace Augustus-Henry Fitzroy | Duke of Grafton | Chancellor of the University. | Set to music by | Dr Randal, | Professor of Music. | Cambridge | Printed for J. Archdeacon, Printer to the University | 1769.' Bradshaw.

The title on the first page of the text is simply *Ode for Music.* It is interesting to notice that Gray's name nowhere appears in this, a thin quarto of eight pages. Phelps.

'After I had quitted the University, I always paid Mr Gray an annual visit; during one of these it was he determined, as he said, to offer with a good grace what he could not have refused if it had been asked of him, viz. to write the *Installation Ode* for the Duke of Grafton[1]. This, however, he considered as a sort of task, to which he submitted with great reluctance: and it was long after he first mentioned it to me before he could prevail with himself to begin the composition. One morning, when I went to him as usual after breakfast, I knocked at his door, which he threw open, and exclaimed with a loud voice:

"Hence, avaunt! 'tis holy ground."

I was so astonished, that I almost feared he was out of his senses: but this was the beginning of the *Ode* which he had just composed.' Nicholls, *Reminiscences.*

Mathias, who tells the story after Nicholls, adds, "Mr Gray in a moment after resumed his pleasant manner, and repeating several verses...said, 'Well, I have begun the *Ode,* and now I shall finish it.'"

That Nicholls correctly interpreted Gray's feelings on writing the

[1] Who had appointed him to the History Professorship

Ode appears from the poet's letter to Beattie (July 16, '69), to the same effect. Of the verses themselves Gray says, "I do not think them worth sending you, because they are by nature doomed to live but a single day; or if their existence be prolonged beyond that date it is only by means of newspaper parodies and witless criticism."

Among Gray's friends at Pembroke, Delaval 'as loud as ever' tried to dissuade him from the task; "he fell upon me," says Gray, "tooth and nail (but in a very friendly manner), only on the credit of the newspaper, for he knows nothing further: told me of the obloquy that waits for me; and said everything to deter me from doing a thing that is already done. Mason sat by and heard it all with a world of complacency." (To Brown, March, 1769.) Mason's complacency may have been due to the fact that *he* had written the *Ode* (at the Installation, July 1, 1749) of the previous Chancellor, the Duke of Newcastle, and since Gray had forestalled him this time, was not displeased that the task would be troublesome. It is thus that Mason concluded his praise of '*Fobus*, the old *fizzling* Duke, the old *hubble-bubble* Duke,' as he and Gray delighted to call Newcastle:

"Meanwhile the Muse shall snatch the trump of Fame,
And lift her swelling accents high,
To tell the world that Pelham's name
Is dear to learning as to liberty."

Gray's task was completed by the 20th of April [1769]. "I know it will bring abuse enough upon me," he wrote to Wharton in announcing the fact. It *had* to be done: for it was to be set to music, and rehearsed before July 1. "Odicle," he says to Nicholls (24th of June), "has been rehearsed here again and again, and the boys (the undergraduates) have got scraps by heart: I expect to see it torn piece-meal in the *North-Briton* before it is born. the musick is as good as the words: the former might be taken for mine and the latter for Dr Randal's. if you will come, you shall see it and sing in it with Mr Norris and Mr Clerke the Clergyman, and Mr Reinholt, and Miss Thomas, great names at Salisbury and Gloster musick-meeting and well versed in Judas Maccabæus."

This *Ode*—good as it is amongst Installation Odes—is another evidence that Gray never wrote at his best under pressure. In it he sometimes falls back upon his earlier and most conventional manner.

It seems that Stonhewer (Grafton's Secretary) showed the Duke the *Ode* before the ceremony. Gray writes to Stonhewer from Cambridge (June 12):

"I did not intend the Duke should have heard me till he could not help it. You are desired to make the best excuses you can to his Grace for the liberty I have taken of praising him to his face; but as somebody was necessarily to do this, I did not see why Gratitude should sit silent and leave it to Expectation to sing, who certainly would have sung, and that *à gorge déployée* upon such an occasion."

Gray is Gratitude; but who is or might be Expectation? If there is any thought of Mason, whom Gray was wont to flout on his insatiable hunger for preferment, Mason himself either did not see it, or chose to ignore it; for he is our sole authority for this letter.

Gray of course did not escape attack. On July 8, 1769, Junius addresses the Duke of Grafton, and reminding him that the king may discard him without the forms of regret, says, "You will then have reason to be thankful if you are permitted to retire to that seat of learning, which, in contemplation of the system of your life, the comparative purity of your manners with those of their high steward [the Earl of Hardwicke], and a thousand other recommending circumstances, has chosen you to encourage the growing virtue of their youth, and to preside over their education. Whenever the spirit of distributing prebends and bishopricks shall have departed from you, you will find that learned seminary perfectly recovered from the delirium of an installation, and, what in truth it ought to be, once more a peaceful scene of slumber and thoughtless meditation. The venerable tutors of the University will no longer distress your modesty, by proposing you for a pattern to their pupils. The learned dulness of declamation will be silent: and even the venal muse, though happiest in fiction[1], will forget your virtues."

Dr Bradshaw quotes 'a parody on the Epitaph in the *Elegy* in a newspaper in 1769, which is to be found cut out therefrom and pasted on the last page of vol. II. of Upcott's edition of Gray in the British Museum. The letter runs as follows: "As a certain Church-yard Poet has deviated from the principles he once profest, it is very fitting that necessary alterations should be made in his Epitaph.—*Marcus*.

"Epitaph.

Here rests his head upon the lap of earth,
One not to fortune nor to fame unknown;
Fair science frown'd not on his humble birth,
And smooth-tongued flatt'ry mark'd him for her own.

[1] An allusion to Waller's answer, when Charles II. asked him, why he had praised the Protector so much better than he had praised *him*.

Large was his wish—in this he was sincere—
Fate did a recompence as largely send,
Gave the poor C . . r four hundred pounds a year,
And made a d . . y Minister his friend.

No further seek his deeds to bring to light,
For, ah ! he offer'd at Corruption's shrine;
And basely strove to wash an Ethiop white,
While Truth and Honour bled in ev'ry line."'

The first notes to the Ode were by Mason; and are here printed from his edition of 1775.

1. It is obvious to compare, with Mitford, 'Procul, O procul este profani,' Virg. *Æn.* VI. 258, and a great many other classical instances in which the profane are warned off holy ground.

2. "Meanwhile, welcome joy and feast,
Midnight shout and revelry,
Tipsy dance and jollity."
Milton, *Comus*, 102. (Wakefield.)

Comus himself thus speaks in Milton. His name signifies 'Revel.' He was personified in *later* antiquity, but I think his *parentage* from Circe and Bacchus is the invention of Milton (*Comus*, 46—58).

When we remember Gray's description of the state of Cambridge in 1747 with 'the Fellow-commoners (the Bucks) run mad' etc. and the practical joke played upon the already famous author of the *Elegy*, by the young gentlemen of Peterhouse, which caused his migration to Pembroke College in 1756; his *Hymn to Ignorance* (*q. v.*) and his description of Cambridge in 1764 as 'a silly, dirty place,' we may picture the poet writing these opening lines with something like a grim smile.

11. **Science.** See *Eton Ode*, l. 3.

14. **indignant lay,** 'the previous verses which the poet feigns to have heard said by sages and bards as they look down on their old University, "indignant" lest Comus, Ignorance &c., should profane the "holy ground".' Bradshaw.

17. "Hail, bards triumphant! born in happier days,
Immortal heirs of universal praise,
Nations *unborn* your mighty name shall sound
And *worlds* applaud *that must not yet be found.*"
Pope, *Essay on Criticism*, l. 193. (Wakefield.)

18. *accomp.* 'This means that though the recitative was held the next nine lines were also accompanied.' Phelps.

21. "Spread the young thought and warm *the opening heart.*"
Education and Government, l. 12. Bradshaw.

22. 'the genuine ardour' is an instance of relapse into the conventional diction of Gray's century.

24. **shell.** See on *Progress of Poesy*, l. 15.

26. **Meek Newton.** The humility of Newton was exhibited not only in his famous comparison of himself to a child picking up shells beside the ocean of Truth, but in his habitual demeanour; it was an essential part of his character. Gray wisely forgets that he had no appreciation of poetry, which he described as 'ingenious nonsense.'

Ib. **his state sublime,** his chair of state, as often in Shakespeare. Phelps. This is possibly correct, cf. l. 15, and *Macbeth*, III. 4. 5, 'Our hostess keeps her state;' *Twelfth Night*, II. 5. 5, 'sitting in my state.' But one cannot be sure. The expression has certainly passed into our poetic diction in a less particular sense, e.g.

"If in thy second *state sublime*
Thy ransom'd reason change replies
With all the circle of the wise,
The perfect flower of human time."
Tennyson, *In Memoriam*, LXI. 1.

26. "E'en mitred Rochester would *nod the head.*"
Pope, *Prologue to the Satires*, l. 140. Wakefield.

"See Rochester approving nods the head,
And ranks one modern with the mighty dead."
Gay, *Mr Pope's Welcome from Greece* (1720), ll. 111, 112. Pattison.

27. This stanza being supposed to be sung by Milton is very judiciously written in the metre which he fixed upon for the stanza of his Christmas hymn

"'Twas in the winter wild," &c. Mason.

27. '**brown**' with shadows, as Milton teaches, whose diction, as Bradshaw points out, Gray tries to repeat:

"...when the sun begins to fling
His flaming beams, me, Goddess, bring
To *arched* walks of twilight *groves*,
And shadows *brown.*" *Il Penseroso*, ll. 131—134.

29. **'willowy.'** 'rushy' is Gray's epithet in *Hymn to Ignorance*, l. 39, *q. v.* corresponding to Milton's 'arundifer' and 'juncosus'; but these epithets were not meant to be complimentary. Hall, Milton's contemporary, quoted by Mitford, writes

"Nought have we here but *willow-shaded* shore
To tell our *Grant* his banks are left forlore."

(*Grant* is the Cam.) *Sat.* B. I. i.

30 sq. Bradshaw collects the Miltonic passages which Gray had in mind in this imitation, ll. 27—34:

"Together both, ere the high *lawns* appeared
Under the opening eyelids of the *morn*,
We drove afield." *Lycidas*, 25, 26.

(Milton, as Bradshaw remarks, is here speaking of his life at Cambridge.)

"After short *blush of morn.*" *Par. Lost*, XI. 184.

"The shepherds on the *lawn*
Or ere the point of *dawn.*" *Christmas Hymn*, 85.

"I did not err: there does a sable cloud
Turn forth her *silver* lining on the night,
And casts a *gleam* over this tufted grove."
Comus, ll. 223—225.

And *Il Penseroso* (l. 54), the Cherub *Contemplation* (cf. l. 28 here); and the rhyme, *Ib.* 61, 62,

"Sweet bird, that shunn'st the noise of *folly*,
Most musical, most *melancholy*!"

(cf. ll. 33, 34); also 'the studious cloister's pale.' *Ib.* l. 155.

silver-bright (l. 32) is Shakespearian:

"Their armours, that march'd hence so *silver-bright.*"
K. John, II. I. 315.

In this 'airy pageant' first is seen the session of the 'few whom *genius* gave to shine,' and Milton, a son of Granta, speaks as their representative. Then comes a procession through the heavenly portal of royal or noble founders and patrons. The conception is striking; its only defect is that Milton's song, even by its form, seems to be the beginning of a new turn in the poem, instead of the end of the first part; we are expecting Milton to go on, when he is interrupted, without ceremony, by the appearance of these important personages.

38. **mitred fathers.** Among these Hugh de Balsham, Bishop of

Ely, founder of Peterhouse, the oldest of Cambridge colleges, Gray's college up to 1756, and the college to which the Duke of Grafton's name was attached. Gray escapes the necessity of paying any distinct tribute to Peterhouse[1] by connecting Grafton's name with that of his ancestress, 'the venerable Margaret,' l. 66.

39. **Edward the Third**; who added the fleur de lys of France to the arms of England. He founded Trinity College. (Mason.) Trinity College was consolidated by Henry VIII. out of several earlier foundations, including King's Hall, founded by Edward III. in 1337.

41. **sad Chatillon.** Mary de Valentia, Countess of Pembroke, daughter of Guy de Chatillon, Comte de St Paul in France: of whom tradition says, that her husband Audemar de Valentia, Earl of Pembroke, was slain at a Tournament on the day of his nuptials. She was the Foundress of Pembroke College or Hall, under the name of Aula Mariae de Valentia. Mason.

To this tradition Gray's words are accommodated, but Phelps notes the facts as far as known to history. "Aymer de Valence married, as his third wife, Marie de Castillon (Châtillon), daughter of Guy IV., Count of St Pol, 5 July, 1321; he died suddenly (murder was suspected) near Paris, 23 June, 1324. His widow, who founded Pembroke Hall in 1343, long survived him."

5. **Clare.** Elizabeth de Burg, Countess of Clare, was wife of John de Burg, son and heir of the Earl of Ulster, and daughter of Gilbert de Clare, Earl of Gloucester, by Joan of Acres, daughter of Edward the First. Hence the Poet gives her the epithet of 'Princely.' She founded Clare Hall. Mason. Phelps says, "She rebuilt Clare Hall (which had been founded by Dr Richard Badew in 1326 under the name of University Hall) and gave it this name about 1342. See Dugdale, *Baronage of England*, 1675, I. 209, 217."

43. **Anjou's heroine.** Margaret of Anjou, wife of Henry the Sixth, foundress of Queens' College. The Poet has celebrated her conjugal fidelity in the *Bard*, l. 89. Mason.

Ib. **the paler Rose.** Elizabeth Widville [or Woodville] wife of Edward the Fourth (hence called the paler rose, as being of the House of York). She added to the foundation of Margaret of Anjou. Mason. See on *Bard*, l. 92.

[1] Gray to Wharton, March 25, 1756, "I left my lodgings, because the rooms were noisy and the People of the house dirty." See on l. 2.

44. **her woes.** Cf. Shakesp. *Rich. III.* Act IV. sc. 4, where Margaret of Anjou and Queen Elizabeth [Woodville] balance their woes, see especially ll. 38—44 where Margaret says to Elizabeth:

> "If sorrow can admit society,
> Tell o'er your woes again by viewing mine:—
> I had an Edward, till a Richard killed him:
> I had a Harry, till a Richard kill'd him:
> Thou hadst an Edward, till a Richard kill'd him,
> Thou hadst a Richard, till a Richard kill'd him."

45. **either Henry.** Henry the Sixth and Eighth. The former the founder of King's, the latter the greatest benefactor to Trinity College. Mason.

Add. "King Henry VI. was so liberal a benefactor to *Pembroke* College, as to obtain the name of a second Founder." *Cambridge Calendar.*

46. **saint.** Cf. *Eton Ode*, l. 4; *Bard*, l. 90.

Ib. **the majestic lord** &c. "I do not think it would be possible for bluff King Hal to be more happily characterised by any one who wished to make rather a complimentary mention of him, without any sacrifice of truth." Earl of Carlisle.

Ib. **little,** because insignificant to them in their present state.

53. **awful,** stately, venerable.

54. 'come' is here *present indicative*, not the past participle.

61—64. *Par. Lost*, IV. 641—646:

> "Sweet is the breath of Morn, her rising sweet
> ...fragrant the fertile earth
> After soft showers." (Wakefield.)

62. Cf. *Descent of Odin*, l. 44; *Death of Hoel*, l. 17; in both places used however of mead. Mitford compares Theocritus, VIII. 83, κρέσσον μελπομένω τεῦ ἀκουέμεν ἢ μέλι λείχειν. [Better is it to listen to thy singing, than to taste the honeycomb. Lang.]

63. **melting fall.** Shakespeare, *Twelfth Night*, I. I. 4:

> "That strain again! it had a dying fall:"

Milton, *L'Allegro*, 142:

> "The *melting* voice through mazes running;"

and *Comus*, l. 251:

> "At every *fall* smoothing the raven down
> Of darkness till it smil'd."

64. 1 Kings xix. 12, "and after the fire a still small voice." Cf. the

third of rejected stanzas in the *Elegy* quoted in note after l. 72 there. The hint for lines on *Gratitude* in Gray's *Pocket Book* for 1754, quoted on the *Vicissitude* Fragment (Introductory note) is more or less adopted here. But West, whom Gray never forgot, had in his Monody on the Death of Queen Caroline (given in *Gray and His Friends*, pp. 110—114) personified Gratitude much in the same way, describing her however as '*descending* from the skies.'

65. "...a voice from midst *a golden cloud*
Thus mild was heard." *Par. Lost*, VI. 28. Luke.

66. **Marg'ret**, Countess of Richmond and Derby, the mother of Henry the Seventh, foundress of St John's and Christ's Colleges.

"Although *Christ's College* was originally founded in the reign of King Henry VI. by the name of God's House, yet its foundation is usually dated from its second and more ample establishment, by Margaret, Countess of Richmond, in 1505." Lysons, *Magna Britannia*, I. 120. "The foundation of *St John's College* was projected and begun by Margaret Countess of Richmond a short time before her death, which happened in 1509." *Ibid.*, I. 121. (Phelps.)

70. **A Tudor's fire** &c. The Countess was a Beaufort, and married to a Tudor: hence the application of this line to the Duke of Grafton, who claims descent from both these families. Mason.

The pedigree is traced through Charles II., of whom the first Fitzroy, Duke of Grafton, was an illegitimate son. Cf. note on the *Bard*, l. 116.

71. **judging eye.** Mitford compares Pope, who, *Prologue to the Satires* (Ep. to Arbuthnot), l. 246, says bitterly of 'full-blown Bufo' (Montagu):

"Dryden alone escaped this *judging eye*."

72—76. The thought of *Elegy*, ll. 53—56, was in Gray's mind when he wrote thus.

78. Taken from *Par. Lost*, VIII. 504—the description of Eve on her creation and first appearance to Adam:

"Her virtue, and the conscience of her worth,
That would be wooed, and not unsought be won,
Not obvious, not obtrusive, but retired" &c.

'Obvious' is used in the Latin sense 'coming to meet one' and with Gray here is nearly synonymous with 'obtrusive,' thrusting herself forward.

83. **thy youthful brow.** The Duke of Grafton was born in 1735, and was at his installation about 34 years old.

84. **laureate wreath.** The leaves of the bay tree, sacred to Apollo, were used to crown poets and men of letters generally (hence 'poet laureate'), and are therefore appropriate to the chief dignitaries in a great University. But William Cecil was, besides, himself a man of intense application to study when at Cambridge. Laurels were also used to crown conquerors; in this sense Milton uses the phrase which Gray has taken from him: *Sonnet to Cromwell*, l. 9,

> "While Darwen stream, with blood of Scots imbrued,
> And Dunbar field, resounds thy praises loud,
> And Worcester's *laureate wreath*."

Ib. **Cecil.** Lord Treasurer Burleigh was Chancellor of the University in the reign of Queen Elizabeth. Mason.

He was elected Chancellor of the University early in 1559. 'He was not made Lord Burghley until 1571.' Phelps. His college was St John's, the Venerable Margaret's foundation. See Froude, *Hist. of Eng.* vol. VII. c. 43, pp. 203 sq. for the pains Cecil took, as Chancellor, to disguise from Elizabeth on her visit to the University the confusion and disorder into which the place had fallen; and for 'the rashness of a few boys, which marred all.'

86. The fasces were a bundle of rods in the centre of which was an axe; they were borne by the lictors before the Roman consuls, and were a symbol of authority. Mitford quotes the last lines of Dryden's *Threnodia Augustalis*,

> "[The asserted Ocean rears his reverend head,
> To view and recognise his ancient lord again:]
> And with a willing hand, restores
> The *fasces of the main*."

And the same expression, *Annus Mirabilis*, st. 50:

> "And shook aloft the *fasces of the main*."

89. Milton, *Comus*, 87:

> "Well knows to still the *wild* winds *when they roar*,"

and Shakesp., *Temp.* I. 2. 379:

> "Courtsied when you have and kiss'd
> The *wild waves* whist."

Dryden, *Annus Mirabilis*, st. 94:

> "The *wild waves* master'd him and suck'd him in."

92. The figure is of course of Grafton helming the ship of state: 'the wild waves' are the domestic troubles centering round Wilkes, and

the various other discontents treated in Junius' letters. But though Gray has Horace in mind:

"neque altum
Semper urguendo, neque dum procellas
Cautus horrescis, nimium premendo
Litus iniquum.
[Not always tempt the distant deep
Nor always timorously creep
Along the treacherous shore. Cowper]

he departs from him, and not for the better. Who would tell a pilot not to be afraid of rocks? Gray means 'do not, because you fear the rocks, keep too far out to sea.' But contrast with his feeble and obscure use of this hint from Horace, Dryden's lucid and vigorous description from the same source of:

"...a daring pilot in extremity,
Pleased with the danger when the waves went high,
He sought the storms, but for a calm unfit
Would steer too nigh the sands, to boast his wit."
Absalom and Achitophel, Pt. I. ll. 159 sq.

93. **Brunswick.** The guiding star of George III. and the House of Brunswick generally. George I. was son of the Duke of Brunswick-Luneburg, who became Elector of Hanover.

ADDITIONAL NOTES.

P. x, l. 6. That William Antrobus was Gray's *cousin* not his *uncle* s certain. The two daughters of William are expressly named in Gray's will as his *second* cousins.

As early as 21 Dec., 1726, William Antrobus was instituted to the living of Everdon, in Northamptonshire. If he commenced residence at once, he was clearly not Gray's tutor at all at Eton. But he probably did not. He had three children christened at Everdon, the eldest, a boy, not till 1731.

That Robert Antrobus was ever Gray's Eton tutor in any sense, I much question. He died in 1729 and I think quitted Eton for the neighbourhood before then. He may have superintended the child's earlier education. Probably William succeeded Robert at Eton and they were never assistant-masters together; perhaps seldom or never seen together at the school. William might easily be supposed by the boys to be a younger brother.

P. 88, at end of n. on l. 42, add :—

Byron best interprets Gray:

"Childe Harold bask'd him in the noon-tide sun
Disporting there like any other fly."

P. 100, at end of n. on l. 16, add :—

Cf. also *Odyssey* XVIII. (Pope's), where Telemachus says

"Yet taught by time, my heart has learn'd to glow
For others' good, and melt at others' woe."

(This 18th book was Broome's, and he borrows this of Pope.)

P. 141, l. 38, add :—There was some precision required as to the rhyme of 'toil,' as Steele shows in the *Tatler* no. 11, "Avail and toil" he says "will never do for rhymes."

P. 144, note on l. 41.

41. 'Storied.' Milton perhaps first used the word in *Il Penseroso* —'storied windows,' that is representing ancient story. Pope has, *Essay on Man* IV. 303, 'the trophy'd arches, story'd halls.' Pattison says this is a Miltonic epithet misapplied—since it can only mean 'halls famed in story.' Why may it not mean 'halls adorned with painted records,—genealogical trees &c.'?

P. 147. For the thought from ll. 45 to 51 (incl.) of the *Elegy*, cf. Addison, *Spectator*, no. 215, "The philosopher, the saint, or the hero, the wise, the good, or the great man, very often lie hid and concealed in a plebeian; which a proper education might have disinterred and have brought to light."

P. 149, at end of n. on l. 55, add :—Cf. also Racine, *Athalie* Act II. Sc. 9

"Tel en un secret vallon,
Sur le bord d'une onde pure,
Croît à l'abri de l'aquilon,
Un jeune lis, l'amour de la nature.
Loin du monde élevé, de tous les dons des cieux
Il est orné dès sa naissance, et du méchant l'abord contagieux
N'altère point son innocence."

Pope, Thomson and Gray had all read Racine, and this perhaps is the true succession after all.

P. 151, at end of long note on ll. 57 sq., add :—

In Table-talk, *Guardian* Newspaper of Jan. 25, 1871, under the head "Stanzas published in great poems and afterwards rejected" there are given besides the well-known lines "There scattered oft," &c. which Gray indeed wrote but never published, the following which he certainly neither wrote nor published :

"Some rural Laïs, with all conquering charms,
Perhaps now moulders in this grassy bourne,
Some Helen, vain to set the fields in arms,
Some Emma dead, of gentle love forlorn."

(I owe this quotation to the Rev. Lewis Hensley, Vicar of Hitchin.)

There is no trace whatever, as far as I can discover, connecting these lines with Gray. They seem to be the work of some early champion of the claims of Womanhood.

The stanza in Fraser MS. follows l. 48 of present text.

P. 155, l. 2. Cf. Richardson's *Clarissa* (1749) vol. II. Letter XI., "Friday, midnight, I have now a calmer moment: *Envy, ambition*, high and selfish resentment, and all the violent passions are now, most probably, *asleep* around me; and shall not my own angry ones give way *to the silent hour* and subside likewise?" Is this mere coincidence?

P. 168, l. 18. I am inclined to suspect this identification of Miss Speed in Bentley's design. She may be the more robust of the two ladies.

P. 179, at end of n. on ll. 17–24, add:—It is noteworthy that Collins in his Ode on the Poetic Character despairs of following the guiding steps of Milton. The imagery differs from Gray's, but the spirit is the same.

P. 255, at end of n. on l. 51, add:—Gray's version is best explained by supposing that he gave to Bartholin's Latin a conjectural meaning. B. is substantially correct, and so is my English version.

Professor Kittredge kindly points this out to me.

P. 255, at end of n. on l. 55, add:—Bartholin interprets after Honoratum Fratrem 'sc. se ipsum'—but this is wrong. The right version is Hoder bears (or shall bear) thither a tall splendid sapling [i.e. the mistletoe].

P. 277, 2nd par. ad fin. add:—It is certain that Dyson was not dubbed *Mungo* until 1769. It was a nickname given him by Colonel Barré, from a black slave, employed in all kinds of jobs, in a farce, *The Padlock*, of 1708. (See Walpole's *Mem. of George III.* vol. 3, p. 211.)

For EU product safety concerns, contact us at Calle de José Abascal, 56–1°, 28003 Madrid, Spain or eugpsr@cambridge.org.

www.ingramcontent.com/pod-product-compliance
Ingram Content Group UK Ltd.
Pitfield, Milton Keynes, MK11 3LW, UK
UKHW020320140625
459647UK00018B/1947

* 9 7 8 1 1 0 7 6 6 5 6 8 2 *